Magnus Magnusson is an Icelander who has spent most of his life in Scotland. Educated at The Edinburgh Academy, he won an Open Scholarship to Jesus College, Oxford (1948–53), from where he graduated in English and Old Icelandic literature.

He became a journalist in Scotland before moving to current affairs television on programmes like *Tonight*. Best-known for his 25-year reign as quizmaster of *Mastermind*, his main interest, however, was in making historical documentaries. He was the founder-presenter of *Chronicle* (1966–80), a monthly series on world archaeology and history.

As a writer and historian, Magnus has published thirty books, dealing with archaeology, Iceland, Scottish history, Irish history and Lindisfarne, as well as translating Icelandic sagas and modern novels and editing the 1995 *Chambers Biographical Dictionary*.

Magnus was the founder-chairman of Scottish Natural Heritage (1992–99), the government's environmental agency in Scotland. He has been awarded honorary doctorates by seven universities, and the honorary Fellowship of his old college. He was also awarded an honorary knighthood (KBE) for services to the heritage of Scotland.

Christine Moorcroft is a former teacher, lecturer, school inspector and publisher, and now writes educational books and courses for schools and colleges. She was a contestant on *Mastermind* twice, in 1988 and 1996, taking Vincent van Gogh and Perfume as her specialised subjects. She also appeared on the revived *Mastermind* programme on the Discovery Channel.

Christine is a member of the Mastermind Club (the refuge for survivors of the Black Chair) and was the editor of its quarterly journal (entitled *PASS*, of course) from 1996 to 1998.

Also by Magnus Magnusson

INTRODUCING ARCHAEOLOGY
VIKING EXPANSION WESTWARDS
THE CLACKEN AND THE SLATE
HAMMER OF THE NORTH
BC: THE ARCHAEOLOGY OF THE BIBLE LANDS
LANDLORD OR TENANT? A VIEW OF IRISH HISTORY
ICELAND
VIKINGS!
MAGNUS ON THE MOVE
TREASURES OF SCOTLAND
LINDISFARNE: THE CRADLE ISLAND
READER'S DIGEST BOOK OF FACTS (Editor)
ICELAND SAGA
CHAMBERS BIOGRAPHICAL DICTIONARY (Editor-in-Chief)
THE NATURE OF SCOTLAND (Editor)
RUM: NATURE'S ISLAND
SCOTLAND: THE STORY OF A NATION
MAGNUS MAGNUSSON'S QUIZ BOOK

Magnus Magnusson's Family Quiz Book

Magnus Magnusson

and

Christine Moorcroft

A *Time Warner* Paperback

First published in Great Britain in 2002
by Time Warner Books

Reprinted in 2004

The authors gratefully acknowledge permission to quote from the following:
For the Fallen by Laurence Binyon, from *The New Oxford Book of English Verse* published by Oxford University Press
Anthem for St Cecilia's Day by W. H. Auden, from *Collected Poems* published by Faber & Faber
Leopards at Knole by Vita Sackville West
The Dolly on the Dustcart by Pam Ayers, from *I Like this Poem* published by Puffin
Cinderella, from *Revolting Rhymes* by Roald Dahl published by Puffin
Colonel Fazackerley, from *Going to the Fair* by Charles Causley published by Puffin
Eye Sore, from *Sky in the Pie* by Roger McGough published by Puffin
Loveliest of Trees, the Cherry Now, from *A Shropshire Lad* by A. E. Housman published by Jonathan Cape
Mushrooms, from *The Colossus* by Sylvia Plath published by Faber & Faber

A CIP catalogue record for this book is
available from the British Library.

ISBN 0 7515 3279 7

Typeset in Sabon by M Rules
Printed and bound in Great Britain by
Clays Ltd, St Ives plc

Time Warner Paperbacks
An imprint of
Time Warner Book Group UK
Brettenham House
Lancaster Place
London WC2E 7EN

www.twbg.co.uk

Contents

Authors' Foreword

Magnus Magnusson's Family Quiz Book is a natural sequel to the highly successful *Magnus Magnusson's Quiz Book (An A–Z Quiz for All the Family)*, which was published in 2000. But it is more than just a follow-up, or a follow-on: it is a continuation of the noble pastime of Finding Things Out – and Finding More Things Out.

Nor is it just another quiz book designed to provide lists of simple questions-and-answers with which to swot for a pub quiz or a big-money prize on television. Quizzes are much more than that. Quizzes are about the pleasure of knowing things. Quizzes are purposeful fun – even if only for the display of conspicuous knowledge!

Magnus Magnusson's Family Quiz Book is inspired by this ethos: to spark, and to satisfy, people's curiosity about how things happened, why things happened, when things happened – to encourage people who want to find out more for themselves. So that's what happened! So that's why, or how, it came about! So that's who invented it! Shakespeare's roguish Autolycus in *The Winter's Tale* could not have been more assiduous in his snapping up of unconsidered trifles. All along the way, questions were constantly being sparked off by chance encounters or visits: unexpectedly finding Dante Gabriel Rossetti's painting of *Dante's Dream* in an art gallery in Scotland (Visual Arts, Question 19); spotting a plaque in the vestibule of a Manchester hotel which commemorates a historic meeting between a designer and a financier to set up one of the world's most famous car companies (Engineering, Q8); stopping to contemplate an intriguing cast-iron statue of a mummified *Iron Man* in an English city square (Gods and Goddesses General Knowledge, Q15); darting across a busy London thoroughfare to a triangular traffic island opposite Marble Arch to track down a half-forgotten plaque commemorating centuries of London history (Cathedrals GK, Q17).

This is a Family Quiz Book, just like the first Quiz Book. It uses the same classic twin formula (from *Mastermind*) of specialised subjects arranged alphabetically, with accompanying General Knowledge sets. The questions in each set are graded into four bands, ranging from 'family easy' to 'professional stinkers'; and each General Knowledge set echoes the theme of the preceding specialised set in its first and last questions.

Compiling a book of quizzes is an endlessly fascinating exercise in serendipity ('the faculty of making fortunate discoveries by accident'). The pursuit of knowledge for its own sake is a pastime which can easily become an obsession. Everything and everyone is grist to that insatiable mill. A programme on the car radio often demands a halt in the nearest lay-by in order to scribble some notes for further investigation. All those weighty Sunday newspaper magazines, which all too often are consigned to the wastebasket unread, become an irresistible source of esoteric information. Obituaries and birthday lists in newspapers gain a new significance, recalling important lives or events which deserve to be remembered. Even crossword puzzles can be a lucky source of unusual words.

Indeed, many of the 2,000 questions in this book are concerned with orismology – the study and explanation of definitions and terminology. It is such a pleasure to know how words came about and how their modern meanings have developed from earlier times – words like 'boycott' or 'pundit', for instance. Words – all words – are such precious objects, the building blocks of language, of thought, of expression: they should all be cherished and protected and kept in good working order.

In the ultimate resort of definition, perhaps, this book is a paean to opsimathy, the pleasure of learning late in life. You're never too old (or too young, for that matter) to learn. And what better than to combine edification with fun?

In the compilation of this book we were given help and inspiration by a great many people, many of them complete strangers – clergy, librarians, museum curators, press officers, secretaries of agencies and organisations, tourism officers, university officials. A host of people all over the country went to considerable trouble to answer e-mails or telephone calls asking for facts and figures to be checked. Annette Atherton of the Lawn Tennis Association personally checked a fascinating tennis fact which could not be found on a website (Tennis,

Q11); Dianne Egan of Slough checked and double-checked information about an embalmed dog named 'Station Jim' (Geology GK, Q19); John Hardacre, curator of Winchester Cathedral, kindly clarified confusions about the mortuary chests containing the bones of early kings of England (Cathedrals GK, Q1); Anthony McBirnie of Sainsbury's delved into the mystery of the real name of the fish sold in their supermarkets as 'Antarctic icefish' (Zoology GK, Q20); David Marriott of the City of Edinburgh Council provided a personal guided subterranean tour of a long-forgotten warren of buildings under the City Chambers (Edinburgh, Q14); Paul Reece, rector of St Lawrence, Little Stanmore, sent information about the subject of Handel's fifth harpsichord suite, and even a photograph of the grave (Bible GK, Q18); and Naomi Robins of the Environment Agency tracked down some obscure information about 'tickling and groping' (Pastimes, Q13). The list could go on and on . . .

At the risk of being invidious we would like to single out some direct contributions made by friends and colleagues: Bunny Campione, of BBC TV's *The Antiques Roadshow*, for her help with antique toys; Anita Myatt, of the Sutton Central Library, for questions in many fields; Iain Orr, of the Foreign and Commonwealth Office, for an intriguing selection of questions on biodiversity; Virginia Smith, Christmas Quiz-setter for the Imperial Cancer Research Fund (now Cancer Research UK); David Taviner, of BBC TV's *Songs of Praise*, for help on the connection between Lewis Carroll and a cathedral; Des Thompson, of Scottish Natural Heritage, for expert advice on ornithology; Marion Whitelaw, for invaluable assistance throughout; and Susie Wong, of the Chinese Cultural Centre (and Jeanette Greenfield), for help with matters Chinese.

Many former Masterminders (all members of the Mastermind Club) gave unstintingly of their expertise, including Kevin Ashman (*Mastermind* 1995, Champion) on films; Norman Izzett (*Mastermind* 1984) on Latin and classical subjects; Leo Stevenson (*Mastermind* 1997) on art; Ray Ward (*Mastermind* 1978), who once devised a special Mastermind Club quiz at our request; and innumerable others who have helped to set quiz questions over the years in the Club's quarterly publication (called, of course, *PASS!*) and whose labours of love sparked new questions on related subjects.

Above all, we owe a huge debt of gratitude to Geoff Thomas (*Mastermind* 1994), who checked every single question (and answer) with painstaking patience and unfailing courtesy.

Finally, our thanks go to our friends and colleagues at Time Warner

Books: Richard Dawes, who scrutinised the manuscript; our editor, Catherine Hill; and our publisher Alan Samson (himself a Masterminder in 1985). Between them they encouraged and nurtured this new offering with exemplary diligence.

Magnus Magnusson
Christine Moorcroft
June 2002

Astronomy Questions

1 For what does the acronym NASA stand?
2 On which planet was the film and comic strip hero Superman born?
3 What is the Russian word for 'astronaut'?
4 The word 'planet' is derived from the Greek *planetes* – meaning what?
5 What was the name (meaning 'peace') of the space station launched by the USSR in 1986, which was replaced by the International Space Station and brought back to earth on 22 March 2001?
6 What was the name of the world's first 'space tourist', a sixty-year-old Californian financier, who paid the Russian space agency $20 million to travel with the crew of a Soyuz spacecraft to the International Space Station in April 2001?
7 What was the name of the astronaut in David Bowie's first Top Ten hit, *Space Oddity*, released in 1969 to coincide with the landing of *Apollo 11* on the moon?
8 Which is the densest planet in the solar system?
9 In 1675 who was appointed the first Astronomer Royal?
10 What are Lyrids, Perseids and Leonids?
11 Which sixteenth-century Danish astronomer, who made his name by discovering a new star (which was named after him) in the constellation of Cassiopeia, wore a false nose made of a gold and silver alloy, having lost most of the original in a duel at the age of nineteen?
12 What name is given to a streamer of glowing gas (mainly hydrogen) which can be seen in the outer layers of the sun's atmosphere?
13 In 1930 which self-taught US astronomer discovered Pluto?
14 How long is the period of Halley's comet?
15 In 1609 which German astronomer discovered that planets move in elliptical, rather than circular, orbits?
16 Who were the commander and pilot of the first US Space Shuttle flight (*Columbia*) on 12 April 1981?
17 Which satellite of Jupiter is named after the mother of Arcas (whose father was Zeus), who was turned by Artemis into a she-bear and, later, by Zeus into a constellation?
18 In 1979 who commented that 'Space isn't remote at all. It's only an hour's drive away if your car could go straight upwards'?
19 Which was the first variable star to be discovered?
20 On 3 August 2000 the International Astronomical Union announced the discovery of a Jupiter-sized planet orbiting which star?

1 **National Aeronautics and Space Administration** (founded in 1958).
2 **Krypton.** Superman was created by Jerry Siegel and Joe Shuster in 1933 and turned down by every magazine to which they offered it. The first Superman story was published in Action Comics in 1938.
3 **Kosmonavt** (cosmonaut), from the Greek *kosmos* (space) and *nautes* (sailor).
4 **Wanderer.** To the ancients the planets appeared to wander among the stars instead of having fixed places.
5 ***Mir.***
6 **Dennis Tito.**
7 **Major Tom.**
8 **Earth** (its density is 5.5 times that of water).
9 **John Flamsteed** (1646–1719).
10 **Annual meteor showers.** Lyrids (radiating from the constellation Lyra) occur from 19 to 22 April; Perseids (from the constellation Perseus) from 27 July to 17 August; and Leonids (from the constellation Leo) from 15 to 17 November.
11 **Tycho (or Tyge) Brahe** (1546–1601). He discovered the star (Tycho's nova) in 1572 and published his observations of it in *De nova stella* in 1573.
12 **Prominence.**
13 **Clyde Tombaugh** (1906–97). After finishing high school, Tombaugh built a telescope and used it to make observations of Jupiter and Mars. He sent sketches of them to the Flagstaff (Lowell) Observatory, hoping for some advice about his work. Instead, in 1929, he was offered the job of continuing the search for the expected ninth planet, which had been initiated in 1905 by Percival Lowell (1855–1916), the founder of the observatory.
14 **Between 74.4 and 79.6 years** (the average is usually given as 76 years). Its periodicity was worked out by Edmund Halley, who saw it in 1682 and correctly predicted that it would return in 1758–9. Since then it has been seen in 1835, 1910 and 1985–6.
15 **Johannes Kepler** (1571–1630).
16 **John Young** (commander) and **Robert Crippen** (pilot). They were the first astronauts to land on the ground, rather than in the sea, on their return to earth (at Edwards Air Force Base in California).
17 **Callisto.** According to the legend, Callisto remained a she-bear until her son Arcas grew up and met her while out hunting; he would have killed her with an arrow had not Zeus turned them both into constellations (Ursa Major and Arcturus).
18 **Fred Hoyle** (1915–2001), quoted in the *Observer*, 9 September 1979.
19 **Algol** (Beta Persei). The variation in the star's brightness was first noticed in 1667 by the Italian astronomer Geminiano Montanari, but it was not until 1782 that the young Dutch-born English astronomer John Goodricke (1764–86) measured it or explained its cause as originating in a 'binary'. He showed that the variation was the result of eclipses, caused by the star's movement in a binary system in which one star comes between the other and the earth.
20 **Epsilon Eridani.** The orange-red dwarf star, much younger than the sun, is in the constellation Eridanus, which is 10.5 light-years from the earth.

General Knowledge Questions

1 Which planet was the birthplace of Mr Spock of the BBC TV series *Star Trek*?
2 What is Cockney rhyming slang for 'whisky'?
3 The name of which small puff-pastry case comes from the French for 'flight in the wind'?
4 Soft solder is an alloy of which two metals?
5 What is the name of the eponymous Bogeyman in the 1977 book by Raymond Briggs?
6 Which writer was once known as 'the Great Unknown'?
7 Which condition, sometimes called 'post-viral (fatigue) syndrome', 'chronic fatigue syndrome' or 'yuppy flu', is known by the initials ME?
8 In Greek legend, who was the long-suffering wife of Odysseus and mother of Telemachus?
9 The name of which Jewish festival, celebrated from 15 to 21 Tishri, September/October, means 'arbours' or 'tabernacles'?
10 What is the highest point in the Peak District National Park?
11 What name is given to a wheel placed in a gear train to alter the direction of another wheel and which has no effect on the ratio of the drive?
12 In Mozart's opera *The Magic Flute*, who is the mother of Pamina?
13 What type of substance is gutta-percha?
14 In which collection of 'dramatic scenes' by Robert Browning does a young girl from an Italian silk mill sing, on New Year's Day, the following lines?

The year's at the spring
And day's at the morn;
Morning's at seven;
The hillside's dew-pearled;
The lark's on the wing;
The snail's on the thorn:
God's in his heaven –
All's right with the world!

15 To whom is attributed the design of the ceremonial uniform of the Swiss Guards of the Vatican City?
16 What was the name of the horse on which Colonel Harry Llewellyn rode a clear round, which helped Britain's show-jumping team to win the gold medal in the 1952 Olympics in Helsinki?
17 In 1959 which car manufacturer was the first to fit seat belts, designed and patented by Nils Bohlin, one of its engineers?
18 What is the common name for *Latrodectus mactans*, the arachnid which has distinctive red markings on its abdomen in the shape of an hourglass, stripes or spots?
19 Whose last words after a nurse had commented that 'he seemed to be little better', are said to have been 'On the contrary'?
20 In 1671 which Italian-born French astronomer was appointed the first Director of the Paris Observatory, founded by Louis XIV?

General Knowledge

1 **Vulcan.**
2 **Gay and frisky.**
3 **Vol-au-vent.**
4 **Tin and lead.** Hard solders (brazing solders) are alloys of copper, silver and zinc.
5 **Fungus.**
6 **Sir Walter Scott** (1771–1832). He published *Waverley* (1814) anonymously and his subsequent novels were published under the name of 'The Author of *Waverley*'. He did not publicly acknowledge authorship until 1827.
7 **Myalgic encephalomyelitis.** It is a prolonged form of encephalomyelitis (inflammation of the brain and spinal cord), usually occurring after a viral infection and characterised by flu-like symptoms: headaches, fever, localised muscular pain and weakness.
8 **Penelope.**
9 **Sukkot** (the plural of sukkah). Sukkot begins on 15 Tishri and lasts for seven days. It marks the end of the agricultural year, and commemorates the portable tabernacles erected by the Israelites during their forty years in the desert after they escaped from slavery in Egypt and followed Moses to find the Promised Land (Leviticus 23:39–43).
10 **Kinder Scout.** It is an upland plateau whose highest point is 636 metres above sea level.
11 **Idle wheel** (or idler).
12 **The Queen of the Night.**
13 Latex or **rubber** from Malaysian trees. It is used in dentistry and as an electrical insulator, and was once used for making golf balls. The name comes from the Malay words *getah* (gum) and *perca* (strips of cloth), which it resembles.
14 ***Pippa Passes*** (1841).
15 **Michelangelo** (Michelangelo di Lodovico Buonarroti Simoni, 1475–1564). The guards normally wear blue doublets and berets, but on ceremonial occasions they wear uniforms designed in about 1506, consisting of tunics with stripes in the Medici family colours (red, dark blue and yellow), white ruffs and high plumed helmets, and carry pikes and swords.
16 **Foxhunter.**
17 **Volvo.** The three-point adjustable safety belt was first fitted in the PV544. Volvo did not enforce the patent, in the belief that all motorists should benefit from it.
18 **Black widow spider.** It is found mainly in North America. The female's markings are either two small spots or an hourglass. The male often has four pairs of reddish stripes on the sides of its abdomen as well as the hourglass.
19 **Henrik Ibsen** (1828–1906).
20 **Giovanni Domenico** (Jean Dominique) **Cassini** (1625–1712). Three subsequent generations of his family also held the post. He discovered Cassini's division, the dark gap between two of the rings of Saturn.

1 What is the final word of Revelation, the last book of the New Testament?

2 What is the collective term for the first five books of the Old Testament, known in Hebrew as the Torah (Law)?

3 Who, on a visit to King Solomon, gave him 'an hundred and twenty talents of gold, and of spices very great store, and precious stones'?

4 According to Genesis 4:16, to which land was Cain exiled after killing his brother Abel?

5 The wife of which Egyptian captain of the guard (and master of Joseph) attempted to seduce Joseph and claimed that he had tried to rape her, leading to his imprisonment?

6 Under Mosaic law, what animal was laden with the sins of the people on Yom Kippur (the Day of Atonement), which it symbolically carried into the desert to a place of no return?

7 In which present-day country is Mount Sinai, where Moses received the Ten Commandments engraved on two stone tablets?

8 William Tyndale published the first English translation of the New Testament in 1525, but was executed (in 1536) before he could complete the Old Testament. Who (in Zurich in 1535) published the first English translation of the entire Bible?

9 In which two languages were the Dead Sea Scrolls written?

10 Who was the father of the disciples James and John?

11 In the early seventeenth-century painting by Artemisia Gentileschi depicting a scene from the book of Judith in the Apocrypha, whom is Judith beheading?

12 In the gospel of St John, which miracle did Jesus perform near the Pool of Siloam, outside Jerusalem?

13 To which priest of David did Handel dedicate an anthem for the coronation of George II in 1727, which has been performed at every coronation of a British monarch since then?

14 Which giant, according to Deuteronomy, 'remained of the remnant of the Rephaim' and had a basalt bedstead which was nine cubits long and four cubits wide 'after the cubit of a man'?

15 In which city did Joshua command the sun to stand still and condemn its inhabitants to be 'hewers of wood and drawers of water'?

16 St Paul (Saul of Tarsus), like most other rabbis of the time, offered his services free and made his living from other, manual work. What kind of work did he do?

17 With which Persian king is King Ahasuerus in the book of Esther identified?

18 After which six characters in the Bible are champagne bottles named?

19 Which couple, members of the temple in Jerusalem, violated the principle of redistribution of wealth 'unto every man according as he had need' by bringing to the Apostles only part of the money from the sale of their land?

20 Where did St John the Divine, in Revelation, say that Armageddon, the last battle on the Day of Judgement, would be fought?

Answers

1 **Amen** (Revelation 22:21: 'The grace of our Lord Jesus Christ be with you all. Amen.').

2 **Pentateuch**, from the Greek *pente* ('five') and *teukhos* ('tool', later 'scroll'): Genesis, Exodus, Leviticus, Numbers and Deuteronomy.

3 **The Queen of Sheba** (I Kings 10:1).

4 **The Land of Nod**. The term, which might mean 'a land of wandering' rather than a specific location, came to be used to mean 'going to bed' after Jonathan Swift, in *A Complete Collection of Genteel and Ingenious Conversation* (1738), wrote that he was 'going into the land of Nod', meaning that he was going to sleep.

5 **Potiphar**. His wife is not named in the Bible (Genesis 39).

6 **Goat**. The Scapegoat was used in the annual ritual of Yom Kippur – hence the term 'scapegoat' for a person made to bear the blame for others (Leviticus 16:7–10).

7 **Egypt** (Exodus 19:18–25, 20:1–17).

8 **Miles Coverdale** (1488–1568).

9 **Aramaic** and **Hebrew**. In late 1946 or early 1947 a Bedouin goatherd, Muhammad Khalil, and his friend Muhammad el-Hamed found, in a cave at the north-west end of the Dead Sea, some pottery jars containing the first of the scrolls to be discovered since biblical times.

10 **Zebedee** (Matthew 4:21, 10:2, Mark 1:19–20).

11 **Holofernes** (*Judith Beheading Holofernes*, in the Uffizi Gallery, Florence). Judith liberated her people by killing the Assyrian general Holofernes, who was besieging her town (Bethulia of Samaria).

12 **He gave a blind man sight** (John 9:1–11).

13 **Zadok** (2 Samuel 8:17, 1 Kings 1:39).

14 **Og, King of Bashan** (Joshua 9:10, Deuteronomy 3:11). According to tradition Og lived for 3000 years and walked beside the Ark during the Flood. The cubit varied between 45 and 59 centimetres, different places having their own 'standard cubit'.

15 **Gibeon** (Joshua 9:27, 10:13), the present-day site of el-Jib, a few kilometres north of Jerusalem.

16 **Tent-making** (Acts 18:3).

17 **Xerxes I** (r. 486–65 BCE). Ahasuerus chose Esther, the orphaned ward of Mordecai, as his queen, not knowing that she was Jewish. When Haman, the king's vizier, issued an edict to have all Jews in the kingdom slaughtered, Esther pleaded for them to be spared. The king granted her request, and Haman and his sons were hanged instead. The deliverance of the Jews from the massacre is celebrated at the festival of Purim.

18 **Jeroboam**, first king of Israel after it had broken from Judah (four times the size of a normal bottle); **Rehoboam**, son of Solomon (six bottles); **Methuselah**, the longest-living ancestor of the Hebrews (eight bottles); **Salmanazar** (Shalmaneser), an Assyrian king mentioned in II Kings 17:3 (twelve bottles); **Balthazar**, one of the Magi, named in later sources but not in the Bible (sixteen bottles); and **Nebuchadnezzar**, king of Babylon (twenty bottles).

19 **Ananias and Sapphira** (Acts 4:37, 5:1–10).

20 **Megiddo**, on the plain of Jezreel. Armageddon means 'Hill of Megiddo' (1 Kings 9:19, Revelation 16:16).

General Knowledge Questions

1 What is the meaning of the word 'bible'?
2 Who wrote the early stories for the 1980–88 ITV series *Tales of the Unexpected*?
3 Who was the manager of the Scottish national football team from 1978 until his death in 1985 from a heart attack, only minutes after he had led the team to qualification for the World Cup finals with a 1–1 draw against Wales at Ninian Park, Cardiff?
4 In slang parlance, especially in the West Country, what is a 'grockle'?
5 What is the name of the seat of the Duke and Duchess of Devonshire?
6 What name is given to the poetic form, originating in Japan and meaning 'amusement verse', of three unrhymed lines whose syllable pattern is 5–7–5?
7 Where, in London, are the Grace Gates, designed by Herbert Baker?
8 What is the meaning of Punjab?
9 *The Silence of the Lambs* was the second film based on books by Thomas Harris to feature Hannibal Lecter; what was the first?
10 What kind of animal is a cachalot?
11 Which artist painted the nude prostitute *Olympia*, which had to be hung high up on the wall when it was first exhibited in Paris at the 1865 Salon in order to prevent infuriated visitors attacking it?
12 In dressmaking, what type of pleat consists of two parallel creases folded inwards towards one another?
13 Who was the Archbishop of Canterbury when Edward VIII abdicated in December 1936?
14 Which imperial unit of measurement is equivalent to $\frac{1}{20}$ of a pint?
15 What is the name of the eye disease, a severe form of conjunctivitis, which causes the eyelids to turn inwards so that the eyelashes scratch the cornea, resulting in blindness?
16 What is the meaning of '-thwaite' in place names such as Haverthwaite, Langthwaite and Linthwaite?
17 Which Scottish king was married to Joan Beaufort (the granddaughter of John of Gaunt), with whom he fell in love after seeing her from a window during his captivity in Windsor Castle?
18 By what nickname (erroneously linked to the influence of the sounds of a forge near the church where Handel was organist for the Duke of Chandos) are the air and variations of Handel's fifth harpsichord suite commonly known?
19 What were 'chapbooks', which were popular from the seventeenth to the nineteenth century?
20 What name was given to an 1810 edition of the Bible because of a misprint in Luke 14:26 which read: 'If any man come to me, and hate not his father . . . yea, and his own wife also'?

General Knowledge

Answers

1 **The books** (from the Greek *ta biblia* through medieval Latin *biblia*).

2 **Roald Dahl (1916–90)**. The series began in 1979 as *Roald Dahl's Tales of the Unexpected*, hosted by the author, but the title was shortened the following year, and John Houseman took over as host.

3 **Jock Stein** (1922–85). He had previously been manager of Dunfermline Athletic, Hibernian, Celtic and Leeds.

4 **A tourist** (or an unpleasant outsider).

5 **Chatsworth House**, Derbyshire. It was built by Bess of Hardwick (c. 1527–1608), and her second husband, Sir William Cavendish, and redesigned by their descendant the 1st Duke of Devonshire, William Cavendish (1640–1707).

6 **Haiku**. An example is *Proverbial Logic* by Debjani Chatterjee:

Where there are pandas
there's bamboo, but the converse
is sadly not true.

7 **Lord's Cricket Ground**. They were erected at the Members' Entrance in July 1923 and are named after W.G. Grace (1848–1915).

8 **Five rivers**, from the Persian *panj* (five) and *ab* (water). It refers to the five tributaries of the Indus: Beas, Chenab, Jhelum, Ravi and Sutlej.

9 ***Manhunter*** (1986), directed by Michael Mann and based on the novel *Red Dragon* (also known as *Red Dragon: The Pursuit of Hannibal Lecter*).

10 **Sperm whale**. Herman Melville's 'Moby Dick' is thought to have been an albino cachalot.

11 **Édouard Manet** (1832–83). The painting is now in the Musée d'Orsay, Paris.

12 **Box pleat.**

13 **Cosmo Gordon Lang** (1864–1945).

14 **One fluid ounce.**

15 **Trachoma**, caused by the virus-like bacterium *Chlamydia trachomitis*.

16 **Clearing, meadow or paddock** (from the Old Norse *þveit*).

17 **James I** (1394–1437). James wrote the long love-poem *The Kingis Quair* (King's Book), which was later illustrated in a series of murals in Penkill Castle, near Girvan, by the Pre-Raphaelite artist William Scott Bell.

18 **The Harmonious Blacksmith**. The grave of the blacksmith, at the church of St Lawrence, Little Stanmore, near Edgware, is marked 'Sacred to the memory of William Powell, the Harmonious Blacksmith, who died Feb. 27, 1780, aged about 78. He was parish clerk at the time the immortal Handel was organist of this church'.

19 **Cheap paperback booklets**, containing ballads, romances, jokes, riddles, news (both true and fabricated) and so on, usually sold for a halfpenny or a penny by 'chapmen' (itinerant traders).

20 ***The Wife-hater Bible***. The word 'wife' was a misprint for 'life'.

Cathedrals

Questions

1 Which English cathedral is depicted, with Edward Elgar, on the back of the current Bank of England £20 note?
2 Who was the sculptor of the bronze figure of St Michael trampling the Devil on the façade of Coventry Cathedral?
3 What is the name of the largest bell (weighing almost 17 tons) in St Paul's Cathedral, London?
4 Which cathedral contains the tomb of the Venerable Bede (c. 673–735)?
5 A cathedral is defined as a church containing the 'cathedra'. What is a cathedra?
6 Which cathedral in Wales is reputed to be the smallest ancient cathedral in Britain?
7 Which English cathedral has a late fifteenth-century central tower called 'Bell Harry' after the single bell 'Harry' which it houses?
8 In which cathedral were Catherine of Aragon (in 1536) and Mary Queen of Scots (immediately after her execution in 1587) buried?
9 Which saint's shrine is in the crypt of Glasgow Cathedral?
10 Which French Gothic cathedral, whose foundation stone was laid in 1163, stands on the original site of a sixth-century church of the same name and a basilica dedicated to St Étienne and, before that, a Roman temple to Jupiter?
11 Which writer was Dean of St Patrick's Cathedral in Dublin from 1713 to 1745, and is buried close to the entrance?
12 Who designed the dome of Santa Maria del Fiore, the cathedral of Florence?
13 Which still unfinished US cathedral, said to be the largest in the world, houses the Chapels of the Seven Tongues?
14 To which sainted Norse earl of the Orkneys is the cathedral in Kirkwall dedicated?
15 In which cathedral is the sumptuous tomb of Bess of Hardwick (c. 1527–1608)?
16 Who was the architect of the Roman Catholic Cathedral of Christ the King in Liverpool?
17 In which Norwegian cathedral did the uncorrupted body of St Olav Haraldsson (King of Norway from 1015 to 1030 and patron saint of Norway) find its final resting place in the twelfth century?
18 The cloister of which cathedral houses the oldest mechanical clock on record in Britain, now restored to working order?
19 Which English cathedral claims a share in the inspiration for Lewis Carroll's *Alice's Adventures in Wonderland*?
20 What is the name of the thirteenth-century master mason who designed and built the west façade of Wells Cathedral with its eighty full-sized sculptured figures?

1 **Worcester.**
2 **Jacob Epstein** (1880–1959).
3 **Great Paul.** It is the bourdon (the bell with the lowest note in the peal), housed in the South West Tower.
4 **Durham.** Bede, the 'Father of English History' spent most of his life as a monk at Jarrow (now in Tyne and Wear).
5 **The bishop's chair.** In Early Christian times it was situated behind the altar and in medieval times in the choir. Hence the term *ex cathedra* ('with authority'), defined by the Pope as being doctrinally infallibly true.
6 **Llanelwy (St Asaph)**, Clwyd, Wales.
7 **Canterbury.** The present Bell Harry, cast in 1635, was named after the original bell hung in the central tower by Prior Henry Eastry (1285–1331) of the Benedictine community there.
8 **Peterborough.** James VI and I had his mother, Mary Queen of Scots, reinterred in Henry VIII's Chapel in Westminster Abbey in 1612.
9 **St Mungo** (also known as St Kentigern, 'the Apostle of Cumbria', c. 520–612). The cathedral was built in the thirteenth century on the traditional site of his cell near the Molendinar burn.
10 **Notre Dame.**
11 **Jonathan Swift** (1667–1745).
12 **Filippo Brunelleschi** (1377–1446).
13 **The Cathedral Church of St John the Divine**, New York City. The seven chapels are named St Ansgar (dedicated to the Scandinavian people), St Boniface (German), St Columba (British), St Savior (Eastern Christians), St Martin (French), St Ambrose (Italian) and St James (Spanish).
14 **Earl Magnus Erlendsson** (1075–1117). St Magnus was treacherously done to death on the island of Egilsay in 1117. His nephew, Earl Rögnvald *kali*, vowed that if he were appointed earl he would build in memory of his martyred uncle 'the most magnificent minster in the Northern Isles'.
15 **Derby.** It is in the Cavendish chapel. As a result of four judicious marriages, Elizabeth Hardwick became one of the richest people in Elizabethan England. She spent much of her wealth creating Hardwick Hall, near Chesterfield, in the 1590s.
16 **Sir Frederick Gibberd** (1908–84). Edwin Lutyens had previously designed a domed building in the Mannerist style, and part of the crypt from his plans was built between 1933–41. However, the work was abandoned during the Second World War and in the 1960s Gibberd's design for a modern concrete clad structure was built instead.
17 **Trondheim.** The cathedral was established on the site of St Olav's Church, which had been built by King Magnus *góði* ('the Good', r. 1035–47) to house his father's remains.
18 **Salisbury.** The clock was originally installed in the bell tower of the cathedral in 1386. It has no face – its purpose was only to strike the hours.
19 **Ripon.** Lewis Carroll's father (Charles Dodgson) was Canon-in-Residence at the newly established Ripon Cathedral from 1852 to 1868. The carvings on the misericords on the choir stalls depict a griffin chasing a rabbit down a tunnel, a turtle, pigs playing bagpipes and 'blemyas' (creatures with faces on their torsos, such as Mr Nobody and Mr Somebody).
20 **Adam Lock** (active 1215–29).

General Knowledge Questions

1 Which English cathedral houses the scattered bones of the great Danish king of England, Canute (Cnut, r. 1016–35)?
2 What is the name of the galaxy in which our solar system lies?
3 What was Mahatma Gandhi's first name?
4 Which Mediterranean island, on which St Paul was shipwrecked for three months on his way to Rome, is called 'Melita' in the Bible?
5 What was the name of the massive African elephant which lived at London Zoo from 1865 to 1882 and gave rise to the generic term for outsize things?
6 According to the novel by Douglas Adams, what type of establishment can be found at the end of the universe?
7 Who is the patron saint of television?
8 Which songwriter recorded *It Never Rains in Southern California* and *Free Electric Band* in 1973 and wrote hits such as *Little Arrows* (for Oliver and the Overlord) and, with Mike Hazlewood, *The Air That I Breathe* (for The Hollies)?
9 What is depicted on the badge of Rover cars?
10 What is the collective term for a flock of goldfinches?
11 Which English actor's autobiographies were entitled *Blessings in Disguise, My Name Escapes Me: the Diary of a Retiring Actor* and *A Positively Final Appearance*?
12 Which seventeenth-century German physician discovered the therapeutic quality of crystallised sodium sulphate, and by whose name it is commonly known?
13 In which Scottish city do bronze sculptures of Desperate Dan and his pet Dawg stride along the High Street, stalked by Minnie the Minx with a catapult loaded with a tomato?
14 Hieroglyphics on the walls of the Temple of Amun at Karnak in Egypt record a peace treaty made after the inconclusive Battle of Kadesh in 1275 BCE between Ramses II ('the Great') and the king of which people?
15 What is the Japanese festival dedicated to children, celebrated annually on 5 May by attaching to bamboo poles huge banners in the form of swimming carp?
16 Which was the first property donated to the National Trust, in 1895?
17 What historic site in London is commemorated by a circular plaque set into the paving of the triangular traffic island at the junction of Bayswater Road and Edgware Road, opposite Marble Arch?
18 Which Canadian soldier-poet made the Flanders poppy a potent emblem of remembrance?
19 In medieval castles, what was the work of a 'gong farmer'?
20 In which Welsh cathedral is the tomb of Edmund Tudor, the father of Henry VII and grandfather of Henry VIII?

General Knowledge Answers

1 **Winchester.** In the 1520s the exhumed bones of several kings and bishops had been placed in mortuary chests, some of which were destroyed by Cromwell's troops during the Commonwealth. Six surviving chests have been placed on top of the screens in the Presbytery aisles, but no one can now be sure if the bones were correctly identified.
2 **The Milky Way.**
3 **Mohandas.** His full name was Mohandas Karamchand Gandhi. The name 'Mahatma', by which he became known, means 'Great Soul'.
4 **Malta** (Acts 28:1).
5 **Jumbo.** 'Jumbo' weighed 6.5 tons. He was sold in 1882 to Barnum's *Greatest Show on Earth* in the USA, and was accidentally killed by a railway engine in 1885.
6 **A restaurant** (*The Restaurant at the End of the Universe*).
7 **St Clare.** According to some sources, she is also the patron saint of needlewomen and laundry workers.
8 **Albert Hammond** (b. 1943).
9 **A viking longship.**
10 **A charm.**
11 **Alec Guinness** (1914–2000).
12 **Johann Rudolf Glauber** (1604–68). The mineral Glauber's salt (also known as *sal mirabile* or mirabilite) forms naturally in salt lakes, or results from the action of volcanic gases on sea water.
13 **Dundee.** Desperate Dan has appeared in the *Dandy* since its first issue in 1937, while Minnie the Minx appears in the *Beano*; both comics are published in Dundee by D.C. Thomson.
14 **Hittites.** The treaty, with Hattusilis III, was cemented by Ramses II's marriage to the Hittite princess Matnefrure.
15 **Kodomono-hi.**
16 **Dinas Oleu**, above Barmouth on the Cardigan Bay coast. The National Trust was founded in January of that year by Octavia Hill, Sir Robert Hunter and Canon Hardwicke Rawnsley.
17 **'The Tyburn Tree'.** 'The Tree' was the gallows. Tyburn was a place of execution from the early fourteenth century to 1783, when the gallows were moved to Newgate. The name comes from the tributary of the Thames, the Tyburn, which meandered from the heights of Hampstead down to Whitehall.
18 **Lieutenant-Colonel Dr John McCrae** (1872–1918). His war poem *In Flanders Fields* was written at the Ypres Salient on 3 May 1915:

In Flanders fields the poppies blow
Between the crosses, row on row,
That mark our place; and in the sky
The larks, still bravely singing, fly
Scarce heard amid the guns below.

19 **Cleaning the privies and drains.**
20 **St David's Cathedral.**

Dogs

1 What kind of dog is Snoopy, created by Charles Schulz in 1950?
2 Which breed of dog are the English springer and the Welsh springer?
3 Which organisation for the registration of pedigree dogs was founded on 4 April 1873 at 2 Albert Mansions, Victoria Street, London?
4 In J.M. Barrie's play *Peter Pan: or The Boy Who Wouldn't Grow Up*, what was the name of the Darling family's dog, which was also the children's nurse?
5 In Greek mythology, what was the name of the three-headed dog which guarded the entrance to Hades?
6 The embalmed body of which famous greyhound (the first to win the English Greyhound Racing Derby twice – in 1929 and 1930) is on display at the Tring Zoological Museum?
7 What name is given to a crossbreed dog (usually the offspring of a greyhound and a collie or retriever) used by poachers for pursuing hares and rabbits?
8 In Homer's *Odyssey*, what was the name of Odysseus' dog, which recognised its master when he returned from his travels, and then died?
9 What are the seven categories in which the Kennel Club classifies pedigree dogs according to their origins?
10 What are the Dog Days?
11 The name of which type of hound comes from a French word meaning 'low'?
12 At the inaugural greyhound meeting at Wembley Stadium on 10 December 1927, how did a dog named Palatinus cause the third race to be rerun?
13 What breed of dog was Greyfriars Bobby, whose statue stands opposite Greyfriars Kirk in Candlemaker Row, Edinburgh?
14 In Hungary, what is the traditional work of the puli, which is now kept almost exclusively as a show dog in other countries?
15 In Shakespeare, who said, 'Cry "Havoc", and let slip the dogs of war'?
16 To whom did Alexander Pope give a dog, inside whose collar he is said to have written the following lines: 'I am his Highness' dog at Kew; Pray tell me, sir, whose dog are you?'
17 According to Muslim legend, what is the name of the dog of the Seven Sleepers which is one of the ten animals allowed into Heaven?
18 What breed of dog was Maida, Sir Walter Scott's dog, which is represented at his feet on the Scott Monument in Princes Street, Edinburgh?
19 What was the name of the original royal corgi, a Pembrokeshire, bought in 1933 by the future King George VI?
20 What was the name of the Pekingese dog, the first of the breed to reach Britain, which was found during the sack (by the British Army) of the Imperial Palace of Yuen-Ming-Yuan – the 'Summer Palace', near Beijing – in 1860, and presented to Queen Victoria by Captain John Hart Dunne of the 99th Regiment?

Dogs

Answers

1 **Beagle.** The *Peanuts* cartoon strips first appeared in seven US newspapers on 2 October 1950. Snoopy made his first appearance on 4 October.
2 **Spaniel.**
3 **The Kennel Club.** The meeting was called by Mr S.E. Shirley, MP for Ettington, Warwickshire.
4 **Nana.** She was based on Barrie's own dog, a Newfoundland named Luath.
5 **Cerberus.**
6 **Mick the Miller.** Its record was equalled by Patricia's Hope (1972 and 1973).
7 **Lurcher.** Lurcher was also a term for a petty thief or swindler.
8 **Argus** (*The Odyssey*, Book XVII).
9 **Hounds, gundogs, terriers, utility, working, pastoral** and **toy.**
10 **The hottest days of the summer**, which the Romans named *caniculares dies*. They believed that the Dog Star rising with the sun added to its heat. The dates vary depending on whether the Greater Dog Star (Sirius) or Lesser Dog Star (Procyon) is considered, but are generally accepted as 3 July to 15 August.
11 **Basset hound.**
12 **It caught the hare before the race was over.**
13 **Skye terrier.** There are several versions of the story of a Skye terrier which was often to be seen in the kirkyard of Greyfriars, where, it was believed, its owner had been buried in 1858. When the dog died, it, too, was buried there; its epitaph reads: 'Let his loyalty and devotion be a lesson to us all.'
14 **Herding flocks**, especially sheep.
15 **Mark Antony** (*Julius Caesar*, Act III, scene i).
16 **Frederick Louis, Prince of Wales** (1707–51). He was the eldest son of George II (and elder brother of William Augustus, Duke of Cumberland, who destroyed the Jacobite army at the Battle of Culloden in 1746). He would have succeeded his father as King Frederick in 1760 had he not been killed in 1751 by a ball while playing cricket; his eldest son, George, succeeded in his place, as George III.
17 **Katmir** (also known as Ketmir or Kratim). During the Diocletian persecution (in 303) the dog followed seven Christian youths of Ephesus to a cavern in which they were walled up and fell asleep for two hundred years. The dog remained standing until they awoke, without moving, eating, drinking or sleeping. According to Muslim legend, the nine other creatures allowed into heaven are: Jonah's whale, Noah's dove, Muhammad's horse, Al Borak (some lists include his camel, Al Adha), the ram sacrificed by Abraham, the ox of Moses, Solomon's ant, the lapwing of Balkis, Saleh's camel and Balaam's ass.
18 **Deerhound.**
19 **Dookie.** The Queen's present corgis (Phoenix, Kelpie and Swift), however, are tenth-generation descendants of the bitch Susan, which was given to the then Princess Elizabeth on her eighteenth birthday.
20 **Looty.** According to the *Illustrated London News*, 15 June 1861: 'No other dog like it was found, and it is supposed to have belonged to the Empress or to one of the ladies of the Imperial Family . . .'. However, other sources reveal that Looty was one of five Pekingese dogs found there; Admiral of the Fleet, Lord John Hay, took the other four, and gave two to the Duchess of Wellington and two to the Duchess of Richmond, who bred them at Goodwood. A portrait of Looty by Friedrich Wilhelm Keyl is in the Royal Collection.

General Knowledge Questions

1 Which breed of dog is featured in the Dulux paint advertisements?
2 In the children's story by Carlo Collodi (Lorenzini), what kind of creature acted as Pinocchio's conscience?
3 In which 1960 film did Elvis Presley sing *Wooden Heart*?
4 Which English football club is nicknamed the Hatters?
5 The recipe for which liqueur, the name of which means 'the drink which satisfies', did Bonnie Prince Charlie give to Captain John MacKinnon of Strathaird in gratitude for sheltering him at his home on Skye after the Battle of Culloden in 1746?
6 Where, in the human body, is the pisiform bone?
7 In text messaging, what does 'PCB' mean?
8 In the book of Genesis, to whom did God say: 'Two nations are in thy womb, and two manner of people shall be separated from thy bowels; and the one people shall be stronger than the other people; and the elder shall serve the younger.'?
9 From which 1925 musical does the song *Tea for Two* come?
10 In *Notes From a Small Island*, which English city did Bill Bryson describe as 'a perfect little city'?
11 What is *Alcyonium digitatum*, commonly known as 'dead men's fingers'?
12 Which word, meaning a long, rambling story, is derived from a term used to describe the returns of each Hundred to Edward I's inquest, and also the roll of Homage and Fealty made by the Scottish clergy and barons to Edward I?
13 Who designed *The Angel of the North*, the largest sculpture in Britain, which stands on a hilltop beside the A1 near Gateshead?
14 Who, in a poem by Charles Causley, had 'ears like bombs and teeth like splinters'?
15 Who struck the first blow in the murder of Thomas à Becket on 29 December 1170?
16 Which form of transport, first marketed by Enrico Piaggio in 1946, was designed specifically for travelling on roads damaged during the Second World War?
17 What is the real name of the veteran crossword-setter for the *Guardian*, 'Araucaria'?
18 Which play opens with the following lines?
'You've missed the point completely, Julia:
There were *no tigers*. That *was the point.'*
19 What name is given to diacritic marks such as the dot on a lower-case 'i'?
20 What was the name of Edward VII's wire-haired fox terrier which followed the coffin during his funeral procession in 1910?

1 **Old English sheepdog.** Dogs bred from the original Dulux dog have appeared in the advertisements for many years. The present one is called Max; he has a noticeable black marking, and all dogs born with that marking are reserved as the 'Dulux Dog' by the owners.
2 **A cricket** (in the 1940 Disney film he was called Jiminy Cricket).
3 ***GI Blues.*** The film was made just after Elvis had served in the US Army in Germany, and he sang part of the song in German.
4 **Luton Town.** Luton is known for the manufacture of straw hats.
5 **Drambuie.** The name comes from the Gaelic *An Dram Buidheach*, the name coined for the liqueur in 1893 at the Broadford Inn, Skye. The MacKinnons had passed on the recipe for generations for their own private consumption. It was first produced commercially in 1909 by Malcolm MacKinnon, who was in the whisky trade. He sold twelve cases of it that year.
6 **Wrist.** Pisiform means 'pea-shaped'.
7 **Please call back.**
8 **Rebecca,** the mother of Isaac's twin sons, Esau and Jacob (Genesis 25:23).
9 ***No, No, Nanette*** (composed by Vincent Youmans).
10 **Durham** (*Notes From a Small Island*, Chapter 24).
11 **A form of soft coral** found attached to rocks and seaweed which has finger-like projections.
12 **Rigmarole** (from Ragman Rolls). The term was given to the scrolls because of the ragged appearance created by the numerous pendant seals attached to them. There was a popular game named 'ragman' involving a roll with strings attached to it.
13 **Antony Gormley** (b. 1950). Digital technology was used to calculate the measurements for each piece of the 20-metre-high sculpture with its 54-metre wingspan, which was assembled in 1998.
14 **Timothy Winters.**
15 **Reginald FitzUrse.** His accomplices were William de Tracey, Richard le Breton and Hugh de Moreville.
16 **Motor scooter.** Piaggio had asked one of his aeronautical engineers, Corradino d'Ascanio, to come up with a simple, two-wheeled personal form of transport; he produced the Vespa.
17 **John Graham,** who took the name from the monkey puzzle tree. One of his inspired anagrams is 'synthetic cream' (from 'Manchester City').
18 ***The Cocktail Party*** by T.S. Eliot. The lines are spoken by Alex (Alexander MacColgie Gibbs).
19 **Tittle.** The noun comes from the Latin *titulus*, little stroke, accent. It came to mean 'a very small amount', as in the biblical phrase 'not one jot or tittle' (Matthew 5:18).
20 **Caesar.** The dog was bred by the Duchess of Newcastle and presented to the king by Lord Dudley in 1902. Caesar died in 1914 and was buried in the Dog Cemetery at Marlborough House, London; his image was later carved at the feet of Edward VII on his tomb in St George's Chapel, Windsor.

1 What is the name of Scotland's international rugby football stadium in Edinburgh?

2 Which Scottish poet wrote the following lines in his *Address to Edinburgh*?

Edina! Scotia's darling seat.
All hail thy palaces and tow'rs,
Where once beneath a monarch's feet,
Sat Legislation's sov'reign pow'rs . . .

3 What are the 'wynds' in Edinburgh and other Scottish towns?

4 What is the name of the mighty fifteenth-century cannon now on display in Edinburgh Castle?

5 By what name is the former North British Hotel (opened in 1902 by the North British Railway Company above Waverley Station) now known?

6 Edinburgh has three universities – what are they called?

7 What was the name of the stagnant loch which was drained in 1759–63 to facilitate the extension of Edinburgh into the New Town, and is now the site of Princes Street Gardens and the main railway line?

8 To whom is the tiny chapel at the highest point of the Castle Rock dedicated?

9 Which Battle of Britain fighter squadron, regarded as the city's own, was based at Turnhouse Airport during the Second World War?

10 When the Old Tolbooth, which served as Edinburgh's Council Chambers and prison, was demolished in 1817, which Scottish writer acquired its door and key for his own house?

11 Which princes are commemorated in the name of Princes Street?

12 Which popular museum, founded in 1955 in Lady Stair's House by a bachelor town councillor, is now housed in Hyndford House in the High Street?

13 Which renowned TV cook opened, in Edinburgh's West Bow in 1995, a bookshop devoted solely to cookery books?

14 Which narrow Edinburgh alley, now 'buried' under the City Chambers, was abandoned and walled up after an outbreak of the plague in 1645?

15 Which two First World War poets, recovering from shell shock, convalesced at Craiglockhart Hospital after returning from the Western Front?

16 A seated bronze sculpture of which Edinburgh philosopher wearing a toga was unveiled in 1997 in front of the High Court of Justiciary?

17 Which dockyard was the birthplace of the massive *Great Michael*, launched in 1511 by King James IV during his naval arms race with his brother-in-law, Henry VIII?

18 In 1840 which Swiss-born geologist identified, at the foot of Blackford Hill, grooves and striations on an overhanging rock which proved his theory of a series of Ice Ages and the effect of glaciation on landscape?

19 Which pioneering Scots-born botanist and town planner established a 'sociological laboratory' in the Outlook Tower at the top of Castlehill, which now houses the Camera Obscura?

20 During the Scottish Enlightenment in the late eighteenth century, which English visitor is recorded as saying, 'Here I stand at what is called the Cross of Edinburgh, and can, in a few minutes, take fifty men of genius by the hand'?

1 **Murrayfield.**
2 **Robert Burns** (1759–96).
3 **Narrow lanes or alleys.** Sir Walter Scott, for instance, was born in College Wynd.
4 **Mons Meg.** It was presented to James II by Philip the Good, Duke of Burgundy, after the marriage of James to Philip's niece, Marie of Gueldres.
5 **Balmoral Hotel.**
6 **Edinburgh** (founded 1583), **Heriot-Watt** (1966) and **Napier** (1992).
7 **The Nor' Loch** (North Loch).
8 **St Margaret** (c. 1046–93), wife of Malcolm III (Canmore). It is the oldest surviving building in Edinburgh.
9 **603 Squadron of the RAF.**
10 **Sir Walter Scott.** His novel *The Heart of Midlothian* (1818) was named after the iron box in the centre of the building which served as the condemned cell. Scott built the door into an upper wall of Abbotsford, near Melrose.
11 **Duke of Rothesay** (the future George IV) and **Duke of York**, the sons of King George III. The name first proposed for the new thoroughfare was 'St Giles Street', but George III objected because the name reminded him of a slum area in London.
12 **Museum of Childhood.** Councillor Patrick Murray (d. 1987) always claimed he did not like children.
13 **Clarissa Dickson Wright**, one of television's *Two Fat Ladies* (the other was Jennifer Paterson, who died in 1999).
14 **Mary King's Close.** The surviving buildings form an 'underground' warren of rooms, which crime writer Ian Rankin used as the setting of the opening murder in his 1994 novel *Mortal Causes*. One of the rooms, known simply as 'the little girl's room', is reputed to be haunted by the ghost of a child; since the area was opened to tourists, the room has become a shrine to her memory and many visitors leave toys and money for her there.
15 **Wilfred Owen** (1893–1918) and **Siegfried Sassoon** (1886–1967).
16 **David Hume** (1711–76), sculpted by Alexander Stoddart. The inscription describes him as 'a Scot and European, man of the Enlightenment'.
17 **Newhaven**, at the western extremity of Leith Docks. The *Great Michael* was the largest and most powerful warship in the world at the time; it took six years to build, and 'wasted all the woods in Fife', according to a contemporary writer.
18 **Louis Agassiz** (1807–73). The scratches on the underhang of the Agassiz Rock, by the Braid Burn, are still clearly visible.
19 **Patrick Geddes** (1854–1932).
20 **'Mr Amyat, King's Chemist'.** The remark was reported by the printer and antiquary William Smellie in *Literary and Characteristic Lives of Gregory, Kames, Hume and Smithy*, 1800. 'The Cross of Edinburgh' was the Mercat (Market) Cross beside St Giles.

General Knowledge Questions

1 What is the name of the Edinburgh café in which J.K. Rowling scribbled her first draft of *Harry Potter and the Philosopher's Stone*?
2 By what name is a Cub Scout pack leader known?
3 What is the French term for their ultra high-speed trains?
4 Who won the title of European Footballer of the Year in 2001?
5 Which is the only one of New York's five boroughs to be on the mainland?
6 Which pop-singing duo produced a hit World Cup single in 2002 with their version of an old Arsenal song, *We're on the Ball?*
7 In web-speak, for what do the initials html stand?
8 In a children's book, who gave directions to his home as 'second to the right and straight on till morning'?
9 Which French Impressionist artist depicted a firing squad and its victim in the painting *The Execution of Emperor Maximilian*?
10 Which Dutch-born former songwriter and music producer restored the 'Lost Gardens of Heligan', near Mevagissey, Cornwall, in the 1990s, and masterminded the Eden Project ('the world's largest greenhouse') near St Austell, which went on public view in 2000?
11 From the Latin name for which small mammal is the word 'muscle' derived?
12 Who was the architect of the Expiatory Church of the Sagrada Familia (Holy Family) in Barcelona?
13 What is the common name of the amber-coloured berry *Rubus chamaemorus*, commonly used in northern Scandinavia in tarts, preserves and other confections?
14 What was the occupation of a bummaree?
15 What kind of animal is the American-Indian 'wishtonwish'?
16 What was the name of the elite corps, meaning 'New Soldiers', in the Ottoman Empire from the fourteenth century to 1826?
17 What, in music, is a paradiddle?
18 The 'Alfred Jewel', which was found near Athelney in Somerset in 1693, was part of an Anglo-Saxon *æstel*; what was the function of an *æstel*?
19 From whom was the word 'grog' (for 'rum') derived?
20 Which twentieth-century Scottish poet, whose real name was Christopher Murray Grieve, was once a pupil-teacher at Broughton Higher Grade School in Edinburgh?

1 **Nicolsons** (Nicolsons Restaurant) in Nicolson Street. It is owned by her restaurateur brother-in-law Roger Moore.
2 **Akela.** Akela was a wolf in Rudyard Kipling's *Jungle Book* (1894).
3 **TGV** (Train à Grande Vitesse).
4 **Michael Owen** (Liverpool FC).
5 **The Bronx.** Jonas Bronck, a Scandinavian, bought the 200-hectare plot from the Dutch West India Co in 1641, and it became known as 'Bronck's Land', which in turn became 'Bronx'.
6 ***Ant and Dec*** (Anthony McPartlin and Declan Donnolly, from Fenham in Newcastle).
7 **HyperText Mark-up Language**, a code in which web pages are created.
8 **Peter Pan** (in J.M. Barrie's *Peter and Wendy*, 1911). That, Peter had told Wendy, was the way to the Neverland.
9 **Édouard Manet** (1832–83). Ferdinand Joseph Maximilian (1832–67), Archduke of Austria and Emperor of Mexico, was defeated by the Mexican patriotic leader Benito Juárez at Querétaro and executed.
10 **Tim Smit** (b. 1954). He took a degree in archaeology and anthropology at Durham University before playing with the band The Shake. He wrote the song *Midnight Blue* (1983).
11 **Mouse** (Latin *musculus* – little mouse). The movements of some muscles apparently suggest the way a mouse moves.
12 **Antonio Gaudí** (1852–1926). He directed the building operation from the 1880s until his death. The church is still unfinished.
13 **Cloudberry.** It is also called bakeberry, baked apple berry, malka, salmonberry and yellowberry.
14 **Market porter.** A bummaree was a middleman at Billingsgate Fish Market, London; the word is also used for a self-employed porter at London's Smithfield Meat Market.
15 **Prairie dog.**
16 **Janissaries.** They were originally Christian conscripts from the Balkans who were converted to Islam. They became a powerful political force and engineered many palace coups, but came to an end when they rebelled and were massacred.
17 **A basic drum roll produced by beating with alternate drumsticks.**
18 **An *æstel* was a pointer for following the text of a manuscript.** The 'Alfred Jewel' (now in the Ashmolean Museum in Oxford) is inscribed with the words 'AELFRED MEC HEHT GEWYRCAN' ('Alfred ordered me to be made'). King Alfred sent an *æstel* to each bishopric with a copy of his translation of Pope Gregory the Great's *Pastoral Care.*
19 **Admiral Edward Vernon** (1684–1757). As Commander-in-Chief, West Indies, he diluted with water the daily issue of neat rum to officers and ratings. He was known as 'Old Grog' from his coat of grogram (from the French *gros grain*, a coarse fabric stiffened and made waterproof with gum), and the name was transferred to the new beverage. The grog ration for Navy ratings was abolished in 1970.
20 **Hugh MacDiarmid** (1892–1978).

Fashion Questions

1 By what name did Lesley Hornby (now Lawson) come to prominence as a fashion model in the 1960s?
2 Which British fashion designer, who built up the clothing chain Next in the 1980s, created a clothing range for Asda between 1990 and 2000 and another (Per Una) for Marks & Spencer in 2001?
3 Which fashion designer and photographer won two Academy Awards (for Colour Costume Design and Colour Art Direction) for the screen version of *My Fair Lady*?
4 For which article of clothing is the Malaysian-born designer Jimmy Choo renowned?
5 Who was the designer of the silk crêpe dress held together with safety pins which Elizabeth Hurley wore for the premiere of the 1994 film *Four Weddings and a Funeral*?
6 Which Paris fashion designer launched the 'Space Age Look' in the late 1960s?
7 Which Algerian-born couturier founded a world-famous fashion house in Paris in 1962 and designed the 'Mondrian' dress for his winter collection of 1965?
8 Which 1966 film was about a hip fashion photographer, played by David Hemmings, who inadvertently photographed a murder which was revealed in a series of enlargements?
9 What name was given to the brief shorts worn over tights, sometimes with an open-fronted skirt, which were popular in the 1970s?
10 In 1963 who founded the London boutique Biba?
11 Which fashion house designed the 'Kelly Bag', named after Princess Grace of Monaco, who popularised it in the 1950s?
12 In Elizabethan and Jacobean England, what could be worn in styles such as *pique devant*, screw, hammercut, sugar-loaf and swallow-tail?
13 In 1907 who designed the 'Delphos', a flowing dress made from a tube of finely pleated silk fastened with a cord drawn through the neckline?
14 In medieval academic and clerical dress, what was a liripipe?
15 In 1974 who was the first black fashion model to be featured on the cover of US *Vogue*?
16 In 1936 who designed the 'Desk Suit' featuring vertical true and false pockets made to look like desk drawers, and based on Salvador Dalí's *City of Drawers* and *Venus de Milo of Drawers*?
17 In seventeenth-century England what name was given to a very long lock of hair (worn by men) falling forward on to the chest and tied with a ribbon?
18 Which former assistant of Nino Cerruti came to the fore after designing the clothes worn by Richard Gere in the 1980 film *American Gigolo*?
19 Which editor-in-chief of US *Vogue* from 1963 to 1971 wrote the 'Why don't you . . .?' column in *Harpers Bazaar* using phrases which became fashion clichés, such as 'Fashion is refusal' and 'Pink is the navy blue of India'?
20 Who, in a Gilbert and Sullivan operetta, had 'a swallowtail coat of a beautiful blue, a couple of shirts and a collar or two'?

Fashion

Answers

1 **Twiggy** (b. 1949).
2 **George Davies** (b. 1942).
3 **Cecil Beaton** (1904–80).
4 **Shoes.**
5 **Gianni Versace** (1946–97).
6 **Pierre Cardin** (b. 1922).
7 **Yves Saint Laurent** (b. 1936). He retired at the age of sixty-five in 2002.
8 *Blow Up*, directed by Michelangelo Antonioni.
9 **Hot pants.**
10 **Barbara Hulanicki** (b. 1936).
11 **Hermès.** The bag was modelled on the 'high handle' bag used as a carrying case for saddles. Thierry Hermès was a master saddler and harness maker who set up his Paris workshop in 1879. His grandsons now run the fashion house, which produces a range of leather goods as well as clothing and perfumes.
12 **Beards.**
13 **Mariano Fortuny** (1871–1949). The 1909 patent for the dress stated, 'This invention is related to a type of garment derived from the classical robe but its design is so shaped and arranged that it can be worn and adjusted with ease and comfort.'
14 **A very long tail, or tippet, of a hood.** The word also means a lesson committed to memory, or a foolish person.
15 **Beverly Johnson.**
16 **Elsa Schiaparelli** (1890–1973).
17 **Love lock.**
18 **Giorgio Armani** (b. 1935). Every scene was choreographed to show the clothes to their best advantage, prompting Richard Gere to ask, 'Who's acting in this scene – me or the jacket?'
19 **Diana Vreeland** (1906–89).
20 **The Judge**, in *Trial by Jury*.

1 What is the name of Gianni Versace's sister, who took over as head of the fashion house in 1997 when her brother was murdered?
2 In 1986 which former Page 3 model in the *Sun* newspaper recorded the single *Touch Me* which reached No. 3 in the UK charts?
3 Which North African dish is prepared by steaming semolina grains in the upper compartment of a large covered pot in whose lower part a stew is cooked simultaneously?
4 In which Spanish city is the Prado Museum?
5 Which Hebridean island was the location for the 2000 BBC TV series *Castaway*?
6 Which president of Chile was overthrown in September 1973 in a military junta by General Pinochet and died in the presidential palace in Santiago during the fighting?
7 One of the names for which US state is the 'Valentine State', so called from the day on which it was admitted as a state of the USA?
8 The declaration of which faith is known as the Shahada?
9 The role of which English missionary in China was played by Ingrid Bergman in the 1958 film *The Inn of the Sixth Happiness*?
10 In which sport is the Corbillon Cup awarded to women's teams?
11 Which post was held by Robert Greene (for Elizabeth I), Archie Armstrong and Thomas Derrie (for King James VI and I) and Muckle John (for Charles I)?
12 From which medieval student song do the following lines come?

Post jocundam juventutem,
Post molestam senectutem,
Nos habebit humus.

13 What was the name of the Swedish writer of children's stories who created Pippi Longstocking?
14 In which British city did the Gala Theatre open on 15 January 2002 with Alan Ayckbourn's new trilogy *Damsels in Distress* (*GamePlan*, *FlatSpin* and *RolePlay*)?
15 In Greek mythology, which hero slew the Gorgon Medusa?
16 Which US theoretical physicist won the Nobel Prize for physics in 1969 for his work on predicting the existence of 'quarks'?
17 Which idiom, meaning 'the centre of attention', arose from a device made in 1816 by the Scottish engineer, Thomas Drummond (1797–1840), for use as a marker for map-making in poor weather conditions?
18 What type of fabric is 'prunella'?
19 What popular name was given to the Prisoners (Temporary Discharge for Ill-Health) Act 1913, whereby suffragettes on hunger strike in prison could be freed for health reasons and subsequently rearrested when they recovered?
20 Which Paris fashion designer introduced the 'Sack Look', also known as the 'H-line', in 1954?

General Knowledge Answers

1 **Donatella Versace** (b. 1955).
2 **Samantha Fox** (b. 1966). She had formed a band at the age of fourteen and was offered a recording contract, but instead started modelling for the *Sun*. Afterwards she returned to singing.
3 **Couscous**. Semolina, from which pasta products are also made, is the endosperm of durum wheat (*Triticum durum*).
4 **Madrid**.
5 **Taransay**. It lies off the west coast of the island of Harris.
6 **Salvador Allende** (1908–73).
7 **Arizona**. It was admitted on 14 February in 1912. It is also known as the 'Aztec State', 'Apache State' and 'Grand Canyon State'.
8 **Islam**. It is the First Pillar of Islam and states, 'I declare that there is no god except Allah. Muhammad is the Messenger of Allah. He is One and has no partner. And I also declare that Muhammad is His Servant and His Messenger.'
9 **Gladys Aylward** (1902–70). With the Scottish missionary Jeannie Lawson, she founded the Inn of the Sixth Happiness in Yangcheng as a base from which to preach. They used to tell Bible stories to travellers. The film was based on the book *The Small Woman* (1957) by Alan Burgess.
10 **Table tennis**. The Swaythling Cup for national men's teams has been awarded since 1926, when the International Table Tennis Federation was founded. In 1933 the equivalent Corbillon Cup for women was donated by Marcel Corbillon, president of the French association. Both awards are now biennial.
11 **Court fool**.
12 ***Gaudeamus Igitur*** ('Let us then rejoice'). The lines mean: 'After the pleasures of youth, after the travails of old age, the earth shall hold us.' The words are of medieval origin; the traditional melody forms the final theme in Brahms's *Academic Festival Overture*.
13 **Astrid Lindgren** (1970–2002).
14 **Durham**. The theatre is part of the 'Millennium City' project.
15 **Perseus**. Medusa's eyes turned to stone anyone she looked at, but Perseus borrowed the helmet of Hades, which made him invisible.
16 **Murray Gell-Mann** (b. 1929). The word 'quark' has no meaning of its own: it was plucked by Gell-Mann from a phrase in James Joyce's *Finnegans Wake*: 'Three quarks for Muster Mark.'
17 **In the limelight**. The marker lamps burned calcium oxide (lime), which gave off a soft, yet brilliant, white light when heated, and could be seen from long distances. The 'Drummond light' was first used in a theatre in 1837, to draw attention to the central character on stage.
18 **A worsted cloth**, formerly used for clergymen's gowns and the uppers of women's boots. The name is thought to have come from the colour of the cloth (from the French *prune*, plum).
19 **Cat and Mouse Act**.
20 **Christian Dior** (1905–57).

Geology Questions

1 What is measured on the Richter scale?
2 Of what type of geological feature is 'The Witch's Kitchen' in the Mendip Hills an example?
3 What name do geologists give to rocks such as granite and basalt formed from cooled and crystallised magma?
4 By what name are the extinct volcanic cones in the Dore mountains in the Auvergne region of France known?
5 What unique variety of fluorite (calcium fluoride) is found only near Castleton in the Peak District National Park and is used for making jewellery and ornaments?
6 In 1912 what name was coined by the German meteorologist Alfred Wegener for the supercontinent which was thought to have split into the present continents?
7 On which Antarctic island is the active volcano Mount Erebus?
8 What type of rock used to be quarried from the Llechwedd caverns in Blaenau Ffestiniog in the Parc Cenedlaethol Eryri (Snowdonia National Park)?
9 Alabaster is a form of which mineral, composed of hydrated calcium sulphate?
10 What is the Hoba West, which was found in 1920 near Grootfontein in what is now Namibia?
11 On Mohs' scale, developed in 1812 by the German mineralogist Friedrich Mohs, which mineral is the softest?
12 What name is given to the fossilised marine arthropod with a distinctive three-lobed, three-segmented form which is commonly found around the shores of Britain?
13 Which non-metallic mineral is mined using the Frasch process?
14 Which eighteenth-century Edinburgh scientist and philosopher is regarded as 'the father of modern geology'?
15 What name is given to the weathered sandstone outcrops found across the North York Moors, the most famous of which is on Grime Moor?
16 By what name is the mineral ferric oxide commonly known because of its red colour, arising from its high iron content?
17 What is the name of the 137-metre-high sandstone sea stack off Rora Head in the Orkneys?
18 What is the main characteristic of a 'logan' – for example, Logan Rock, near Land's End?
19 What name is given to a depression in a glacial outwash made by the melting of a detached mass of glacial ice which became wholly or partly buried?
20 Which Scottish stonemason and journalist from Cromarty on the Black Isle made a major contribution, in 1841, to the development of the study of geology with his collection of essays entitled *The Old Red Sandstone*?

1 **The strength or magnitude of earthquakes.** The scale, which was introduced in 1935, is named after the US seismologist Charles Richter (1900–85), who devised it with his German-born colleague Beno Gutenberg (1889–1960).
2 **Cavern.** It is part of a network of caverns worn in the limestone by the River Axe in which there is a stone formation with the appearance of a witch's head. According to legend, a witch who terrorised the local people lived there. A monk named Father Bernard was called in to exorcise her spirit from the cavern; when she ran off, screaming curses at him, he blessed the pool there and threw a handful of its water at the witch, who was immediately turned into stone.
3 **Igneous rocks** (from the Latin *ignis*, fire).
4 **Puys.** The largest are the Puy de Sancy (1885 metres) and the Puy de Dôme (1464 metres).
5 **Blue John** (from the French *bleu jaune*, blue yellow. Blue John was discovered by miners searching for lead in the eighteenth century.
6 **Pangaea.** The splitting is thought to have begun during the Triassic Period (between 245 and 208 million years ago).
7 **Ross Island.** Mount Erebus is the highest point on the island.
8 **Slate.**
9 **Gypsum.**
10 **The largest known meteorite.** The estimated weight of the nickel-and-lead meteorite is 60 tons.
11 **Talc.** Mohs' scale grades minerals from 1 to 10, according to hardness. Each mineral will scratch those of lower hardnesses: talc = 1, gypsum = 2, calcite = 3, fluorite = 4, apatite = 5, orthoclase = 6, quartz = 7, topaz = 8, corundum = 9, diamond =10.
12 **Trilobite.** Trilobites appeared at the beginning of the Cambrian Period, about 540 million years ago, when they dominated the seas.
13 **Sulphur.** The process was patented in 1891 by the German-born US chemist Herman Frasch (1851–1914); it produces sulphur of a very high degree of purity by forcing superheated water into the sulphur deposit.
14 **James Hutton** (1726–97). His *Theory of the Earth* (1788) challenged the creation theory of the earth embodied in the Bible. 'Hutton's Section' at the south end of Salisbury Crags in Edinburgh, now a magnet for visiting geologists, is where he demonstrated that the rocks of the Crags were formed by the intrusion and cooling of hot molten rocks.
15 **Bridestones.**
16 **Haematite,** from *haima* (Greek, blood).
17 **The Old Man of Hoy.** The stack, on a basalt base, was separated from the island by erosion.
18 **It rocks.** It is a boulder, perched on top of another rock, which can be rocked backwards and forwards without overturning. A logan is also known as a 'rocking stone'.
19 **Kettle,** or **kettle hole.**
20 **Hugh Miller** (1802–56). His birthplace (Hugh Miller's Cottage), a low, thatched cottage in Cromarty, north of Inverness, is now a museum dedicated to his memory and is in the care of the National Trust for Scotland.

1 The geological term magma for molten rock below the surface of the earth is derived from a Greek verb meaning what?
2 In which South American city is the Maracana Stadium, the holder of the world record for the highest official attendance at a football match?
3 The seeds of which plant form the principal ingredient of hummus (hummous)?
4 In about 1568–9 who painted a banquet of peasants entitled *Peasant Wedding* which featured bagpipers and a pair of men bearing a huge wooden tray carrying bowls of soup?
5 During the Second World War, what was the government-recommended depth for a hot bath, in order to save fuel?
6 What is the derivation of the word 'journeyman', as applied to a craftsman?
7 In Greek mythology, who was 'the first woman'?
8 What did the Metropolitan Police carry as an alarm signal before they finally adopted whistles towards the end of the nineteenth century?
9 Which solid, white, waxy hydrocarbon with the chemical formula $C_{10}H_8$ is obtained from coal tar and gives mothballs their distinctive smell?
10 In 1947 which French mime artist created the sad, white-faced clown Bip?
11 Where in Scotland is the birthplace of the historian and essayist Thomas Carlyle (1795–1881)?
12 Which instrument represents the cat in Prokofiev's *Peter and the Wolf*?
13 What was the name of the spiritualistic medium played by Margaret Rutherford in both the 1941 stage and 1945 film versions of Noel Coward's *Blithe Spirit*?
14 In 1794 which old code did the French engineer Claude Chappe use in his mechanical visual telegraph?
15 What is the term for a unit of astronomical distance equivalent to 3.262 light-years?
16 What did the Ancient Greeks and Romans call northern Afghanistan, between the Hindu Kush mountains and the River Oxus?
17 'The best thing since sliced bread' – who patented the first bread-slicing and wrapping machine?
18 The world's first multi-coloured postage stamp was issued in Switzerland in July 1845; by what name is it known to philatelists?
19 At which railway station in England is there a stuffed and mounted mongrel collie, known as 'Station Jim', displayed in a glass case on Platform 5?
20 Which technical word for volcanic ash was coined from the Greek by the Icelandic vulcanologist Sigurður Þórarinsson?

General Knowledge Answers

1 **To knead** (*massein*).
2 **Rio de Janeiro** (199,854). The match, in which Uruguay beat Brazil 2–1, took place on 16 July 1950. In addition to the official attendance, some 5000 spectators broke into the stadium without paying.
3 **Chick pea** (*Cicer arietinum*). The boiled chick peas are mashed to a paste and mixed with lemon juice, olive oil, garlic and sesame paste.
4 **Pieter Bruegel the Elder** (c. 1525–69). The painting now hangs in the Kunsthistorisches Museum in Vienna.
5 **Five inches.**
6 **Someone qualified to work at his trade for a day's wages** (from the French *jour*, day).
7 **Pandora**. She was fashioned by the gods as punishment on the human race for obtaining fire from Prometheus; she was endowed with all attributes of grace, beauty, cogency and dexterity, as well as lying and deceit.
8 **A rattle.**
9 **Naphthalene.**
10 **Marcel Marceau** (b. 1923).
11 **Ecclefechan**, Dumfriesshire ('The Arched House'). The house was built by his father and uncle, who were stonemasons. It is now a museum run by the National Trust for Scotland.
12 **Clarinet.**
13 **Madame Arcati.**
14 **Semaphore**. The name *télégraphe* (far-writer) was coined by Chappe (1763–1805). His work was developed in Britain by Charles Pasley (1780–1861), who created the Universal Telegraph, which incorporated oil lamps into the mechanical arms so that the system could be used at night.
15 **Parsec** (the term is a contraction of 'parallax second').
16 **Bactria**, the country invaded by Alexander the Great in 329 BC. The Bactrian (two-humped) camel, used as a beast of burden in the cold deserts of central Asia, derives its name from the region.
17 **Otto Frederick Rohwedder**. He began work on his machine in 1912. After being told by his doctor, in 1915, that he had only a year to live, he went on to replace the prototype which he lost in a fire in 1917 and, still alive in 1928, he produced and patented the machine. He first sold one to his local bakery in Battle Creek, Michigan, and then several to the Continental Bakery of New York for its pre-sliced, pre-wrapped Wonder Bread.
18 **'Basle Dove'**. It was issued in Basle, and depicted a dove in flight with a letter in its beak.
19 **Slough**. For many years, until his death in November 1896, 'Station Jim' worked as the Canine Collector for the Great Western Railway Widows' and Orphans' Fund, with leather collection boxes strapped across his shoulders. *Station Jim* was also the title of a 2001 BBC TV film about a dog (a Jack Russell) which helps to save a Victorian rural railway station from the clutches of developers.
20 **Tephra** (literally, 'ashes').

Horses

Questions

1 What was the name of the horse which the Duke of Wellington rode at the Battle of Waterloo on 18 June 1815?
2 Which nineteenth-century English novelist wrote the children's classic *Black Beauty: The Autobiography of a Horse* (1877)?
3 In which 1944 film did Elizabeth Taylor play the part of a young girl who wins an unmanageable horse named Pirate (Pie) in a raffle and goes on to win the Grand National on it?
4 What was the name of Princess Anne's horse on which she won the individual gold medal at the 1971 European Three-Day Event at Burghley?
5 Which Suffolk town is the home of the National Horseracing Museum?
6 What is the proper name for the renowned White Horses of Vienna used in the Spanish Riding School there?
7 In the 1950s television series *The Lone Ranger*, what was the name of Tonto's horse?
8 Which Liverpool-born playwright wrote the 1973 play *Equus* about an psychoanalyst's relationship with a horse-obsessed patient?
9 Which jockey rode the Derby winners Grundy (in 1975), Golden Fleece (in 1982) and Quest for Fame (in 1990)?
10 The name of which breed of horse with a barrel-shaped body and short legs comes from a Neapolitan dialect word for a short, stout person?
11 What are the ingredients of the drink known as a Horse's Neck?
12 What was the name of Tam o' Shanter's grey mare in Robert Burns's ballad of the same name?
13 In the 1870s which nineteenth-century Russian soldier and explorer discovered a rare breed of wild horses, native to the Mongolian steppes, which now bears his name?
14 What were the colours of the horses ridden by the Four Horsemen of the Apocalypse?
15 Who was the most famous rider on the Pony Express in the USA from 1860 to 1861?
16 What is the Argentinian breed of miniature horse evolved at a ranch near Buenos Aires, and recognised as the smallest horse in the world?
17 Which Liberal Prime Minister's horses won the Derby in both years of his premiership?
18 Which 1825 painting by Constable depicts a barge horse being trained to jump stiles on the towpath?
19 Who, according to Homer, designed the Trojan Horse which brought about the downfall of the city of Troy?
20 The Icelandic horse (*Equus scandinavicus*) is unique in having five separate gaits: step (*fetgangur*), trot (*brokk*), gallop (*stökk*), pace (*skeið*) – and which other, which sets the Icelandic horse apart from all other European breeds?

1 **Copenhagen.**
2 **Anna Sewell** (1820–78). Born in Great Yarmouth in Norfolk, she was an invalid for most of her life. *Black Beauty*, her only novel, was written for children as a plea for the more humane treatment of animals.
3 *National Velvet.* Elizabeth Taylor played the part of Velvet Brown.
4 **Doublet.** In 1974 Doublet broke his leg and had to be put down; in the European Championships in 1975, as a member of the British silver-medal-winning team, the princess rode Goodwill.
5 **Newmarket.**
6 **Lipizzaner**, from the Austrian imperial stud at Lipizza, in Slovenia, which used to be part of the Austro-Hungarian Empire.
7 **Scout.** The Lone Ranger's horse was named Silver. The films were based on an original US radio series about John Reid (b. 1850), the sole survivor of a group of ambushed Texas rangers, who was found and nursed back to health by Tonto.
8 **Peter Levin Shaffer** (b. 1926).
9 **Pat Eddery** (b. 1952).
10 **Punch** (as in Suffolk Punch), from Punchinello (Polecinella), the stock character from the *commedia dell'arte*.
11 **Brandy and ginger ale** – a long drink served on ice.
12 **Meg** (also Maggie). She saved her master from an attack by ghosts and witches by crossing a stream ahead of them (witches cannot cross running water), but lost her tail in the process – it was pulled out by one of the pursuing horde.
13 **Nikolai Mikhailovich Przewalski** (1839–88). The Przewalski is the only current breed of wild horse.
14 **White, red, black and pale** (Revelation 6:1–7). The first two riders symbolised war, the third and fourth famine and death.
15 **William (Buffalo Bill) Cody** (1846–1917). The Pony Express delivered mail by continuous horse-and-rider relays from St Joseph, Missouri, to Sacramento, California – a distance of 2900 kilometres. It was superseded by the transcontinental telegraph system in 1861. Bill Cody earned his sobriquet for killing nearly 5000 buffalo for a contract to supply meat for the workers on the Union Pacific Railway (1867–8).
16 **Falabella.** Its average height is 76 centimetres.
17 **Earl of Rosebery,** Prime Minister from 1894 to 1895. He was a keen race-goer, and won the Derby three times – 1894 (Ladas), 1895 (Sir Visto) and 1905 (Cicero).
18 ***Leaping Horse.*** Canal horses had to negotiate obstacles such as boundary fences, stiles, bridges and tunnels.
19 **Epeios.** When the Greeks had apparently given up the siege of Troy, Odysseus thought up the scheme of leaving a huge wooden horse outside the walls as a farewell gift. The Trojans dragged it into their city; but concealed in it were Odysseus, Menelaos and a band of champions, who emerged that night and sacked the city.
20 ***Tölt*** (running walk). The Icelandic horse was brought to Iceland by the original settlers from Norway, and has never been crossbred.

General Knowledge Questions

1 Which seventeenth-century literary character rode a hack named Rosinante?
2 Which pop song was the Christmas No. 1 in the UK in 2001?
3 What is the derivation of the word 'navvy', meaning a labourer?
4 What is the name of the official country residence of the British Prime Minister?
5 Which Victorian novelist is credited with the invention of the Post Office's pillar box?
6 Which biblical character, who complained to Jesus that her sister Mary did not do enough housework, is invoked as the patron saint of housewives?
7 What is the Aboriginal name by which Ayers Rock in the Northern Territory of Australia is once again known?
8 Who succeeded Arnold Wolfendale (b. 1927) as Astronomer Royal in 1995?
9 Which London landmark is bordered by Maple Street, Cleveland Street, Cleveland Mews and Howland Street in the area of central London sometimes known as Fitzrovia?
10 What was the title of Terence Rattigan's 1946 play about the trial of George Archer-Shee, a cadet who was expelled from the Royal Naval Academy accused of stealing a five-shilling postal order?
11 The French region which produces the wine Entre Deux Mers lies between which two rivers?
12 What does Primrose Day (19 April) commemorate?
13 At what public occasions in Ancient Rome would the participants salute the emperor with the words *Morituri te salutant*?
14 In the film of Tolkien's *Lord of the Rings*, which actor plays the part of the hobbit Bilbo Baggins, having taken the role of his adopted young nephew, Frodo Baggins, in Brian Sibley's radio serialisation of the epic in 1981?
15 Sir Arthur Sullivan composed the music for the song *The Lost Chord*; which Victorian feminist poet had composed the following words?

Seated one day at the organ,
I was weary and ill at ease,
And my fingers wandered idly
Over the noisy keys...
But I struck one chord of music
Like the sound of a great Amen.

16 For which major constellation was 'Charles's Wain' a popular name?
17 Which group of architects designed the futuristic new 'submarium', The Deep, an ocean discovery centre at Sammy's Point, a derelict riverside site in Kingston upon Hull?
18 Which Australian bowler's first ball in a Test Match in England was the so-called 'ball of the century' which dismissed Mike Gatting in the England v Australia Test at Old Trafford in 1993?
19 In the textile industry, what did 'preemer boys' do?
20 Which Scottish monarch owned a palfrey named Black Agnes?

1 **Don Quixote**, in the two-part novel by Miguel de Cervantes (1547–1616).
2 ***Somethin' Stupid*** (Robbie Williams and Nicole Kidman). The same song (written by C. Carson Parks) also reached No. 1 in 1967 when Frank and Nancy Sinatra recorded it.
3 **Navigator** (builder of a navigation, i.e., canal).
4 **Chequers**, in Buckinghamshire. It was presented to the nation in 1917 for that purpose by Arthur Hamilton Lee (1868–1947), Conservative MP for Fareham. The first Prime Minister to use it was Lloyd George, in 1921.
5 **Anthony Trollope** (1815–82). Trollope was a professional civil servant in the Post Office until he resigned in 1867; by that time he was earning £70,000 a year from his 'spare-time' occupation of writing.
6 **Martha of Bethany**. She was the sister of Lazarus and Mary. She is represented in art with a bunch of keys at her girdle and holding a ladle or a broom.
7 **Uluru**. It is one of the thirty-six Katajuta ('many heads'), also known as the Olgas, the isolated, weathered, red conglomerate rocks in the Uluru-Kata Tjuta National Park. It was named after Sir Henry Ayers (1821–97), premier of South Australia seven times between 1863 and 1873.
8 **Martin Rees** (b. 1942), Royal Society Research Professor at Cambridge University.
9 **BT Tower**. Work began on the 189-metre tower (designed by the Ministry of Public Building Works) in April 1961 and it was opened on 8 October 1965.
10 ***The Winslow Boy***. Edward Carson, the barrister employed by the boy's father, Martin Archer-Shee, issued a Petition of Right against the College. Edward VII signed the petition 'Let Right be Done', allowing the prosecutor to proceed. The admiralty challenged and won, but Carson appealed and the ruling was overturned. The Archer-Shee family was later awarded £3000 in addition to costs, but no formal apology or withdrawal of charges. George Archer-Shee was killed in action at Ypres in 1914.
11 **Garonne** and **Dordogne**.
12 **Anniversary of the death of Benjamin Disraeli** (1804–81). The primrose was (mistakenly) believed to be Disraeli's favourite flower, from the wreath sent to his funeral by Queen Victoria: 'His favourite flowers from Osborne, a tribute of affection from Queen Victoria.'
13 **Gladiatorial circuses**. It means: 'Those who are about to die salute you.'
14 **Ian Holm** (b. 1931).
15 **Adelaide Ann Procter** (pseudonym of Mary Berwick, 1825–64). Her poem *A Lost Chord* was published in *Legends and Lyrics* (1858). Sullivan composed the music at the bedside of his dying brother Frederick in 1877.
16 **Ursa Major** (the Plough) – probably a contraction of 'Charlemagne's Wagon'.
17 **Terry Farrell & Partners**. The main architect was Aidan Potter.
18 **Shane Warne** (b. 1969). It was a unique and unplayable ball which pitched outside leg stump and fizzed across to hit the top of the off stump.
19 **Removed bits of wool from teasels with a preem** (iron comb). They also ran errands, swept the floor and supplied the croppers (cloth-cutters) with beer.
20 **Mary Queen of Scots**. She was given the mare by her half-brother, James Stewart, Earl of Moray. The palfrey was named after 'Black Agnes', Countess of Dunbar, who in 1338 held Dunbar Castle against a powerful English army for six months.

Iceland

Questions

1 What is the literal meaning of the name of Iceland's capital, Reykjavík?
2 According to early historical tradition, who is hailed as the first permanent settler of Iceland?
3 Before Iceland became fully independent in 1944, it had been under the sovereignty of which Scandinavian country for several centuries?
4 What is the name of Iceland's parliament, claimed to be the oldest in the world?
5 Into what unit of currency is the Icelandic *króna* divided?
6 What is the building named Perlan ('The Pearl') in Reykjavík?
7 Which ice-domed volcano on the west coast, in an area designated in 2001 as Iceland's fourth National Park, was used by Jules Verne as the gateway for his 1864 science-fiction novel *A Journey to the Centre of the Earth*?
8 What name was given to the island off the south coast of Iceland which emerged after a submarine volcanic eruption in 1963?
9 After which Icelandic explorer is the passenger terminal at Keflavík International Airport named?
10 What is the name of the naturally heated spa in the middle of a lava field near Grindavík in south-western Iceland?
11 Who was the first Icelandic historian to write in the vernacular?
12 What is the name of Iceland's second city?
13 What is the literal meaning of the Icelandic word for Saturday?
14 What is the title of Iceland's national anthem?
15 What is the name of the official residence of the President of Iceland?
16 To which seventeenth-century priest and poet is the towering neo-Gothic church which dominates the Reykjavík cityscape dedicated?
17 Under which fjord north of Reykjavík is the road tunnel which was opened in July 1998?
18 What is the name for the traditional form of Icelandic wrestling?
19 Iceland is almost treeless. Where, on the east coast, is the largest area of woodland to be found?
20 What is the name of the nineteenth-century Icelandic scholar-statesman who is hailed as the 'Father of Icelandic Independence'?

1 **'Smoky Bay'**. It was named after the steaming 'reek' from the active hot springs in the area.
2 **Ingólfur Arnarson**, a Norwegian, in 874.
3 **Denmark.**
4 **Alþingi** (Althing – 'National Assembly'). It was established in the open air in 930 in the great geological rift known as Þingvellir and met there annually until 1798, when it was suspended by the Danish authorities. It was re-established in 1845, and now meets in the Alþingishús (Parliament House) in Reykjavík.
5 ***Eyrir*** (plural *aurar*). There are 100 *aurar* in the *króna*.
6 **A glass-domed revolving restaurant.** It is built on Öskuhlíð hill, on top of the six huge tanks which store the natural hot water for Reykjavík's central heating system.
7 **Snæfellsjökull** (Snæfells Glacier). The volcano has been dormant for 1750 years.
8 **Surtsey** (Surtur's Island). It was named after Surtur ('the Black One'), the fire giant of Norse mythology.
9 **Leifur Eiríksson** (Leifur *heppni*, Leif the Lucky).
10 **Bláa Lónið** (The Blue Lagoon). The 'blue' in the name comes from the colour of the silica-rich water, which is the run-off from the nearby Svartsengi geothermal power plant.
11 **Ari *fróði* ('the Learned') Þorgilsson** (1068–1148). In c. 1120 he wrote *Íslendingabók* (Book of Icelanders). He also compiled the original version of *Landnámabók* (Book of Settlements).
12 **Akureyri**, on Eyjafjörður in the north of Iceland.
13 **'Bath Night'** (*laugardagur*), from *laug* (natural hot pool) and *dagur* (day).
14 ***O, guð vors lands*** (O, God of our land). The music was composed in 1874 by Sveinbjörn Sveinbjörnsson at 15 London Street, Edinburgh, where he worked as a piano teacher and composer. The words were written by the poet Matthías Jochumsson to celebrate the granting of Iceland's first constitution in 1874.
15 **Bessastaðir**, on Álftanes, a few kilometres east of Reykjavík. It is an ancient manor farm which once belonged to the saga-historian Snorri Sturluson.
16 **Hallgrímur Pétursson** (1614–74). Hallgrímskirkja (Hallgrímur's Church) was consecrated in 1986. Hallgrímur wrote the *Passíusálmar* (Passion Hymns), a profound meditation on the Crucifixion.
17 **Hvalfjörður** (Hvalfjord).
18 ***Glíma***. This unique style of wrestling involves seizing the opponent by the waist and trousers and trying to throw him by nimble footwork.
19 **Hallormsstaður**. It is now a state-run forestry centre, covering 740 square kilometres.
20 **Jón Sigurðsson** (1811–79). From his home in Copenhagen he led the intellectual independence movement against Denmark and saw the introduction of Iceland's first written constitution in 1874. When Iceland achieved full independence as a republic in 1944, his birthday (17 June) was chosen as Iceland's National Day. His statue stands in the centre of Austurvöllur Square in Reykjavík, facing the Alþingishús.

1 What is the Icelandic word (now also a generic word in English) for the country's spouting hot springs?
2 Where did the eponymous tailor live, in the book by Beatrix Potter?
3 Which Latin words, meaning 'God willing', are abbreviated to 'DV'?
4 The name of which small edible crustacean, especially of the genus *Crangon*, is used as a derogatory term for a small or weak creature?
5 In Robert Louis Stevenson's *Travels with a Donkey in the Cévennes* (1879), what was the name of his donkey?
6 What is measured on the Stanford–Binet scale?
7 Which planet has satellites named after Shakespearian characters, including Miranda, Titania and Oberon?
8 What originally gave 'foolscap' as a size of writing or printing paper its name?
9 Which sixth-century pope is sometimes called the 'Apostle of the English'?
10 Where, according to the old bird woman about whom Mary Poppins sang in the 1964 Disney film, could you feed the birds for tuppence a bag?
11 Who was the only future British monarch to have acted in films?
12 What type of bird was Huitzilopochtli, worshipped by the Aztecs?
13 In the cartoon series *Yogi Bear*, what was the name of the Park Ranger?
14 Which British Second World War base on the Antarctic Peninsula was renovated in 1996 by the British Antarctic Survey for the benefit of tourists?
15 Which ballet by Léo Delibes is subtitled *The Girl with Enamel Eyes*?
16 Who was the first woman MP to be elected to the House of Commons, although she refused to take her seat?
17 To what does the word 'brachylogy' refer?
18 In the New Testament, which two disciples were the candidates for the vacancy in the Apostleship left by the suicide of Judas Iscariot?
19 Which classical Roman author produced the first encyclopedia in the Silver Latin Age, the thirty-seven-volume *Naturalis Historia*?
20 Which English League football club is owned by a consortium of Icelandic businessmen and in 1999 appointed an Icelandic manager (Guðjón Þórðarson, known to his staff as 'Mr G')?

1 *Geysir*. In English the word has become 'geyser'.
2 **Gloucester** (*The Tailor of Gloucester*, 1902).
3 ***Deo volente*.**
4 **Shrimp.**
5 **Modestine.**
6 **Intelligence.** The test was devised between 1905 and 1911 by the French psychologist Alfred Binet (1857–1911), collaborating with Theodore Simon; it was refined by Lewis Terman of Stanford University in the USA.
7 **Uranus.**
8 **The watermark formerly used on this kind of paper.** It was the image of a fool's head wearing cap and bells.
9 **Pope Gregory the Great** (c. 540–604). In 597 he sent St Augustine to Kent to undertake the conversion of the Anglo-Saxons.
10 **The steps of St Paul's.** The title of the song, by Richard M. Sherman and Robert B. Sherman was *Feed the Birds*.
11 **Edward, Prince of Wales** (the future Edward VIII). He appeared in two silent films: *The Power of Right* (1919 – the story of a colonel's son who joins the cadets and kills a German internee) and *The Warrior Strain* (1919 – the story of a cadet who foils a German baron's attempt to signal to the enemy from Brighton).
12 **Hummingbird.** The Aztecs believed that dead warriors were reincarnated as hummingbirds.
13 **John Smith.**
14 **Port Lockroy.** It was established in 1944 as part of a secret naval project, Operation Tabarin, and was occupied continually until January 1962, after which it fell into disrepair. The effects of tourism are being monitored by the British Antarctic Survey.
15 *Coppélia* (1870).
16 **Countess Constance Markievicz** (1868–1927). She was elected as the Sinn Fein member for the St Patrick's division of Dublin in 1918. The first woman MP to take her seat in the Commons was Lady Nancy Astor, who was elected as Coalition Unionist member for the Sutton division of Plymouth in 1919.
17 **Preciseness of speech,** or conciseness of expression. It comes from the Greek *brakhus* (short) and *logia* (words).
18 **Matthias** and **Joseph Barsabbas** (surnamed Justus). Matthias was elected by lot (Acts 1:22–6).
19 **Pliny the Elder** (Gaius Plinius Secundus, AD 23–79).
20 **Stoke City.**

1 In 1925 which jazz musician, nicknamed 'Satchmo' (Satchelmouth), recorded hits such as *Cornet Chop Suey* with the Hot Five studio group?
2 After he enlisted in the army in 1942, which US trombonist and bandleader organised the Army Air Force Band and was on his way to plan engagements on the continent when his plane was lost without trace over the English Channel in 1944?
3 Which term refers to the music style, popular in the 1950s, in which pre-First World War pop tunes were played on out-of-tune pianos?
4 Which US clarinettist and bandleader, who featured on the *Let's Dance* radio series, was known as the 'King of Swing'?
5 Which instrument did the early jazz musician Buddy Bolden play in his band?
6 The life of which US jazz singer (played by Diana Ross) was the subject of the 1972 film *Lady Sings the Blues*?
7 Which US bandleader and clarinettist, who achieved huge success with *Begin the Beguine* in 1938, was born Arthur Arshawsky?
8 After which jazz style did Piet Mondrian name his 1942–3 abstract painting featuring horizontal and vertical yellow lines intersecting one another on a white background, and rectangles and squares of blue, grey and red?
9 Which US jazz musician and composer became the figurehead of the free jazz movement in the 1960s and recorded a series of classic quartet albums between 1959 and 1961 which included *Beauty is a Rare Thing*?
10 Which jazz term, popularised by Louis Armstrong, refers to imitating an instrument with the voice using nonsense words (for example, *doo-bee-doo-bee-doo*)?
11 Which US writer first described the 1920s as the 'Jazz Age'?
12 Which astonishingly versatile Virginia-born jazz singer began her professional career with the Tiny Bradshaw Band and had a memorable cameo role in the 1955 film *Pete Kelly's Blues*?
13 Which US saxophonist, bandleader and composer was the leading exponent of the new bebop jazz style in the 1940s?
14 Which term was coined by the US composer and writer Gunther Schuller in 1957 for a mixture of jazz and classical music?
15 In 1892 who composed the earliest known rag (*Harlem Rag*), which was not published until 1897?
16 Which white US cornettist, one of the most celebrated jazz performers of the 1920s, was the posthumous subject of Dorothy Baker's 1938 novel *Young Man with a Horn* (filmed in 1950 and released in the UK as *Young Man of Music*, starring Kirk Douglas)?
17 According to the US composer and bandleader John Sousa, jazz would endure as long as people hear it through what instead of their brains?
18 In 1920 who was the first female singer to make a commercial recording of what came to be recognised as blues – *Crazy Blues*?
19 Who were the authors of the classic book about the history of jazz entitled *They All Played Ragtime: The True Story of an American Music*, published in 1950?
20 Which US tenor saxophonist was familiarly known as 'Prez'?

1 **Louis Armstrong** (1901–71).
2 **Glenn Miller** (1904–44).
3 **Honky-tonk.**
4 **Benny Goodman** (1909–86).
5 **Cornet.** Buddy Bolden (1877–1931) is generally considered to be the first bandleader to play the improvised music which later became known as jazz.
6 **Billie Holiday** (Eleanora Fagan Gough, 1915–59). She herself appeared with Louis Armstrong and other jazz singers in *New Orleans* (1947), the story of jazz.
7 **Artie Shaw** (b. 1910). He married eight times; his wives included the actresses Lana Turner, Ava Gardner and Evelyn Keyes.
8 **Boogie-Woogie** (*Broadway Boogie-Woogie*, now in the Museum of Modern Art, New York).
9 **Ornette Coleman** (b. 1930).
10 **Scat singing** (scatting).
11 **F. Scott Fitzgerald** (1896–1940), in *Tales of the Jazz Age* (1922).
12 **Ella Fitzgerald** (1917–96). Her recording career lasted from 1935 to 1992, giving her one of the longest recording histories of any artist.
13 **Charlie Parker** (1920–55), known as 'Bird', who is considered the most influential performer in post-1940s modern jazz.
14 **Third Stream** (for the title of the album *Third Stream Music* by the Modern Jazz Quartet). Schuller (b. 1925) played the French horn in symphony orchestras before turning to jazz and writing compositions for several key jazz figures. He has also written books on the history of jazz.
15 **Tom Turpin** (1871–1922).
16 **Bix Beiderbecke** (1903–31).
17 **Their feet.**
18 **Mamie Smith** (1883–1946). *Crazy Blues* sold a million copies in its first six months.
19 **Rudi Blesh** and **Harriet Janis.**
20 **Lester Young** (1909–59). The soubriquet was an abbreviation of 'President of Tenor Saxophonists', a title conferred on him by his great friend Billie Holiday.

General Knowledge Questions

1 In which US city did jazz originate in the late nineteenth century?
2 Which Muslim festival marks the end of Ramadan?
3 Which veteran US comedian was born Nathan Birnbaum?
4 In landscape gardening, what is a ha-ha, as invented by Lancelot 'Capability' Brown in the eighteenth century?
5 In which establishment in a 1964 children's book by Roald Dahl are the Rock Candy Mine, Strawberry Juice Water Pistols and Stickjaw for Talkative Parents?
6 For which Latin words do the letters 'e.g.' stand?
7 What is the name of John Lennon's childhood home in Liverpool which was bought by his widow, Yoko Ono, and presented to the National Trust in 2002?
8 Which nineteenth-century President of the USA had the shortest presidency?
9 About whom did The Kinks sing in 1966:
They seek him here, they seek him there,
His clothes are loud, but never square.
10 What is the name of the valley in north-eastern Arizona and south-eastern Utah, dotted with 300-metre-high sandstone buttes, which John Ford used as a location for *Stagecoach* (1939) and many of his subsequent films?
11 Which battle in September 1651 ended Charles II's attempt to claim the English throne by force?
12 What is a 'mermaid's purse'?
13 What term refers to words which imitate sounds: for example, 'boom', 'squeak' and 'splash'?
14 Which pioneer German bacteriologist discovered the tuberculosis bacillus, in 1882?
15 In distilling, what is known as the 'Angels' Share'?
16 Which Spanish playwright, who was assassinated by nationalist partisans at the beginning of the Spanish Civil War, wrote the Andalusian tragedy *Blood Wedding* (*Bodas de Sangre*, 1933)?
17 In which northern European city is there a unique Phallological Museum (Museum of the Phallus)?
18 Which thirty-year-old divorcée and portrait painter created the London *A–Z* in 1936?
19 What was the name of the demon in medieval Mystery Plays who collected and carried off to Hell the words omitted or mutilated by priests in slipshod celebrations of the Mass?
20 Which Kentucky-born drummer introduced the vibraphone into jazz in the 1930s, recording with Louis Armstrong and Benny Goodman?

General Knowledge

Answers

1 **New Orleans.**
2 **Idul-Fitr**, on 1 Shawwal. As in all Muslim festivals, the date of Idul-Fitr moves back by eleven days each year because it is based on the Islamic lunar calendar.
3 **George Burns** (1896–1996).
4 **A boundary ditch hiding a fence or wall.** It was constructed below ground level so as not to impede the view from the house.
5 **Mr Wonka's Chocolate Factory**, in *Charlie and the Chocolate Factory.*
6 *Exempli gratia* ('for example', 'for instance').
7 **Mendips.** It is a three-bedroomed, semi-detached house in Menlove Avenue, in the suburb of Woolton. John Lennon lived there with his aunt Mimi (Mary Smith, his mother's sister), who looked after him when his mother, Julia, ran into difficulties.
8 **William Henry Harrison** (1773–1841). He caught pneumonia at his inauguration in 1841 and died four weeks later.
9 **The Dedicated Follower of Fashion.**
10 **Monument Valley.**
11 **Worcester.**
12 **The horny egg sac of a skate, ray or shark.**
13 **Onomatopoeia.**
14 **Robert Koch** (1843–1910). He was awarded the Nobel Prize for physiology or medicine in 1905.
15 **The amount of spirit which evaporates through the casks while it is maturing.** About 2 per cent (mainly alcohol) evaporates.
16 **Federico García Lorca** (1898–1936).
17 **Reykjavík** (Hið Íslenzka Reðasafn). It contains a collection of more than eighty penises and penile parts belonging to nearly all the land and sea mammals to be found in Iceland, as well as mycological specimens and *objets d'art.*
18 **Phyllis Pearsall** (d. 1996). She began by selling the book from a handcart and went on to publish *A–Z* guides to other British cities, eventually becoming the head of a publishing company with 250 titles in print.
19 **Titivil** (Tutivillus). In Hell the words were registered as a special sin.
20 **Lionel Hampton** (b. 1909). He did not form a permanent big band until 1940.

K is for Knights

1 Which eighty-year-old radio broadcaster and former singer, known as 'the housewives' choice', was knighted in the 2002 New Year's Honours List?
2 Which British newspaper has as its logo a knight dressed in chain mail and carrying a white shield bearing a red cross?
3 Which Mediterranean island was the headquarters of the Knights Hospitallers of St John of Jerusalem from 1529 to 1798?
4 Who played the part of Sir Lancelot in the 1967 film *Camelot*, in which Richard Harris starred as King Arthur?
5 To which two Orders of Knighthood has the Queen appointed the Princess Royal a Lady?
6 What is the motto of the Most Noble Order of the Garter, the senior order of knighthood in Britain?
7 Which claimant to the British throne was known as the Young Chevalier?
8 Which tragicomedy, attributed to Shakespeare and Fletcher, is closely based on the Tale told by Chaucer's 'verray, parfit gentil knyght' in *The Canterbury Tales*?
9 Who was the 'Knight of La Mancha'?
10 Who was the renowned French knight and national hero who was described in contemporary chronicles as 'le chevalier sans peur et sans reproche'?
11 Which military order of knights, founded during the Third Crusade (1188–92), was crushed by the Poles and Lithuanians at the Battle of Tannenberg in 1410?
12 For what purpose did medieval knights use a quintain?
13 Which fifteenth-century knight was the author of *Le Morte d'Arthur*, the most authoritative version of the Arthurian legend in the English tradition?
14 Upon which real-life figure did Shakespeare base the character of his fat knight Falstaff?
15 Which British city was dubbed the 'City of Dreadful Knights' in the aftermath of the 'honours for sale' scandal which damaged the reputation of David Lloyd George, Prime Minister in the coalition government after the First World War?
16 Which order of knighthood is denoted by the initials KCB?
17 Who was the 'opponent' of Sir Gawain in the alliterative poem of the late fourteenth century which tells of his exploits?
18 What do the French mean by a *chevalier d'industrie*?
19 In Tennyson's *Idylls of the King* (1859–85), which Arthurian knight of the Round Table was married to Enid the Good, daughter of Yniol?
20 Which eighteenth-century French chevalier, a diplomat and secret agent, gave his name as an alternative term for transvestism?

1 **Jimmy Young.** He was one of the launch DJs for BBC Radio 1 in 1967, before moving to the 'JY Prog' on BBC Radio 2.
2 ***Daily Express.***
3 **Malta.** The Knights Hospitallers are the oldest order of Christian chivalry, founded in c. 1048 by merchants of Amalfi for pilgrims, whose travel routes the knights defended against the Saracens.
4 **Franco Nero.**
5 **Order of the Garter** (1994) and **Order of the Thistle** (2000).
6 'Honi soit qui mal y pense' ('Shame on him who thinks ill of this'). The Order was originated by Edward III in c. 1348. Members of the Order (officially known as 'Knights Companions') are limited to twenty-four.
7 **Charles Edward Stuart** (1720–88), Bonnie Prince Charlie, the 'Young Pretender'. He was the son of the exiled James Francis Edward Stuart (1688–1766, the 'Old Pretender') and grandson of King James II and VII.
8 ***The Two Noble Kinsmen*** (c. 1613). It tells the story of the love of Palamon and Arcite for Emelye, sister of Hippolyta (queen of the Amazons).
9 **Don Quixote**, the eponymous hero of the novel by Cervantes.
10 **Chevalier de Bayard** (Pierre Terrail, c. 1473–1524), 'the fearless and irreproachable knight'. He made his name in the Italian campaigns of Charles VIII, Louis XII and Francis I, and was killed in action Italy.
11 **The Teutonic Knights.**
12 **To practise jousting at speed.** It was a dummy figure mounted on a post and used as a target for tilting at the lists.
13 **Sir Thomas Malory** (d. 1471). He has been identified with a knight of the same name, of Newbold Revel in Warwickshire and Winwick in Northamptonshire, who was tried and imprisoned for a number of crimes of violence, including theft and rape, some time after 1450.
14 **Sir John Oldcastle** (c. 1378–1417), a Wycliffite who served with gallantry in France during the reign of Henry IV; a boon companion of the young Prince Hal, he was condemned as a heretic in 1413 after Hal's accession as Henry V. Shakespeare introduced Falstaff in *Henry IV*, described his heart-broken death in *Henry V*, but brought him back to life by public demand in *The Merry Wives of Windsor*.
15 **Cardiff.** Three people connected with South Wales newspapers were among the recipients of these honours. The accolade was a pun on the title of the poem *The City of Dreadful Night* by James Thomson (1834–82).
16 **Knight Commander of the Order of the Bath.**
17 **The Green Knight.** *Sir Gawain and the Green Knight* tells how a huge green man enters Camelot during a New Year's feast and challenges a knight to cut his head off, on condition that the knight agrees to have his own head cut off a year hence.
18 **An adventurer or swindler**, someone who lives by his wits and calls himself a gentleman.
19 **Sir Geraint**, prince of Devon.
20 **Charles Éon de Beaumont**, known as the Chevalier d'Éon (1728–1810). As a secret agent in Russia in 1755 he stayed at the court of Elizabeth (Empress of Russia) dressed as a woman. He tried to claim a pension in France as a woman, and was sentenced to wearing women's clothing for the rest of his life: hence the term eonism.

General Knowledge Questions

1 In medieval times, what name was given to a knight's attendant and shield-bearer?
2 Which fictional 1960s Yorkshire village is the setting for the popular ITV series *Heartbeat*?
3 What collective term is applied to a group of moles?
4 How much did Edward Lear's Owl and Pussycat pay for their wedding ring?
5 Osteoporosis is the thinning and weakening of which components of the human body?
6 Which literary character in a 1905 novel lived at Blakeney Manor?
7 What is the name of the Jewish Festival of Lights, on 25 Kislev, which usually coincides with the end of December?
8 Which Latin words are commonly abbreviated to q.v.?
9 Which English cathedral houses the bodies of King John and Prince Arthur (eldest son of Henry VII), and the ashes of Stanley Baldwin?
10 Who is the sculptor of the 2.5-metre-high marble statue (complete with marble handbag) of the 'Iron Lady', Margaret Thatcher, unveiled in the House of Commons in February 2002?
11 Which tenth-century Archbishop of Canterbury, the patron saint of goldsmiths, is sometimes depicted carrying a pair of red-hot tongs with which, according to legend, he seized the devil by the nose?
12 What was the political song (with words by Lord Thomas Wharton) which influenced popular pro-Orange sentiment at the time of the 'Glorious Revolution' of 1688?
13 Which English ironmaster invented the 'puddling' process for purifying iron?
14 What kind of creature is a dik-dik?
15 Where in Scotland is J.M. Barrie's birthplace, now owned by the National Trust for Scotland?
16 Who played the part of the determined former prostitute (Mrs MacBain) in Sergio Leone's 1969 'spaghetti Western' *Once Upon a Time in the West*?
17 Which slang word for prison came into use from the name of a notorious gaol in Southwark in London?
18 What is the distinctive type of mathematics which developed in Japan during the seventeenth century and whose results were originally displayed on wooden tablets called *sangaku* hung under the roofs of shrines and temples?
19 Which three historic industrial sites in Britain, all connected with mill works, were awarded World Heritage status by UNESCO's World Heritage Committee in December 2001?
20 According to Malory's *Le Morte d'Arthur*, which three of King Arthur's Knights of the Round Table achieved the quest for a sight of the Holy Grail (the cup used by Jesus at the Last Supper)?

General Knowledge

Answers

1 **Esquire** (from the Old French *esquier*, from the Latin *scutarius*, shield-bearer). The esquire ranked immediately below a knight, and often was subsequently knighted himself.

2 **Aidensfield**, set in Goathland, a village on the remote moors above Whitby, North Yorkshire.

3 **A labour.**

4 **One shilling:**

'Dear Pig, are you willing to sell for one shilling
Your ring?' Said the Piggy, 'I will.'

5 **Bones.** It is a reduction in the protein and mineral content of the bones.

6 **The Scarlet Pimpernel** (Sir Percival Blakeney, in the novel by Baroness Orczy, 1865–1947).

7 **Hanukkah.** It commemorates the rededication of the Temple in Jerusalem by Judas Maccabeus.

8 ***Quod vide*** ('which see').

9 **Worcester.**

10 **Neil Simmons.** An anonymous donor provided £50,000 for the statue to be commissioned.

11 **St Dunstan** (c. 909–88).

12 ***Lilliburlero.*** The 'lilli' of the title is said to have been the orange lily, which was the symbol of the Irish supporters of William of Orange.

13 **Henry Cort** (1740–1800). In the process of 'puddling', molten pig iron is stirred on the bed of a reverberatory furnace (one in which the heat comes from the flames and hot gases swirling above the metal, preventing the metal from coming into contact with the fuel). The circulating air removes carbon from the iron.

14 **Antelope** (any small antelope of the genus *Madoqua*). The name is said to derive from the sound of its call.

15 **Kirriemuir**, in Angus (9 Brechin Road). It was acquired in 1937, allegedly to stave off a threat by Barrie enthusiasts in the USA to transport the house stone by stone to the States. It is now a museum of Barrie memorabilia, including the little washhouse which inspired Peter Pan's 'Wendy House'. Kirriemuir appears in several of Barrie's works as 'Thrums'.

16 **Claudia Cardinale.**

17 **Clink.** The prison was destroyed in the anti-Catholic Gordon Riots of 1780.

18 **Wasan.** It was developed early in the Edo period (1603–1867), when Japan cut itself off almost completely and developed its own cultural activities, including Noh and Kabuki theatre and the writing of haiku.

19 **New Lanark village** (Lanarkshire), **Saltaire** (West Yorkshire) and **Derwent Valley Mills** (Derbyshire). New Lanark was founded as a model cotton-spinning centre in 1785 by the Scottish entrepreneur David Dale; Saltaire was the brainchild of Sir Titus Salt, who began building the town in 1850; Derwent Valley Mills are described as 'the definitive model of the English mill system'.

20 Sir **Galahad** (the son of Sir Lancelot and Elaine of Ascolot), **Sir Percival** and **Sir Bors de Ganis** (Lancelot's nephew).

Latin Phrases

1 For which Latin words do the letters 'i.e.' stand?
2 What is the Latin motto of the RAF?
3 What does the Latin phrase *modus operandi* mean?
4 Why is a stand-in doctor called a 'locum'?
5 Which three-word Latin phrase means 'in blazing crime', and refers to being caught in the act of committing an offence?
6 What is the Latin derivation of 'ad-libbing'?
7 Which Latin word is used to mean 'letter by letter' or 'literally'?
8 In printing, what is the opposite of 'verso'?
9 What is the Latin phrase for 'a passing remark'?
10 By which Latin phrase is the Canticle of Simeon (from Luke 2:29) better known?
11 In academic examinations, what does an *aegrotat* signify?
12 *Volens nolens* is the Latin version of which common English expression?
13 What is the meaning of the abbreviated Latin phrase *infra dig*?
14 To which groups of people are the plural terms *alumni* and *alumnae* applied?
15 A species of which common garden flower, characterised by its large blue or violet flowers, has the Latin name *Delphinium belladonna*?
16 Which Roman poet wrote the following lines?
Dulce et decorum est
Pro patria mori
('Sweet and honourable it is to die for one's country')?
17 What is the meaning of the 1951 film title *Quo Vadis*?
18 What is the Latin motto of the Crown of Scotland?
19 To which victory was Julius Caesar referring with his celebrated claim '*Veni, vidi, vici*' ('I came, I saw, I conquered')?
20 Which television quiz programme had as its unofficial slogan '*Ludus non nisi sanguineus*'?

1 *Id est* ('that is'), meaning 'That is to say'.
2 *Per ardua ad astra* ('Through hardships to the stars'). It was adopted as the official motto of the Royal Flying Corps in 1913.
3 **Method of operation.**
4 **From the Latin *locum tenens*** ('one holding a place', 'a stand-in').
5 ***In flagrante delicto.***
6 ***Ad libitum*** ('at pleasure', 'extemporaneously').
7 ***Literatim.***
8 ***Recto.*** A recto is a right-hand page of a book, and bears an odd number; a verso is a left-hand page.
9 ***Obiter dictum*** ('a saying by the way').
10 ***Nunc Dimittis***, from the opening of the Latin (Vulgate) version, '*Nunc dimittis servum tuum, Domine*' ('Lord, now lettest thou thy servant depart in peace'). It forms part of the Anglican liturgy at evensong and compline.
11 **A certificate allowing a candidate to pass an examination** although he or she has missed all or part of the examination through sickness (literally, 'he/she is ill').
12 **Willy-nilly** ('whether willing or unwilling').
13 **Beneath one's dignity** (*infra dignitatem*).
14 **Men and women graduates of a school or college** (singular *alumnus* and *alumna*), meaning 'nurseling', 'foster child', from the Latin *alere*, 'to nourish'.
15 **Larkspur.**
16 **Horace** (65BC–8AD), in his *Odes*, Book 3, No. 2. The phrase '*Dulce et decorum est*' is the title of a poem by Wilfred Owen (1893–1918), in which he stigmatised it as 'The old Lie'; the concept was also rejected in a poem (*Amours de Voyage*) in 1858 by Arthur Hugh Clough (1819–61).
17 **'Whither are you going?'** It was derived from the words of the Apostle Peter to Jesus on the Appian Way: '*Quo vadis, Domine*?' The film was based on the 1896 novel of that name by the Polish Nobel Prize-winner Henryk Sienkiewicz (1846–1916).
18 ***Nemo me impune lacessit*** ('No one provokes me with impunity', or 'Wha daur meddle wi' me'). It is also the motto of the Order of the Thistle and all the Scottish regiments.
19 **The Battle of Zela** (47 BC), in Asia Minor, over Pharnaces, the son of Mithridates, at the conclusion of Caesar's Pontic campaign. According to Plutarch, that was how Caesar announced his victory to his friend Amintius.
20 ***Mastermind*** (1972–97): a loose translation (by Dr Gerald Mackenzie, Life Vice-President of the Mastermind Club) of the encouragement traditionally given to contenders on the programme, 'It's only a bloody game!'

General Knowledge Questions

1 Which Latin phrase means, literally, 'for the rate' – that is, proportionally?

2 In which 1968 Beatles song, a No. 1 hit in 1969 for the Scottish group Marmalade, did Desmond have 'a barrow in the market place'?

3 Who was elected Speaker of the House of Commons, amid some controversy, in October 2000, in succession to Betty Boothroyd?

4 Where has Crufts dog show been held since 1991?

5 Which songwriter composed the unofficial national anthem of the USA, *God Bless America*?

6 Which 1960s BBC TV series about the clothing industry starred Reg Varney, Sheila Hancock and Miriam Karlin?

7 At which Scottish castle did the pop superstar Madonna marry film director Guy Ritchie in December 2000?

8 Which battle on 22 May 1455 marked the start of the Wars of the Roses?

9 Which writer of children's books lived at Hill Top Farm at Sawrey, in the Lake District?

10 Which cocktail, originally made from rum and lime juice, is named after a small town on the east coast of Cuba?

11 About which Egyptian pharaoh did Shelley write the following lines?

'My name is Ozymandias, King of Kings:
Look on my works, ye Mighty, and despair!'
Nothing beside remains. Round the decay
Of that colossal wreck, boundless and bare
The lone and level sands stretch far away.

12 What term is used for the sugary substance exuded by aphids after they have been feeding on sap?

13 Which caring organisation was founded by the Rev Chad Varah, rector of St Stephen Walbrook in London, in 1953?

14 Which was the first National Nature Reserve to be declared in Britain, in November 1951?

15 Which Hindu deity is worshipped as the goddess of wealth and good fortune, especially during Divali, on the eve of the New Year (the first day of the bright half of the month of Kaartik, which usually corresponds with October-November)?

16 What is the literal meaning of the word 'xylophone'?

17 What is the ancient name of the volcanic island in the Cyclades whose violent eruption in the fifteenth century BC is thought to have brought about the decline of the Minoan civilisation of Crete?

18 Who was the writer and illustrator of the 1952 sporting classic *Confessions of a Golf Addict* – the first of some fifty books on addiction to the sport?

19 Which two Cambridge writers and linguists introduced 'Basic English' as an international language in the 1920s?

20 What is the meaning of the sardonic Latin epigram '*Sed quis custodiet ipsos custodies*'?

1 **Pro rata.**
2 ***Ob-La-Di Ob-La-Da.*** Paul McCartney, who wrote the song, first heard the expression used by the singer Jimmy Scott (Jimmy Anonmuogharan Scott Emuakpor). Scott was from the Yoruba tribe in Nigeria, in whose language it apparently means 'Life goes on'.
3 **Michael Martin**, Labour MP for Glasgow Springburn.
4 **The National Exhibition Centre, Birmingham.** Charles Cruft organised his first annual dog show at the Royal Agricultural Hall, London, in 1891. After his death in 1939 his widow continued to run it until 1948, when the Kennel Club took over and changed the venue to Earls Court in London.
5 **Irving Berlin** (1888–1989). He wrote it in 1939.
6 ***The Rag Trade.***
7 **Skibo Castle**, Sutherland. Skibo was formerly the holiday home of the Scots-born industrialist and philanthropist Andrew Carnegie (1835–1919), who bought it in 1897.
8 **Battle of St Albans.** The Lancastrians, led by Edmund Beaufort, Duke of Somerset (who was killed in the battle), were defeated by the Yorkists, led by Richard, Duke of York. Henry VI, the Lancastrian king, was captured.
9 **Beatrix Potter** (1866–1943). She moved there in 1905, and six of her later books were set there.
10 **Daiquiri.** Its invention has been credited to a US engineer, Jennings Cox, who went to Daiquiri in the late nineteenth century to work in the iron mines, but other sources suggest that the Cubans had been enjoying it for years before Cox popularised it.
11 **Ramses II.**
12 **Honeydew.**
13 **The Samaritans.**
14 **Beinn Eighe**, three kilometres north of Kinlochewe in Wester Ross. The 4800-hectare reserve was purchased for just £4000 by Dr John Berry, the first Scottish director of the Nature Conservancy (a predecessor body of Scottish Natural Heritage).
15 **Lakshmi.** The celebration and the date of the New Year vary in different Hindu traditions.
16 **'Wood voice'** (from the Greek *xulon* and *phone*).
17 **Thera** (Santorini). The island has been excavated to reveal three-storey houses and remarkable frescos.
18 **George Houghton** (1905–93). He was a cartoonist and caricaturist, an advertising copywriter and a much-travelled and prolific author, whose golf handicap was never better than thirteen.
19 **Charles Kay Ogden** (1889–1957) and **Ivor Armstrong Richards** (1893–1979). 'Basic' in 'Basic English' was an acronym for 'British, American, Scientific, International, Commercial'. It was a simplified form of English for teaching as an auxiliary language, consisting of 850 English words (600 nouns, 150 adjectives and only 18 verbs, along with operative words such as,'across', 'after', 'can', 'do', and 'very').
20 **But who is to guard the guards themselves?** It was written by the Roman lawyer and satirist Juvenal (c. 55–c. 130) in his mordant verse *Satires*.

Money

1 In which town is the British Royal Mint?
2 In 1976 which pop group had a hit with *Money Money Money*?
3 What is the name of BBC Radio 4's award-winning personal finances programme?
4 What is Maundy Money?
5 Which country's unit of currency is the *dong*?
6 What name is given to the chest at the Royal Mint in which specimen gold and silver coins are kept for annual 'trial' by weight and assay?
7 In Scotland, what does the term 'bawbee' mean when applied to coins?
8 Which book by L. Frank Baum, published in 1900 and turned into a Hollywood musical in 1939, was a satire on the USA joining the Gold Standard?
9 In pre-decimal UK currency, for which Latin words did 'LSD' stand?
10 In Greek mythology, how much did the spirits of the dead have to pay Charon the ferryman to take them across the River Styx to Hades?
11 What name was given to the barter currency of the Native North Americans composed of shells of *Venus mercenaria* strung together to form belts or 'fathoms' worth five shillings?
12 In J.K. Rowling's *Harry Potter* books, which three currency units are issued by Gringotts Bank?
13 What is the origin of the phrase 'Penny plain, tuppence coloured'?
14 Which piece of real estate in North America did Peter Minuit, the first director of the Dutch colony of New Amsterdam, buy in 1626 for sixty guilders (the equivalent of $24)?
15 What is the derivation of the word 'money'?
16 On which small island off Nova Scotia is the 'Money Pit', alleged to be the repository of a fabulous treasure?
17 After whom was the old silver threepenny piece once colloquially called a 'Joey' in Britain?
18 In medieval England, what were 'Pentecostals', also known as 'Whitsun farthings'?
19 Which nineteenth-century British coin was known as a 'bun penny'?
20 For which occasions are 'agonistic' coins struck?

Money

Answers

1 **Llantrisant**, in the Rhondda Valley in South Wales. It was located there in 1968.

2 **Abba.**

3 ***Money Box*** (also *Money Box Live* and *Inside Money*). *Money Box* has frequently won the Broadcast category of the Bradford and Bingley Personal Finance Media Awards.

4 **Gifts in money given by the monarch on Maundy Thursday** to the number of impoverished men and women corresponding to the monarch's age. It is specially struck in silver coins to the face value of one, two, three and four pence. Each person receives a set of coins for each decade of the monarch's age, with the additional years made up with coins to the appropriate value.

5 **Vietnam.** The *dong* is divided into ten *hao* (100 *xu*).

6 **Pyx** (from the Greek *puxis*, box). In ecclesiastical terms, a pyx is the vessel in which the consecrated bread of the Eucharist is kept.

7 **Any coin of low value.** A bawbee was originally a silver coin worth three (later six) Scottish pennies; it was minted by James V's mint master, Alexander Orrock of Sillebawby.

8 ***The Wonderful Wizard of Oz*** (hence the 'yellow brick road').

9 **Librae, solidi, denarii** (pounds, shillings, pence).

10 **One obol.** It represented one-sixth of a drachma.

11 **Wampum** was used as currency until 1704 in the American colonies. Its value varied from three to six individual shells to one English penny.

12 **Galleons, sickles and knuts.** A golden galleon is worth twenty-seven silver sickles; a silver sickle is worth twenty-nine bronze knuts.

13 **Toy theatres.** An East London maker of toy theatres printed scenery and characters on sheets of thick paper for cutting out. They were sold at 1d (one pre-decimal penny) if plain (black and white), 2d if coloured.

14 **Manhattan Island.** Minuit purchased Manhattan from Native Americans (the Manhattan) for trinkets which were valued at sixty guilders.

15 **Latin *moneta*** ('she who alerts the people') one of the epithets applied to the goddess Juno. The first Roman mint was attached to the temple of Juno *moneta* at Arx, on the Capitol in Rome, and was called *moneta* as a result. *Moneta* came to mean 'coin' or 'money'.

16 **Oak Island.** The 'Money Pit' is a complex circular shaft blocked by a series of oak platforms and booby-trapped by tunnels which flood it. The pit was discovered by a sixteen-year-old game-hunter, Daniel McInnes, in 1795. In 1804 a wealthy Nova Scotian, Simeon Lynds, formed a treasure company to excavate the pit, but his efforts only made him bankrupt.

17 **Joseph Hume** (1777–1855), MP and monetarist. He advocated the usefulness of a small coin for paying cab fares and the like, and suggested the introduction of the silver Britannia groat (fourpence) which were struck between 1836 and 1855. The nickname was later transferred to the silver threepenny piece.

18 **Offerings** made to the parish priest at Whitsuntide, or paid by the parish church to the cathedral of the diocese.

19 **A Victorian penny**, issued between 1860 and 1894, depicting on the obverse Queen Victoria with her hair in a bun.

20 **Sporting events** (from the Greek *agonistes*, contestant).

General Knowledge Questions

1 On a standard British Monopoly board, how much does each of the four railway stations cost?
2 What was the name of the ranch featured in the ITV western series *Bonanza*?
3 For which country did the group Milk and Honey win the 1979 Eurovision Song Contest with the song *Hallelujah*?
4 Who is the author of the 1969 novel *The French Lieutenant's Woman*?
5 What was the stage name of Harlean Carpenter, the Hollywood actress who was the original 'platinum blonde'?
6 What does the Latin abbreviation *ult* signify when referring to a date?
7 Announced in 2002, what name was given to the first cat to be cloned, by a team led by Dr Mark Westhusin at Texas A&M University?
8 Who created the cartoon character Oor Wullie in the *Sunday Post* in 1936?
9 What are the three main courts of justice in England and Wales?
10 Which twentieth-century poet wrote *maggie and milly and molly and may*, a poem about three girls who went down to the beach to play one day?
11 In mathematics, what is the name for a square array of numbers arranged in such a way that the sum of the numbers is the same when added vertically, horizontally or diagonally?
12 After the 2001 General Election in Britain, which Scottish Labour MP succeeded Edward Heath as Father of the House of Commons?
13 Which was the last food to be rationed because of shortages during and after the Second World War, and was also the first to come off rationing?
14 Which Tasmanian-born writer won the £10,000 Commonwealth Writers' Prize in 2002 with his novel *Gould's Book of Fish*?
15 What is the common name for the plant *Mentha pulegium*, which was used in ancient times as a flea repellent?
16 According to Muslim belief, on which mountain near Mecca was the Qur'an revealed to Muhammad by the angel Jibreel (Gabriel)?
17 In which British city is the Blue Carpet, a public square opened in January 2002, made from tiles of recycled and reconstituted blue glass?
18 Other than its archaic meaning of a woman who kept an alehouse, what kind of creature is an alewife?
19 Where in northern Sweden do the Sami hold their four-hundred-year-old winter market every February?
20 What is the unit of currency of Venezuela?

General Knowledge Answers

1 £200. The stations are Fenchurch Street, King's Cross, Liverpool Street and Marylebone.

2 **The Ponderosa.**

3 **Israel.**

4 **John Fowles** (b. 1926). It was filmed in 1981 with a script by Harold Pinter and with Meryl Streep in the title role.

5 **Jean Harlow** (1911–37).

6 **'In the last month'** (*ultimo*).

7 cc (nicknamed 'copy cat' or 'carbon copy'), a female calico domestic shorthair cat. She was born in December 2001, but the announcement of the successful cat cloning was delayed until immunisation injections had been completed and her immune system was fully developed. Her genetic donor's name was Rainbow.

8 **Dudley Dexter Watkins** (1907–69). Watkins, born in Manchester, moved to Scotland in 1925 and worked as a part-time illustrator for the publisher D.C. Thomson in Dundee to supplement his income as an art teacher. Oor Wullie, the dungaree-wearing ragamuffin with spiky yellow hair and a rusty, upturned bucket, celebrated his sixty-fifth birthday in 2001.

9 **Crown Court, Magistrates' Court** and **High Court.**

10 **ee cummings** (1894–1962).

11 **Magic square.**

12 **Tam Dalyell** (b. 1932). He entered Parliament as MP for West Lothian in 1962 and has represented Linlithgow since 1983.

13 **Bread** (rationed in July 1946 and taken off rationing in July 1948).

14 **Richard Flanagan.** It revolves around the life of William Buelow Gould, a convict on Sarah Island, Van Dieman's Land (Tasmania), who made a remarkable book of twenty-six paintings of fish in 1828.

15 **Pennyroyal**, derived from the Latin *pulegium* (from *pulex*, flea) and Anglo-Norman *real* (royal). It is a member of the mint family and is also known as 'pudding grass' and 'piliolereial'.

16 **Mount Hira.** The Qur'an is believed by Muslims to be the words of God, revealed to Muhammad from c. 610. Muhammad memorised the words, which became known as the Qur'an ('recitation'), and told them to his followers, one of whom, Abu Bakr, had them written down after the death of Muhammad.

17 **Newcastle upon Tyne.** The Blue Carpet, designed by the Thomas Heatherwick Studio, is at the end of New Bridge Street, on the east side of the city centre.

18 **A fish of the herring family** (*Alosa pseudoharengus*).

19 **Jokkmokk** (population 3500) in Norbotten county. The market was granted a charter by Karl IX of Sweden in 1605.The market is now also a three-day tourist festival attracting 30,000 visitors.

20 **Bolívar.** It was named after the 'Liberator' of Venezuela, Simón Bolívar (1783–1830).

Novels

Questions

1 Who wrote the 2001 Booker Prize-winning novel *True History of the Kelly Gang*?
2 Which Scottish novelist is commemorated by a 61-metre-high monument in Edinburgh's Princes Street?
3 In which country is the home port of the old fisherman Santiago, who is the hero of Ernest Hemingway's 1952 novel *The Old Man and the Sea*?
4 The term 'Aga-saga' was coined to describe the genre of works by which contemporary novelist?
5 Who wrote the 1994 novel *Captain Corelli's Mandolin*, which was made into the 2001 film starring Nicholas Cage and Penélope Cruz?
6 In the jail of which English county town did John Bunyan write the major part of *The Pilgrim's Progress*?
7 Which English novelist created the medieval mystery-solving Benedictine monk Brother Cadfael?
8 In Thomas Hardy's 1874 novel *Far from the Madding Crowd*, who becomes Bathsheba Everdene's second husband?
9 What is the name of the hero of Evelyn Waugh's 1928 novel *Decline and Fall*, who becomes a personal tutor in an eccentric country home and almost marries his pupil's millionaire mother, Margot Beste-Chetwynde?
10 What is the title of F. Scott Fitzgerald's last novel, which was unfinished when he died in 1940?
11 In which Dostoyevsky novel is the student Raskolnikov the central character?
12 Which Oxford philosopher and writer won the 1978 Booker Prize with her novel *The Sea, the Sea*?
13 Whose first novel in 1904 (set in 1984) featured Adam Wayne leading a rebellion against Auberon Quin, who had been chosen by lottery as 'King of London'?
14 Which of Disraeli's novels, with the alternative title of *The New Crusade*, tells the story of a brilliant young English aristocrat who travels to the Holy Land in search of a new faith?
15 In the novel by Charles Dickens, what is the name of 'Our Mutual Friend'?
16 Which Edinburgh historical novelist wrote two major series – about the Lymond family (six volumes) and the House of Niccolò (eight volumes) – as well as a novel about Macbeth and Thorfinn the Mighty, earl of Orkney (*King Hereafter*)?
17 Which Victorian novelist wrote and illustrated the story *The Rose and the Ring* ('A Fireside Pantomime for Great and Small Children') under the pseudonym 'Mr M.A. Titmarsh' in 1855?
18 Which comedienne wrote *Whistling for the Elephants* (1999), the story of a ten-year-old US tomboy who discovers a small, faded zoo on the outskirts of town?
19 In which 1841 novel by Dickens is the narrator of the first two chapters, Master Humphrey, a character based on a clock maker in Barnard Castle, County Durham?
20 Which classic novel by the US writer Harper Lee opens with the words, 'When he was nearly thirteen, my brother Jem got his arm badly broken at the elbow'?

1 **Peter Carey** (b. 1943).
2 **Sir Walter Scott** (1771–1832).
3 **Cuba**. The character was based on Gregorio Fuentes, a fisherman whom Hemingway befriended in Cojimer, near Havana.
4 **Joanna Trollope** (b. 1943).
5 **Louis de Bernières** (b. 1954).
6 **Bedford**. Bunyan spent eleven years (1661–72) there for preaching without a licence.
7 **Ellis Peters** (pseudonym of Edith Pargeter, 1913–95). The first of the series was *A Morbid Taste for Bones* (1977) and the last was *Brother Cadfael's Penance* (1994).
8 **Gabriel Oak**, the shepherd. Her first husband was Sergeant Frank Troy.
9 **Paul Pennyfeather**.
10 ***The Last Tycoon*** (published in 1941), about a Hollywood producer and loosely based on the life of Irving Thalberg (1889–1936).
11 ***Crime and Punishment*** (1866).
12 **Iris Murdoch** (1919–99). She wrote more than twenty novels, starting with *Under the Net* (1954) and ending with *Jackson's Dilemma* (1995); in her latter years she was struck down with Alzheimer's disease. Her story was dramatised in the 2002 film *Iris*, starring Judi Dench, Kate Winslet, Jim Broadbent and Hugh Bonneville, for which Jim Broadbent won an Academy Award for Best Supporting Actor.
13 **G.K. Chesterton** (1874–1936), with *The Napoleon of Notting Hill*. It was a futuristic fantasy about London, full of medieval nostalgia; it adumbrated the themes of his later fiction – glorifying the 'little man' and attacking big business, technology and the monolithic state.
14 **Tancred** (1847). It was the last novel in Disraeli's 'state of the nation' trilogy, after *Coningsby* (1844) and *Sybil* (1845).
15 **John Harmon**. He takes on the identity of John Rokesmith, in which guise he marries Bella Wilfer (which he is required to do in order to qualify for the fortune which his father has bequeathed to him).
16 **Dorothy Dunnett** (1923–2001).
17 **William Makepeace Thackeray** (1811–63). The 'M.A.' stood for 'Michael Angelo' – a reference to Thackeray's drawing skill, on which he greatly prided himself.
18 **Sandi Toksvig** (b. 1958).
19 ***The Old Curiosity Shop***. While staying at the King's Head in Barnard Castle Dickens saw a fine grandfather clock in a nearby clockmaker's shop which had been created by the owner-craftsman Master Humphrey. This inspired the name *Master Humphrey's Clock* for his short-lived weekly publication (1840–1) in which *The Old Curiosity Shop* was to be serialised and linked by the reminiscences of 'Master Humphrey'.
20 ***To Kill a Mockingbird*** (1960). It was her only novel and was made into a 1962 film starring Gregory Peck.

General Knowledge Questions

1 Which writer won the £30,000 Whitbread Book of the Year award in 2002 with his 'children's novel' *The Amber Spyglass*?

2 Forked pieces of wood from which three trees are the most commonly used for dowsing (also known as water divining, but not by its practitioners)?

3 In which 1893 painting, which he inscribed 'This picture must have been painted by a madman', did Edvard Munch depict a figure with cavernous eye sockets, its hands pressed to the sides of its face and its mouth wide open in panic against a background of a dark sea below a vivid orange, red and yellow sunset?

4 Which is the highest waterfall in the world?

5 Which war was the setting for the BBC2 TV series *M*A*S*H*, about a military hospital?

6 Which 1962 UK hit single by Bernard Cribbins was also the name of a group which had a UK No. 2 hit in 1991 with *I'm Too Sexy*?

7 Which English Romantic poet began a poem with the following lines?

'O, what can ail thee, knight at arms,
Alone and palely loitering;
The sedge has withered from the lake,
And no birds sing.'

8 What is the collective term for a group of foxes?

9 In 1953 who composed the opera *Gloriana* for the coronation of Queen Elizabeth?

10 What Latin words were engraved on the golden brooch worn by the prioress in Chaucer's *The Canterbury Tales*?

11 What is the name of the supreme civil court in Scotland?

12 After whom was the Socialist Fabian Society (founded in London in 1883–4) named?

13 Which public school at Horsham, West Sussex, is known as the Blue-Coat School?

14 What are the ingredients of a 'Silver Bullet' cocktail?

15 A few bars of which composer's *Knightsbridge March* provided the opening music for the 1930s BBC Radio programme *In Town Tonight*?

16 Who directed his father to an Academy Award for Best Supporting Actor in 1948?

17 Which mountaineer wrote the acclaimed book *Touching the Void* about his fall on the 6398-metre Siula Grande in the Peruvian Andes and his agonising crawl to safety with a broken leg?

18 Which figure of speech substitutes a word referring to an attribute of something for the thing itself – for example, 'the Crown' for the monarch?

19 Which church in Glasgow's Gorbals displays what are claimed to be some of the relics of St Valentine?

20 Who, in 1907, became the first English writer to be awarded the Nobel Prize for literature?

1 **Philip Pullman** (b. 1946). *The Amber Spyglass* is the third of his epic trilogy *His Dark Materials*; the first two are *Northern Lights* (1995) and *The Subtle Knife* (1997). He was also voted Author of the Year at the 2002 British Book Awards.

2 **Hazel, rowan** and **willow**.

3 ***The Scream*** is now in the National Gallery, Oslo. Munch (1863–1944) based it on a hallucinatory experience about which he wrote, 'The clouds [were] turning blood-red. I sensed a scream passing through nature.'

4 **Angel Falls**, in south-eastern Venezuela (979 metres), discovered in 1935 and named after James Angel, an airman who crash-landed nearby in 1937.

5 **Korean War** (1950–3). It was developed from Robert Altman's 1970 film about the 4077th Mobile Army Surgical Hospital.

6 ***Right Said Fred*** (Richard and Fred Fairbrass, later joined by Rob Manzoli).

7 **John Keats** (1795–1821), in *La Belle Dame Sans Merci* (1819). It tells of a knight who falls into the thrall of a fairy maiden.

8 **A skulk.**

9 **Benjamin Britten** (1913–76).

10 ***Amor vincit omnia*** ('Love conquers all things'). The motto comes from Virgil's *Eclogues*, No. 9.

11 **Court of Session**. Its origins can be traced to the early sixteenth century. The court presently consists of thirty-two judges who are designated 'Senators of the College of Justice' or 'Lords of Council and Session'.

12 **Quintus Fabius Maximus** (c. 260–203 BC). He was a Roman general in the Second Punic War who earned the sobriquet of *Cunctator* ('the Delayer') by refusing to engage Hannibal's stronger forces in pitched battle. The early members of the Fabian society, who included George Bernard Shaw and Sidney and Beatrice Webb, similarly believed in 'long taking of counsel' to achieve their ultimate objective of a democratic socialist state.

13 **Christ's Hospital**. Blue-Coat schools were charity schools for poor children; from the sixteenth century onwards their traditional uniform was a long blue coat. The original Christ's Hospital School was founded in the City of London by Edward VI in 1552. The school moved to Hoddesdon, in Hertfordshire, before being established on its present site in 1902.

14 **Gin with a splash of whisky.**

15 **Eric Coates** (1886–1957). The music, from his *London Suite* (1932), featured traffic noises, street cries and fanfares.

16 **John Huston.** His father Walter Huston won the Academy Award for his role in *The Treasure of the Sierra Madre*.

17 **Joe Simpson** (b. 1960). *Touching the Void* won the Boardman Tasker Award for mountain literature and, in 1989, the NCR Book Award for Non-fiction.

18 **Metonymy.**

19 **Blessed John Duns Scotus Church**, in Ballater Street, formerly named St Luke's. The relics have been on display in a brass-bound wooden casket since 1999. They were brought to Glasgow in 1836, a gift from a French aristocratic family; the rest of St Valentine's relics were divided between Terni, in Italy, and Dublin.

20 **Rudyard Kipling** (1865–1936).

Ornithology

1 What is the common name of the garden bird *Turdus merula* which, according to the nursery rhyme, was baked in a pie as 'a dainty dish for a king'?
2 In birding parlance, what colloquial term is used for someone whose main aim is to collect sightings of rare birds?
3 Which bird is sometimes known as the yaffle?
4 Which former member of *The Goodies* on TV is also a keen birdwatcher and author of *The Little Black Bird Book* (1982) and *Gone Birding* (1983)?
5 Which island in the Bristol Channel is named after its large population of puffins?
6 Which US ornithologist and bird artist produced *Birds of America* (1827–38), a massive collection of eighty-seven portfolios first published in England?
7 Which tiny seabirds are known to sailors as 'Mother Carey's chickens'?
8 Which bird is particularly associated with the village of Abbotsbury, near Dorchester, Dorset?
9 Which bird is traditionally held to have attempted to free Jesus from the Cross?
10 The Latin name of which game bird betrays its change in plumage between summer and winter?
11 In 1955 an act of the legislature honoured which bird as the state bird of Utah to commemorate its role in saving the early Mormon settlers from a plague of crickets in 1848?
12 In 1803 which English poet wrote the following lines?
A Robin Redbreast in a cage
Puts all Heaven in a Rage.
13 If a bird is described as 'fossorial', what is it in the habit of doing?
14 Which eighteenth-century English clergyman and naturalist wrote *Natural History and Antiquities of Selborne* (1789), containing acute observations on the habits of birds living in his parish?
15 On the back of the Bank of England £10 note, introduced in 2000, there is a portrait of Charles Darwin and his ship the *Beagle* and a picture of a bird based on a type found in the Galapagos Islands – which bird?
16 In Greek mythology, which long-legged birds of prey with bronze claws were to be destroyed in the sixth of the Twelve Labours of Herakles (Hercules)?
17 In which Manchester suburb (then an outlying village) was the original Society for the Protection of Birds (later the RSPB) founded in 1889 by a group of women opposed to the destruction of exotic birds for plumage for the millinery trade?
18 Which French composer's interest in birdsong inspired several of his works, including *Catalogue d'oiseaux* for piano (1956–8)?
19 On a bird, what is the technical term for a single, hair-like structure with a downy tuft at the tip?
20 What is the name of the lake in northern Iceland which hosts the largest variety of breeding ducks in the world?

Ornithology Answers

1 **Blackbird**:

Sing a song of sixpence,
A pocket full of rye;
Four-and-twenty blackbirds
Backed in a pie.

2 **Twitcher**.

3 **Green woodpecker** (*Picus viridis*). It was so named in the eighteenth century in imitation of its cry.

4 **Bill Oddie** (b. 1941). The other two 'Goodies' were Graeme Garden and Tim Brooke-Taylor.

5 **Lundy**. The name comes from the Old Norse word for puffin, *lundi*.

6 **John James Audubon** (1785–1851). The National Audubon Society, for the conservation of birds in the USA, was founded in his honour in 1866.

7 **Storm petrels** (*Hydrobates pelagicus*). The name 'petrel' traditionally derives from the Italian *Petrello* ('little Peter') because during storms they seem to 'pat' the waves with alternate feet as if walking on water, like St Peter walking upon the Lake of Gennesaret to join Christ (Matthew 14). 'Mother Carey' is thought to derive from *mater cara* ('mother dear'), with reference to the Virgin Mary, the traditional protector of sailors.

8 **Mute swan** (*Cygnus olor*). Benedictine monks established a swannery at Abbotsbury more than six hundred years ago, and swans have been reared in there ever since.

9 **Crossbill** (*Loxia curvirostra*). It was thought that the curiously shaped mandibles of its beak had become distorted by its frantic efforts to wrench the nails from the hands of Christ; the male bird's plumage was coloured by splashes from Christ's blood.

10 **Ptarmigan** (*Lagopus mutus*), from the Latin *mutare* (to change). In summer it has a grey and brown plumage, which in winter becomes white – the only native British bird to change the colour of its plumage with the winter.

11 **Seagull** (*Larus californicus*).

12 **William Blake** (1757–1827), in *Auguries of Innocence*.

13 **Digging burrows,** typically in preparing nest holes, like sand martins and kingfishers.

14 **Gilbert White** (1720–93).

15 **Humming bird.**

16 **The Stymphalian Birds,** which lived in a dense forest on the shores of Lake Stymphalos in Arcadia, and had become a plague to the surrounding territory. Herakles frightened them out of the forest with the sound of castanets given to him by Athena, and picked them off with his arrows.

17 **Didsbury**. The founder was Mrs R.W. Williamson, of The Croft, Didsbury.

18 **Olivier Messiaen** (1908–92).

19 **Filoplume**. Filoplumes are often mingled with other feathers; they are sensitive to touch, and provide the bird with information on how the feathers are lying on the surface.

20 **Mývatn** (Midge Water), a large, shallow lake in a fascinating lava field reeking with geothermal activity; it gets its name from the massive swarms of midges and blackflies which hatch there. Seventeen species of duck breed there, including the North American species Barrow's goldeneye and the harlequin.

General Knowledge Questions

1 Which bird is sometimes known as the 'sea parrot'?
2 What is the surname of the sisters Joy, Teddie and Babs who formed a singing trio in the 1950s and had hits with songs such as *I Saw Mommy Kissing Santa Claus*, *Little Drummer Boy* and *Little Donkey*?
3 Which element takes its symbol, Hg, from its Latin name, *hydrargyrum*?
4 In Robert Browning's poem *The Pied Piper of Hamelin*, where did the rats make their nests?
5 Through which UK national park does the River Coquet flow?
6 Which Conservative politician was the President of the Board of Education in the wartime coalition cabinet, and is associated with the 1944 Education Act, which reorganised the secondary school system and introduced the 11-plus examination?
7 What was the name of the dog in Jerome K. Jerome's novel *Three Men in a Boat* (1889)?
8 What was the name of the talking supercar featured in the television series *Knight Rider*, which starred David Hasselhof as the detective Michael Knight and William Daniels as the voice of the car?
9 Which 1959 Disney animated film was the first to be made using the widescreen Cinemascope process?
10 Which religious sect was founded in the USA by John Thomas in about 1848?
11 Which cathedral, once the second largest in Scotland, was burned down in June 1390 by Alexander Stewart, the 'Wolf of Badenoch'?
12 Which US industrialist pioneered mass-production techniques for watches and produced a one-dollar watch in 1892?
13 Who was the author of the best-selling book on animal behaviour *King Solomon's Mines* (1949)?
14 What name is given to a strip of land left unploughed at the edge of a field?
15 Who was the first Muslim caliph?
16 What is the origin of the phrase 'spick and span', meaning 'very neat and clean'?
17 In which 1910 opera does Minnie, owner of the Polka Saloon, play poker for the life of her lover, Dick Johnson, who is really a bandit called Ramerrez?
18 Which Roman statesman ended his later speeches in the Senate with the refrain '*Delenda est Carthago*' ('Carthage must be destroyed')?
19 Which English MP was the chief protagonist of the concept of 'daylight saving' early in the twentieth century?
20 Who designed the aviary which was opened at London Zoo in 1965?

1 **Puffin** (*Fratercula arctica*).
2 **Beverley** (the Beverley Sisters).
3 **Mercury** (quicksilver).
4 **Inside men's Sunday hats.** The poem was first published in *Dramatic Lyrics* (1845). It was based on a well-known legend about a rat-catcher, and in the sixteenth century became associated with the alleged disappearance of the children of Hamelin in 1284.
5 **Northumberland.** It rises at Coquet Head on the Scottish border and flows generally eastward through the southern part of the Cheviot Hills to the North Sea at Amble.
6 **R.A. ('Rab') Butler** (1902–82). He was expected to succeed Anthony Eden as Prime Minister in 1957, but became instead 'the best Prime Minister we never had'.
7 **Montmorency.**
8 **KITT** (Knight Industries Two Thousand), a black Pontiac which could reach 300 miles (480 kilometres) per hour (produced by a dying multimillionaire, Wilton Knight).
9 ***Sleeping Beauty*.** It was also the last until *Anastasia* (1997, produced by Don Bluth and Gary Goldman), mainly because of cost and technical difficulties (*Sleeping Beauty* is reported to have cost $6 million to produce).
10 **The Christadelphians.** John Thomas (1805–71) was a British-born physician who emigrated to the USA in 1832. The Christadelphians ('Brethren of Christ') promote a return to primitive Christianity to prepare for Christ's return.
11 **Elgin.**
12 **Robert Hawley Ingersoll** (1859–1928). It was promoted as 'the watch that made the dollar famous'.
13 **Konrad Lorenz** (1903–89). The Austrian ethologist shared the 1973 Nobel Prize for physiology or medicine with Karl von Frisch and Nikolaas Tinbergen.
14 **Headland.**
15 **Abu Bakr** (c. 570–634). He was the father-in-law of the prophet Muhammad, and on the death of the Prophet in 632 he was elected leader of the Muslim community with the title of *Khalifat rasul Allah* ('Successor to the Messenger of Allah').
16 **From 'spick' meaning 'spike, nail', and 'span' meaning 'chip'.** The full phrase was 'spick and span new', referring to a ship in which every nail and chip were new.
17 ***The Girl of the Golden West*** (*La Fanciulla del West*), by Giacomo Puccini (1858–1924), first performed in New York starring Enrico Casus.
18 **Cato the Elder,** the Censor (234–149 BC). He was sent on a mission to Carthage in 153 BC, which so fuelled his fear of Carthaginian power that he thereafter ended all his speeches with this warning. He lived to see the outbreak of the Third Punic War (149–146 BC).
19 **William Willett** (1856–1915). His Bill to introduce daylight saving in 1908 met strong opposition; the measure (British Summer Time) was not adopted until 1916, during the First World War.
20 **Lord Snowdon** (Anthony Armstrong-Jones).

Pastimes Questions

1 In card games, what name is given to a hand in which all cards are from the same suit?
2 How many squares are there on a standard Scrabble board?
3 Who was the first £1 million winner of the television quiz *Who Wants to Be a Millionaire?*, in November 2000?
4 What is the name of the French game in which two players (or two teams) pitch or roll balls named *boules* towards a jack (*cochonnet*)?
5 Which playing card is sometimes called 'the curse of Scotland'?
6 Which chess piece is named *le fou* in French?
7 In Lewis Carroll's *Alice's Adventures in Wonderland*, what were used as mallets in the Red Queen's game of croquet?
8 Which game features twenty-four narrow, wedge-shaped divisions called 'points' on its board?
9 What are the three suits in mah-jong?
10 Which sport gave rise to the phrase 'to win hands down'?
11 What name is given to a hand in bridge or whist which contains no card higher than a nine?
12 Which sport was featured in the 1993 film *Cool Runnings*?
13 In what context have the traditional country skills of tickling and groping been outlawed since 1975?
14 In what game are unplayed pieces gathered in a 'boneyard'?
15 In which sport is an outdoor Bonspiel ('Great Match') held when weather conditions are suitable?
16 Which card game is said to have been invented by the seventeenth-century poet John Suckling?
17 In falconry, what is the name of the short strap fastened round the leg of a hawk and attached to the leash?
18 In philately, what is the name given to the Swiss stamp, first issued in 1843, which was in two halves – the whole stamp for a letter sent from one canton to another, but only half of the stamp for a letter delivered within the canton where it was posted?
19 Which eighteenth-century French composer of operas was also the leading chess master of his day?
20 In October 2001 in which game did Patrick Barrie defeat Dave Lockwood to become World Singles Champion?

Pastimes

Answers

1 **Flush.**
2 225.
3 **Judith Keppel**, the great-granddaughter of Alice Keppel, a mistress of Edward VII. Her final question asked who was the wife of Henry II (Eleanor of Aquitaine).
4 **Pétanque** (or *jeu de boules*).
5 **Nine of diamonds.** The phrase is of dubious origin.
6 **Bishop.** The piece used to represent a court fool dressed in traditional motley.
7 **Live flamingoes.** The balls were live hedgehogs and the playing-card soldiers doubled themselves over and stood on their hands and feet to make the arches.
8 **Backgammon.**
9 **Bamboos, characters and circles.** Each suit of tiles is numbered 1 to 9 and consists of four of each number. There are also two other categories of tile: honours (consisting of four green, four red and four white dragons, four of each of the winds – north, east, south and west) and the optional flowers or seasons (either four flowers and four seasons or eight of one type).
10 **Horse racing.** A jockey with a commanding lead can relax the pull on the reins and win with his or her hands down.
11 **Yarborough.** It is said to be named after Charles Anderson Worsley, the 2nd Lord Yarborough (1809–97), who used to lay odds of 1000–1 against such an occurrence in any named hand.
12 **Bobsleighing** (about the 1988 Jamaican Olympic bobsled team).
13 **Catching trout.**
14 **Dominoes.** The playing pieces are called 'bones'.
15 **Curling.** Traditionally, a Bonspiel is held on the Lake of Menteith in Perthshire between teams representing the North and the South of Scotland – but only if the ice is 10 inches (253 millimetres) thick. The last Bonspiel was held in February 1979.
16 **Cribbage.** The attribution of the invention of 'cribbidge' by Suckling (1609–42) was made by the English antiquary and biographer John Aubrey (1626–97).
17 **Jess.** The word is derived from Latin *jacere* (to throw).
18 **The Geneva Double.**
19 **François-André Philidor** (1726–95). His most popular opera was his adaptation of Henry Fielding's *Tom Jones* (1765). He gained much greater financial rewards playing exhibition chess matches all over Europe, and wrote the best-selling *L'Analyze du jeu des échecs* (1749), the first book to lay down the theoretical and strategical principles of chess.
20 **Tiddlywinks.** It was established as a national competitive sport in 1961 after Prince Philip hanselled a universities championship (whose trophy was, and still is, the 'Silver Wink'), and by the 1960s no fewer than thirty-seven universities were playing. The earliest patent for 'tiddledywinks' was filed by Joseph Fincher in 1888, but the modern game can be traced to a group of Cambridge undergraduates who met at Christ's College in 1955 to devise a sport at which they could represent the university.

General Knowledge

1 In which game do players sometimes use a device called a 'spider'?
2 Which student from Hungerford, Berkshire, singing *Evergreen*, won the national TV vote for *Pop Idol* in February 2002?
3 In the *Punch and Judy* puppet theatre, what was the name of Mr Punch's dog?
4 In the BBC television series *Doctor Who*, from which planet did the Ice Warriors, in the fourth series, come?
5 In the popular song, how much was owed to the bells of St Martins?
6 Which US swimmer equalled Mark Spitz's 1972 record of seven Olympic medals by winning five gold medals, a silver and a bronze at the 1988 Seoul Olympics?
7 Which bird 'booms' in marshes?
8 In which West Indian island group is Mustique, which was a favourite holiday haunt of Princess Margaret?
9 What does the word 'brummagem' describe?
10 Which Swiss-born architect designed Chandigarh, the new capital of the Punjab, which was completed in the 1960s?
11 What is the common name of the wild fruit-bearing flowering plant *Fragaria vesca*?
12 What is the meaning of the Latin phrase *ceteris paribus*?
13 Which endocrine gland, attached by a stalk to the base of the brain, is known as the 'Master Gland'?
14 Which horse won the Derby, the Irish Derby and the King George VI and Queen Elizabeth Stakes in 1975?
15 The name of which variety of peach comes from the drink of the gods in classical mythology?
16 What is the name of the cocktail made from gin, Calvados, apricot brandy, orange juice and a splash of grenadine?
17 A visit to Mexico inspired which US composer to write *El Salón Mexico* (1936)?
18 At which battle of 1798, according to *Casabianca* (a poem by Mrs Felicia Dorothea Hemans in 1829), did the boy stand on the burning deck, when all but he had fled?
19 Which 1976 British film used only Latin dialogue, with subtitles in English?
20 The international governing body of which competitive game has the motto '*Gens una sumus*' ('We are all one people')?

General Knowledge Answers

1 **Snooker**. A 'spider' is a cue rest with a rounded arch with three grooves on which a cue can be rested to raise it above a ball which would otherwise obstruct its movement.

2 **Will Young** (b. 1979). He attracted 4.6 million of the 8.7 million votes cast.

3 **Toby**. References to Punch and Judy can be traced as far back as 1682. In 1828 the journalist John Payne Collier published the 'script' of the traditional puppet show, from an interview with the puppeteer Giovanni Piccini, as *The Tragical Comedy or Comical Tragedy of Punch and Judy*.

4 **Mars**. Ice Warriors were a military race of reptiles who carried sonic guns built into their armour. One hit could shatter victims' bones and destroy their internal organs.

5 **Five farthings**.

6 **Matt Biondi** (b. 1965). He won gold medals for the 50 metres freestyle, 100 metres freestyle and all three relays, silver for the 100 metres butterfly and bronze in the 200 metres freestyle.

7 **Bittern** (*Botaurus stellaris*). The males emit a far-carrying 'booming' or 'thunder-pumping' territorial call.

8 **Grenadines**.

9 **Cheap, tawdry goods, especially jewellery**. 'Brummagem' is a dialect word for Birmingham and was originally used to describe counterfeit coins which were made there.

10 **Le Corbusier** (Charles Édouard Jeanneret, 1887–1965). The US architect Albert Mayer had been appointed architect for the new city in 1949 and he embarked on the designs with a younger partner, Matthew Nowicki. However, after Nowicki's death in a plane crash in 1950, Mayer was not able to continue the project alone, and withdrew. Le Corbusier took it up in 1951.

11 **Strawberry**.

12 **Other things being equal**.

13 **Pituitary**.

14 **Grundy**.

15 **Nectarine** (from the Greek *nektar*).

16 **Golden Dawn**. 3/4 oz gin, 3/4 oz Calvados, 3/4 oz apricot brandy, 3/4 oz orange juice and a splash of grenadine. Shake with ice. Strain and serve in a cocktail glass. Garnish with an orange twist. Enjoy.

17 **Aaron Copland** (1900–90).

18 **Battle of the Nile**. The poem by the Liverpool-born Felicia Hemans (1793–1835) highlights a detail in the battle in which Nelson destroyed a French fleet in Aboukir Bay. The French flagship *L'Orient* caught fire, but Jacques de Casabianca, the ten-year-old son of the wounded captain, refused to leave his father's side and died with him on board.

19 ***Sebastiane***, the first film directed by Derek Jarman (1942–1994). The hero, St Sebastian (played by Leonardo Trevoglio), is banished by the Emperor Diocletian.

20 **Chess** (FIDE – Fédération Internationale des Échecs, established in 1924).

1. What was the name of the galley sailed by Jason from Iolcos to Colchis when he went in search of the Golden Fleece?
2. For what eponymous object was Harrison Ford searching in his role as an archaeologist in the 1981 film directed by Steven Spielberg?
3. Who is officially celebrated on 9 October each year as the discoverer of North America in the year 1000?
4. Which 1979 book by Kit Williams gave clues for a quest to find a hidden jewelled, twenty-two-carat golden hare which he had made?
5. What was the name of the papyrus-reed boat in which the Norwegian adventurer Thor Heyerdahl sailed from Morocco to the West Indies in 1970?
6. Which flamboyant English explorer, linguist and diplomat was sent by the Foreign Office with John Hanning Speke to search for the source of the Nile, which led to the discovery of Lake Victoria in 1858?
7. Who first navigated the so-called Northwest Passage, round the north of the American continent, four centuries after John Cabot began the search for the route in 1497?
8. For what were the fifteen-week expedition of 1954, sponsored by the London *Daily Mail*, and a 1957 expedition led by the Texas oilman Thomas Slick, searching?
9. What was the destination of the NASA space mission launched on 7 April 2001?
10. What was the name of the Dundee-built ship on which Robert Falcon Scott led the first National Antarctic Expedition between 1901 and 1904?
11. Among Native American hunters, part of a boy's initiation was a 'Vision Quest' to find what?
12. Which Elizabethan explorer and buccaneer mounted two unsuccessful expeditions (in 1595–6 and 1617) to South America in a quest for the fabled El Dorado, the supposed source of Spanish gold?
13. In Greek mythology, who was the earth goddess who gave Hera the Golden Apples of the Hesperides at her marriage to Zeus?
14. Which Briton organised the 1979–82 Transglobe expedition which traced the Greenwich meridian crossing both poles, completed the first unsupported crossing of Antarctica on foot and discovered the lost city of Ubar in the Arabian desert?
15. Which renowned explorer, whose discoveries formed the basis for English claims to much of Canada, was set adrift in an open boat with seven others after a mutiny on his ship, the *Discovery*, in 1611?
16. Between 1589 and 1600 which English geographer and historian wrote *Principal Navigations, Voyages, and Discoveries of the English Nation*?
17. In 1968–9 who was the first person to sail single-handed non-stop around the world in a boat named *Suhaili*?
18. Where is the birthplace-museum of the Scottish missionary and explorer David Livingstone?
19. Into whose mouth did Tennyson put the classic definition of a quest: 'To strive, to seek, to find, and not to yield'?
20. What was the name of the ship's cat aboard the *Endurance* during Ernest Shackleton's ill-fated 1914–16 attempt to cross Antarctica from the Weddell Sea to the Ross Sea?

1 *Argo* (from the Greek *argos*, swift).
2 **The Lost Ark of the Covenant** (*Raiders of the Lost Ark*, in which he played the part of Indiana Jones).
3 **Leifur Eiríksson** (Leifur *heppni*, Leif the Lucky).
4 **Masquerade.** It was two years before the hare was discovered by Mike Barker and John Rousseau near Ampthill, Bedfordshire.
5 **Ra II.**
6 **Richard Burton** (1821–90). Speke's claim to have found the source of the Nile was challenged in England and, in 1864, on the day he was to debate the subject publicly with Richard Burton, he was killed by his own gun while hunting.'
7 **Roald Amundsen** (1872–1928). He navigated it in 1903–6.
8 **The Yeti** (Sherpa *yahteh*, 'rock-dwelling animal', from *yah*, rock and *teh*, animal).
9 **Mars.** *Mars Odyssey* is an orbiter equipped to make global observations of Mars to investigate its climate and geological history, including the search for water and evidence of life-sustaining environments.
10 ***Discovery*.** The ship was brought back to Dundee in 1986 and restored, and is now the focal point of 'The City of Discovery'.
11 **His guardian spirit.** He looked for a sign in animal form, or had a dream in which has guardian spirit appeared in animal form and instructed him, took him on a visionary journey and taught him songs.
12 **Walter Raleigh** (c. 1552–1618). El Dorado ('the Gilded One') was said to be a ruler coated in gold, believed to live somewhere in Colombia.
13 **Gaia.** Hera planted them in her garden at the foot of Mount Atlas, protected by the three nymphs of the evening, the Hesperides. Fetching the Golden Apples was the eleventh of the Labours of Herakles (Hercules).
14 **Ranulph Fiennes** (b. 1944). Sir Ranulph Fiennes and Charlie Burton were the first men to reach both poles.
15 **Henry Hudson** (c. 1550–1611). His men mutinied after accusing Hudson of distributing food unfairly when the *Discovery* was trapped for the winter in the ice of Hudson Bay. The castaways were never seen again.
16 **Richard Hakluyt** (c. 1552–1616). He also published *Divers Voyages touching the Discoverie of America* (1582) and *Discourse concerning Western Discoveries* (1584) and introduced the use of globes to English schools.
17 **Robin Knox-Johnston** (b. 1939). Nine sailors started out to accomplish the first non-stop solo circumnavigation but he was the only one to finish (after 312 days).
18 **Blantyre**, Lanarkshire. During his extensive travels in Africa Livingstone (1813–73) discovered the Victoria Falls on the River Zambezi, and Lake Nyasa. He himself was famously 'discovered' by Henry Morton Stanley of the *New York Herald* in Tanganyika in 1871.
19 **Ulysses**, in his dramatic monologue *Ulysses* (1842).
20 **Mrs Chippy.** It was a tabby originally thought to be a female (hence the name) and belonged to the ship's carpenter (Henry McNeish). When the *Endurance* became trapped in the ice, Shackleton ordered his men to get rid of all unnecessary possessions, and Mrs Chippy was put down.

General Knowledge

1 Having joined the British-sponsored archaeological survey of Egypt at the age of seventeen, who went on to discover the tombs of Hatshepsut and Thutmose IV in 1902 and find Tutankhamun's tomb in 1922?

2 Which real Pennine village was the setting for the BBC television series *Last of the Summer Wine*?

3 What do Americans call courgettes?

4 What is the name of the hot, dry wind which blows up from North Africa and often carries dust from the Sahara across the Mediterranean Sea to Europe?

5 Which term for boisterous knockabout comedy is derived from a theatrical prop consisting of a flexible pair of paddles bound together at one end for striking a blow with a loud clapping sound but without causing injury?

6 According to the Gospels, who asked for the body of Jesus after the Crucifixion and placed it in his own garden tomb?

7 Who composed and sang the theme tune for the 1990s BBC television comedy series *One Foot in the Grave*?

8 Who played the part of the petite, 5-foot blonde with whom a 50-foot ape was infatuated in the 1933 film *King Kong*?

9 The theme tune of which jazz band, formed in the 1930s, was *One O'Clock Jump*?

10 In a Sikh *gurdwara* (temple), what is the *langar*?

11 Who was the first person in Britain to hold a flying licence?

12 Which bird walks upstream under water to look for food?

13 What was the original meaning of the word 'carnival'?

14 What two lines follow these opening lines of *The Listeners* by Walter de la Mare?

'Is there anybody there?' said the Traveller,
Knocking on the moonlit door;

15 Which seventeenth-century French army officer's name became an English word for a strict disciplinarian?

16 In Scottish folklore, what is a kelpie?

17 Who was the author of the 'Palliser' novels, featuring Plantagenet Palliser, who was later Duke of Omnium and Prime Minister for a time?

18 Why was Charles Bradlaugh, the social reformer MP for Northampton, excluded from the House of Commons from 1880 to 1886?

19 Which millionaire English eccentric, the builder of Fonthill Abbey (designed by James Wyatt), was buried in 1844 in a folly he had built in 1827 on Lansdown Hill, just north of Bath?

20 Many have sought to find the lost island city of Atlantis, but which classical writer first gave a written account of this fabled place 'beyond the Pillars of Hercules', which was swallowed up by the sea as a result of earthquakes?

1 **Howard Carter** (1873–1939).
2 **Holmfirth**, to the south of Huddersfield, in West Yorkshire.
3 **Zucchini.**
4 **Sirocco.**
5 **Slapstick.**
6 **Joseph of Arimathaea.** 'When the even was come, there came a rich man of Arimathaea, named Joseph . . . He went to Pilate and begged the body of Jesus . . . And when Joseph had taken the body, he wrapped it in a clean linen cloth, and laid it in his own new tomb, which he had hewn out in a rock.' (Matthew 27:57–9).
7 **Eric Idle** (b. 1943).
8 **Fay Wray** (b. 1907).
9 **Count Basie's band** (William Basie, 1904–84). Count Basie had been a member of Bennie Moten's Kansas City Orchestra and, after the death of the band's leader in 1935, formed his own band (originally called the Barons of Rhythm).
10 **Kitchen.** The term is also used for the communal meal which is eaten there after worship; it is always a vegetarian meal, prepared by members of the Sikh community.
11 **Lord Brabazon of Tara** (John Theodore Cuthbert Moore-Brabazon, 1884–1964), who became Minister of Transport in 1940 and of Aircraft Production in 1941, but resigned following public outcry at his criticism of Britain's ally the USSR.
12 **Dipper** (*Cinclus cinclus*). Its nest, a dome of moss in a crevice, is often built behind a waterfall.
13 **Cessation of flesh-eating**, from the Latin *caro* (meat) and *levare* (put away). It denoted the season of revelry immediately preceding Lent.
14 ***And his horse in the silence champed the grasses***
Of the forest's ferny floor.
15 **Jean Martinet** (d. 1672). He became a general in Louis XIV's army as a military engineer and tactician. He achieved notoriety for the brutality of his discipline and was 'accidentally' shot by his own troops at the siege of Duisberg.
16 **A water spirit in the form of a horse.** Kelpies were malevolent creatures which haunted rivers and fords and were said to delight in drowning travellers who accepted a lift on their backs.
17 **Anthony Trollope** (1815–82).
18 **He refused to take the oath of allegiance.** He preferred to affirm, rather than to swear, but was expelled and re-elected regularly until 1886, when he took the oath and his seat.
19 **William Beckford** (1760–1844). He inherited a huge fortune at the age of ten and became a prodigious collector of paintings and *objets d'art*. He wrote (in French) *Vathek* (1787) and several travel books. Beckford's Tower is now a museum housing the Beckford Tower Trust collection.
20 **Plato** (in *Timaeus* and *Critias*).

Radio

Questions

1 What is the name of the Radio 4 series on the History of England from 55 BC to 1999, written and presented by Christopher Lee?
2 In radio technology, what term is used for the distance between the 'crests' of radio waves?
3 In the Radio 4 series *The Archers*, what is the name of the hotel run by Jack Woolley?
4 What was the original 'call sign' of the BBC in 1922 – the introduction with which it began all radio broadcasts?
5 In which radio series did the title character frequently use the phrase 'I'm worried about Jim'?
6 According to the 1979 No. 1 hit for the Buggles, what killed the radio star?
7 After the Second World War, into which three networks did the BBC split its radio broadcasts for national and regional programmes, entertainment and classical music?
8 Which bandleader introduced his Saturday-lunchtime radio programme with a rousing cry of 'Wakey Wakey!', followed by a stirring rendition of *Somebody Stole My Girl*?
9 In radio technology, what is the name of the unit which measures frequency?
10 What was the price of a BBC radio licence when it was introduced in 1922?
11 In which play for radio does Mr Pugh, who keeps his copy of *Lives of Great Poisoners* in a plain paper cover, dream of mixing for his wife a venomous porridge unknown to toxicology?
12 What was the name of the fine wire which was moved to make contact with a crystal in order to receive broadcasts on early 'wireless' sets?
13 'That'll never work on the radio', according to the pundits – but it did. What was the name of the 1950s radio series starring the ventriloquist Peter Brough?
14 From where in Britain were the first transatlantic radio signals sent, in December 1901, to be received by Guglielmo Marconi in St John's, Newfoundland?
15 What was the name of the first daytime music show on BBC radio, introduced in 1940?
16 Which founder member of the zany BBC Radio 4 spoof panel game *I'm Sorry, I Haven't A Clue*, is commemorated by a blue plaque in the ticket hall of Mornington Crescent tube station?
17 In 1932 which Nobel-Prize-winning author scripted George V's Christmas Message broadcast on BBC radio (the first monarch's Christmas Message to be broadcast)?
18 What is the signature tune of Radio 4's *Quote . . . Unquote*, presented by Nigel Rees?
19 Who gave the first Reith Lecture, broadcast on BBC radio on 26 December 1948?
20 Who was the creator and first producer of the Radio 4 programme *Poetry Please*?

Radio

1 *This Sceptred Isle.*
2 **Wavelength.**
3 **Grey Gables.** Jack Woolley (b. 1919) also owns the village shop and the local paper, the *Borchester Echo.*
4 **2LO.**
5 ***Mrs Dale's Diary***, which was first broadcast in January 1948 and continued until April 1969. Mrs Dale was played by Ellis Powell until 1963, when Jessie Matthews took over. 'Jim' was the lovable GP Dr Dale, Mrs Dale's husband, played by the actor James Dale!
6 **Video.** The video which was released to promote the record was used to launch the MTV music channel in 1981.
7 **Home Service** (created in 1939), **Light Programme** (1945) and **Third Programme** (1946). These were rearranged in 1967 as Radio 4 (mainly, although not exclusively, programmes from the Home Service), Radio 1 and Radio 2 (Light Programme) and Radio 3 (Third Programme).
8 **Billy Cotton** (*The Billy Cotton Band Show*).
9 **Hertz**, named after the German radio pioneer Heinrich Hertz (1857–94), the first scientist to broadcast and receive radio waves.
10 **Ten shillings** (50p).
11 ***Under Milk Wood*** (1953, first broadcast 1954) by Dylan Thomas. Mr Pugh is the village schoolmaster.
12 **Cat's whisker.**
13 ***Educating Archie*** (with his dummy, Archie Andrews). The programme was transferred to its more natural medium of television in 1958.
14 **Poldhu**, in Cornwall. The letter 's' in Morse code was transmitted across the distance of nearly 3200 kilometres.
15 ***Music While You Work.***
16 **Willie Rushton** (1937–96). The radio show, hosted by Humphrey Lyttleton, celebrated its thirtieth anniversary in April 2002. The other founder members were Tim Brooke-Taylor, Graeme Garden and Barry Cryer. Since Rushton's death they have been joined by guest celebrities such as Paul Merton, Stephen Fry, Sandy Toksvig and Victoria Wood.
17 **Rudyard Kipling** (1865–1936).
18 ***Duddly Dell.*** It was composed and played by Dudley Moore (1935–2002), and recorded in 1961.
19 **Bertrand Russell** (1872–1970). The subject was 'Authority and the Individual'.
20 **Brian Patten.** It was initially planned as a series of eight programmes in 1979, but proved so popular that it was retained and is still on the air.

General Knowledge Questions

1 For what do the initials CB in CB Radio stand?
2 About which English Cathedral did the New Vaudeville Band sing in 1966, 'You stood and you watched as my baby left town'?
3 In Australia, what name is given to a backwater channel which forms a long, narrow lagoon?
4 What is the name of the one-hundred-and-seventh mayor of New York City, whose eight-year tenure ended on 31 December 2001 and who received an honorary knighthood from the Queen in February 2002?
5 Which historian wrote and presented the BBC television series *A History of Britain*, which was transmitted in three sections in 2000–2?
6 The poem *The Green Eye of the Yellow God* tells of an idol to the north of which city?
7 What is the collective term for a group of crows?
8 What is the name of Britain's first long-distance footpath (now National Trail), opened in 1965 and stretching for 429 kilometres?
9 In 1733–5 which artist created a series of engravings about a character named Tom Rakewell entitled *A Rake's Progress*?
10 In the Bible, on what did the chief priests and elders of the Temple spend the thirty pieces of silver which the repentant Judas Iscariot returned to them before he hanged himself?
11 What is the name of the granular rock, consisting mainly of a mixture of the mineral corundum and iron oxides, used as an abrasive and polishing material?
12 What name is given to the Chinese phonetic alphabet officially approved by the People's Republic in 1979 for transliterating Chinese characters into the Roman alphabet?
13 Which French art nouveau jeweller became a renowned designer of high-quality crystal glassware after being approached by Coty in 1905 to design the company's perfume bottles?
14 Whose 1976 Academy Award for Best Actor for his role in *Network* was awarded posthumously?
15 By what name is Mahler's Symphony No. 8 in E Flat Major (1907) popularly known, because of the number of performers required?
16 What type of plant is the food ingredient dulse (*Rhodymenia palmate*), which can be shredded and added to salads and contains a gelatinous substance sometimes used as a thickening agent?
17 In traditional Scottish marriage custom, what is a 'tocher'?
18 Which Canadian ice-skating pair had their silver medals upgraded to gold at the 2002 Winter Olympics at Salt Lake City after a judge was suspended for rigging the vote?
19 Which former World Chess Champion was arrested in 1981 on suspicion of being a bank robber?
20 Who was the composer of *By the Sleepy Lagoon* (1930), the theme music of Radio 4's *Desert Island Discs*?

1 **Citizens' band.** The Federal Communications Commission in the USA created the first Citizens' Radio Service in the 1940s, for regulating remote-control units and mobile radiotelephones.
2 **Winchester.** The writer Geoff Stephens hired a group of session musicians to record it in the fashion of a 1930s dance band.
3 **Billabong,** from Aboriginal *billa* (water) and *bang* (channel dry except after rain).
4 **Rudolph Giuliani** (b. 1944). He was succeeded by Michael R. Bloomberg.
5 **Simon Schama** (b. 1945), Professor of Art History and Art at Columbia University in New York.
6 **Kathmandu.** The poem was written by J. Milton Hayes (1884–1940):
There's a one-eyed yellow idol to the north of Khatmandu,
There's a little marble cross below the town;
There's a broken-hearted woman tends the grave of Mad Carew
And the Yellow God forever gazes down.
7 **A murder.**
8 **Pennine Way.** It extends from Edale, in Derbyshire, to Kirk Yetholm in the Scottish borders.
9 **William Hogarth** (1697–1764). The prints are in the collection of Sir John Soane's Museum, London.
10 **The Potter's Field** ('Blood Acre'), a burial place for foreigners: 'And they took counsel and bought with them the potter's field, to bury strangers in' (Matthew 27:7).
11 **Emery.** As an abrasive, emery has largely been replaced by synthetic materials such as alumina; its main use now is as a non-slip material for floors, stair treads and pavements.
12 **Pinyin.** After the communist takeover of China in 1949, comprehensive script reform began and the Roman alphabet was chosen. The resulting Chinese Phonetic Alphabet was adopted by the Committee on Language Reform in 1956 and modified in 1958.
13 **René Lalique** (1860–1945). His designs include panels for the Orient Express and fountains on the Champs-Élysées.
14 **Peter Finch** (1916–77). He plays a news anchorman who announces his own impending dismissal and threatens to commit suicide.
15 **'Symphony of a Thousand'.** It calls for a large double choir and a separate boys' choir in addition to a large orchestra and eight soloists.
16 **Seaweed.** It is found along north Atlantic coasts of the UK and North America.
17 **A bride's dowry.**
18 **David Pelletier** and **Jamie Sale.** The French judge, Marie-Reine Le Gougne, was alleged to have 'voted under pressure' for the Russian pair, Yelena Berezhnaya and Anton Sikharulidze, who were nonetheless allowed to keep the gold medals they had been awarded.
19 **Bobby Fischer** (b. 1943). He published a pamphlet about his false arrest entitled *Tortured in a Pasadena Jailhouse* (1982).
20 **Eric Coates** (1886–1957). A plaque commemorates him at Selsey, on the West Sussex coast, where he lived for a time.

Shakespeare Questions

1 From which Shakespeare play did Ray Bradbury cull the title for his 1962 novel *Something Wicked This Way Comes*?

2 In which Shakespeare play does the tinker Christopher Sly awaken from a drunken sleep to be duped into believing that he is a lord who has gone out of his mind?

3 What is the name of Capulet's niece, with whom we are told that Romeo is infatuated before he falls in love with Capulet's daughter, Juliet?

4 Who played the starring roles in John Madden's Academy Award-winning 1998 romantic comedy *Shakespeare in Love*?

5 Who succeeded Terry Hands as Artistic Director of the Royal Shakespeare Company in 1991?

6 What is the name of Katharina's father in *The Taming of the Shrew*?

7 Which Shakespearian character is described as 'the triple pillar of the world transform'd/Into a strumpet's fool'?

8 In Jaques's 'Seven Ages of Man' speech in *As You Like It*, who is 'full of wise saws and modern instances'?

9 Which Shakespeare play ends with the words, 'New joy wait on you! Here our play has ending'?

10 During the performance of which 'Shakespearian' play was the original Globe Theatre burned down in June 1613?

11 In Shakespeare, whose 'flashes of merriment . . . were wont to set the table on a roar'?

12 In *Henry IV Part 2* what did Prince Hal describe as 'polish'd perturbation! Golden care!'?

13 Which former member of the Chamberlain's Men performed in a nine-day Morris dance from London to Norwich, which he described in 1600 in his *Nine Days' Wonder*?

14 Which 1968 musical by Jack Good was based on Shakespeare's *Othello*?

15 In *The Merry Wives of Windsor* which Shakespearian character was disguised as 'the fat woman of Brentford'?

16 In 1769 which English actor, renowned for roles such as Benedick, Richard III, Hamlet, Romeo and King Lear, organised a jubilee in Stratford-upon-Avon to establish the town as a centre for Shakespearian pilgrimage?

17 In *A Midsummer Night's Dream* what name was used by Oberon for *Viola tricolor*, or heartsease, the wild pansy from which he made a love potion for anointing Titania's eyelids?

18 Who played the comic duo of Dogberry and Verges, the 'foolish captains', in Kenneth Branagh's 1993 film version of *Much Ado About Nothing*?

19 On which Shakespeare play was Wagner's 1836 opera *Das Liebesverbot* (*The Ban on Love*) based?

20 Which two fellow actors published in 1623 the so-called First Folio (*Mr William Shakespeare's Comedies, Histories and Tragedies*), the collected edition of thirty-six plays by Shakespeare?

1 *Macbeth* (Act IV, scene i). It is from the witches' scene: 'By the pricking of my thumbs/Something wicked this way comes.'
2 *The Taming of the Shrew* (Induction, scene ii).
3 **Rosaline** (*Romeo and Juliet*, Act I, scene ii).
4 **Joseph Fiennes** (as young Will Shakespeare) and **Gwyneth Paltrow** (as Viola de Lesseps).
5 **Adrian Noble**. He resigned in April 2002.
6 **Baptista** ('a rich gentleman of Padua').
7 **Mark Antony**, in *Antony and Cleopatra* (by Philo, one of Antony's friends, Act I, scene i).
8 **The justice**, 'in fair round belly with good capon lin'd,/With eyes severe, and beard of formal cut.' (*As You Like It*, Act II, scene vii).
9 *Pericles, Prince of Tyre* (spoken by Gower, the 'Chorus').
10 *Henry VIII* (*All is True*). A spark from a cannon set the thatch of the roof alight. Shakespeare is believed to have written parts of *Henry VIII*, possibly in collaboration with John Fletcher.
11 **Yorick**. Said by Hamlet, in *Hamlet* Act V, scene i.
12 **The Crown of England** (Act IV, scene v).
13 **Will Kempe** (c. 1560–c. 1603). The saying 'nine days' wonder', meaning something which arouses great interest but quickly fades, was already well established.
14 *Catch My Soul*. The title comes from words spoken by Othello in Act III, scene iii:

Excellent wretch! Perdition catch my soul
But I do love thee! and when I love thee not,
Chaos is come again.

15 **Falstaff**, in Act IV, scene ii.
16 **David Garrick** (1717–79).
17 **Love-in-idleness**. To mark its 2002 production of *A Midsummer Night's Dream*, the Royal Shakespeare Company commissioned Charles Sell, Fellow of the Royal Society of Chemistry, to recreate the potion. Because it smelled strongly of wintergreen, Dr Sell used a little artistic licence: he added the perfumes of two other flowers found in Titania's bower – sweet musk rose (*Rosa moschata*) and sweet violet (*Viola odorata*).
18 **Michael Keaton** and **Ben Elton**.
19 *Measure for Measure*.
20 **John Heminges** or Hemminge (1556–1630) and **Henry Condell** (d. 1627). It included commemorative verse by, among others, Ben Jonson.

General Knowledge Questions

1 Which denomination of Bank of England notes issued between July 1970 and March 1993 featured a portrait of William Shakespeare?
2 Which comic-book superhero is described as being 'faster than a speeding bullet, more powerful than a locomotive'?
3 Which battle in 1642 was the first armed encounter in the English Civil War?
4 On 1 September each year which English town's mayor sets out by boat with other officials into Pyefleet Creek to read a proclamation, dated 1256, that the oyster beds in the river on which it stands have belonged to it 'from the time beyond which memory runneth not to the contrary'?
5 In the 1956 film *Lust for Life*, Anthony Quinn won an Academy Award for Best Supporting Actor for a nine-minute appearance as which artist?
6 Which Moroccan athlete (nicknamed 'the Moroccan Express') won the gold medal in the 5000 metres in the 1984 Los Angeles Olympic Games and, in 1987, became the first to run that distance in less than thirteen minutes?
7 Whose charitable work is commemorated by the aluminium statue *Angel of Christian Charity* (better known as *Eros*) unveiled in 1893 in London's Piccadilly Circus?
8 Which Asian plant of the genus *Fortunella* produces acid-tasting fruit and has a name deriving from the Chinese for 'golden orange'?
9 Which Latin phrase indicates 'No sooner said than done'?
10 What was the name of the 245-metre-long German airship which caught fire and crashed at Lakehurst, New Jersey, in 1937, just over a year after its launch?
11 To which religion do the scriptures known as the Upanishads belong?
12 What is the name taken by a region of eastern Nigeria, inhabited principally by Igbo (Ibo) people, which seceded in 1967 and fought a three-year civil war, but was overcome by federal forces and ceased to exist as an independent state in January 1970?
13 Which rock group recorded the album *The Piper at the Gates of Dawn* in 1967?
14 From whose poem *The Poplar Field* do the following lines come?

Twelve years have elapsed since I first took a view
Of my favourite field, and the bank where they grew,
And now in the grass behold they are laid,
And the tree is my seat that once lent me a shade.

15 In 1933 which Ohio-born jazz pianist, nearly blind from birth, recorded *Tiger Rag*, which is reported to have sounded like three pianists playing simultaneously?
16 In the grounds of which castle in England were the UK's largest water gardens opened in January 2002?
17 By what name is the wasp *Eumenes fraternus* commonly known because of the vase-like nests of mud which it constructs and attaches to twigs or other objects?
18 The crater of which dangerously active volcano in Java is the site of a huge sulphur quarry?
19 In antiquity, who were known as the Seven Sages of Greece?
20 Which play by Shakespeare contains references to tennis and greyhound coursing?

General Knowledge Answers

1 £20.
2 **Superman**, created in 1938 by Jerry Siegel and Joe Shuster for Action Comics.
3 **Edgehill**, Warwickshire (23 October 1642). Prince Rupert commanded the Royalist army; the Parliamentarians were led by the Earl of Essex. The result was inconclusive.
4 **Colchester**, Essex, which owns all the oyster beds in the River Colne.
5 **Paul Gauguin**. Kirk Douglas played the leading role of Vincent van Gogh.
6 **Said Aouita**, in Rome in July 1987 in 12 minutes 58.39 seconds.
7 **Lord Shaftesbury** (Anthony Ashley Cooper, 1801–85), the social and industrial reformer. The sculptor was Alfred Gilbert (1854–1954).
8 **Kumquat**.
9 ***Dictum factum*** ('spoken – done').
10 ***Hindenburg***. Thirty-six of the ninety-seven people aboard were killed. The fire was generally attributed to a discharge of atmospheric electricity near a hydrogen gas leak from the airship.
11 **Hinduism**. 'Upanishad' means 'to sit down near', from Sanskrit *upa* (near) and *ni-sad* (sit down). The Upanishads feature many dialogues between sages and learners.
12 **Biafra**. The secession was led by the head of the Eastern Region, Lieutenant Colonel (later General) Odumegwu Ojukwu, with the authorisation of a consultative assembly.
13 **Pink Floyd**. The title is that of a chapter in Kenneth Grahame's *The Wind in the Willows* (1908).
14 **William Cowper** (1731–1800).
15 **Art Tatum** (1910–56). His technique was so unorthodox that he could rarely integrate his playing into that of a group; he nearly always played at the head of a trio or as a soloist.
16 **Alnwick**, opened by the Duchess of Northumberland, who commissioned the gardens, which were designed by the Belgian Wirtz International team of Peter, Jacques and Martin Wirtz.
17 **Potter wasp** (also known as the mason or sand wasp), found mainly in North America and Europe. The female lays an egg inside each pot and catches and paralyses caterpillars, which she puts into the pot for the developing larva to feed on. The larva pupates in the pot and emerges fully developed.
18 **Kawa Ijen** (2386 metres). Hundreds of workers toil in the crater cutting slabs of sulphur and carrying them in 100-kilogram loads 600 metres up to the rim of the crater and 3 kilometres to the weighing station on the outer slopes of the volcano.
19 **Bias** of Priene, **Chilon** of Sparta, **Cleobulus** of Lindos, **Periander** of Corinth, **Pittacus** of Mytilene, **Solon** of Athens and **Thales** of Miletus. They were seven men of practical wisdom (statesmen, law-givers and philosophers) who flourished in the seventh and sixth centuries BC. Some sources suggest Anacharsis instead of Periander.
20 ***Henry V***. The Dauphin of France sent Henry V a contemptuous gift of tennis balls when Henry was threatening to invade France (Act I, scene ii). In France, Henry says to his soldiers, 'I see you stand like greyhounds in the slips,/Straining upon the start' (Act III, scene i).

Tennis

Questions

1 For which game was Wimbledon originally designed as a venue?
2 By what name is the International Lawn Tennis Challenge Trophy more familiarly known?
3 What is the new name of the main court at Melbourne Park (one of the four 'Grand Slam' locations)?
4 Which wild-card entry from Croatia won the men's singles championship at Wimbledon in 2001, after three previous defeats in the Final?
5 Which unseeded seventeen-year-old was the youngest to win the men's singles title at Wimbledon in 1985?
6 Which former Wimbledon male champion was defeated by Billie Jean King in a 'Battle of the Sexes' challenge match at the Houston Astrodome, Texas, in 1973, in front of a crowd of more than 30,000 and a worldwide TV audience of nearly fifty million?
7 Named after a former US Wimbledon champion, what is the name of the main stadium at Flushing Meadow where the Finals of the US Open are held?
8 Which US tennis player was, in 1938, the first player to win the 'Grand Slam'?
9 Which member of the British royal family played in the All-England championship at Wimbledon in its Jubilee year of 1926?
10 Which four tennis players, who helped to establish French domination of world tennis in the mid-1920s, were known as 'The Four Musketeers'?
11 Which former British Wightman Cup player was the mother of the British tennis champion of the early 1980s, Buster Mottram?
12 Which ice-hockey player for the 1948 Czech Olympic team won the Wimbledon men's singles title playing as an Egyptian in 1954?
13 Which US player, who won eight Wimbledon singles titles between 1927 and 1938, was nicknamed 'Poker-Face'?
14 Who was the first black player to play for (and win) a Wimbledon singles title?
15 Which survivor of the *Titanic* disaster in 1912 went on to win a Wimbledon title?
16 Who patented the game of lawn tennis in 1874, based on the first *Book of Rules*, which he had published in 1873?
17 Which group of people took the 'Tennis Court Oath' in a tennis court at Versailles in June 1789?
18 What is the old Greek word, meaning 'skill in playing at ball', which was used for an early form of lawn tennis?
19 Which fifteenth-century king of Scotland introduced 'real' (royal) tennis to Scotland and lost his life as an indirect result of his attempts to prevent the tennis balls in his private court being lost?
20 Who is the only tennis player to have competed in both the men's and the women's singles competitions at the US Open Championship?

1 **Croquet.** The All-England Croquet Club (founded in 1868) held its first official tennis tournament in 1877. In 1882 it changed its name to the All-England Lawn Tennis and Croquet Club.

2 **Davis Cup.** It was for the first international team competition in 1900, in which the USA beat Great Britain 3–0. The cup was donated in 1900 by Dwight Davis (1879–1945), the US men's doubles champion (1899–1901).

3 **Rod Laver Arena.** Melbourne Park used to be known as Flinders Park.

4 **Goran Ivanisevic** (b. 1971). He beat Britain's Tim Henman in the semi-finals and defeated Australia's Pat Rafter in a rousing Final.

5 **Boris Becker** (b. 1967).

6 **Bobby Riggs** (1918–95). He had won the Wimbledon singles and doubles titles in 1939.

7 **Arthur Ashe Stadium.** Arthur Ashe (1943–93) was the first black man to win the US Open Championship (1968) and Wimbledon (1975).

8 **Donald Budge** (1915–2000).

9 **The future George VI** (Prince Albert, Duke of York). He played in a first-round doubles game with his partner, Louis Greig, but was defeated in three straight sets by Arthur Wentworth Gore and Herbert Roper Barrett.

10 **Jean Borotra** ('the Bounding Basque', 1898–1994), **Jacques Brugnon** (1895–1978), **Henri Cochet** (1901–87) and **René Lacoste** (1904–96).

11 **Joy Gannon,** who was one of the first players to break the 'all-white' convention by wearing a dress with purple hemlines created by Teddy Tinling.

12 **Jaroslav Drobny** (1921–2001). He defected to Egypt in 1949.

13 **Helen Wills Moody** (1905–98). The nickname arose from her imperturbable and expressionless demeanour.

14 **Althea Gibson** (b. 1927), in 1957. She had already won the Wimbledon doubles title in 1956, and won the singles title again in 1958. She also won the French championship in 1956, and the US title in 1957 and 1958.

15 **Norris Williams** (1891–1968). In 1920, with Charles Garland, he won the men's doubles by beating the British pair A.R.F. Kingscote and J.C. Parke.

16 **Major Walter Clopton Wingfield,** of Nantclwyd in North Wales.

17 **Representatives of the Third Estate** (*Tiers État*, the Commoners). The deputies had been excluded from the assembly hall by Louis XVI (r. 1774–93). They declared themselves to be the National Assembly, and swore never to disband until a constitution had been established.

18 ***Sphairistike.*** It was the name used by Walter Clopton Wingfield in his 1874 patent.

19 **James I** (r. 1406–37). When he was staying at Blackfriars in Perth, he played tennis during the day in the court outside his bedroom. When a group of would-be assassins broke into the house one night the king tried to escape through a sewer running under the floor of his bedroom; but only a few days earlier he had blocked the opening of the sewer at the corner of the court, and he was trapped and killed.

20 **Renée Richards** (b. Richard Raskind, 1934). As Richard Raskind he lost to the defending champion, Neale Fraser, in the first round of the US Open in 1960. After a sex-change operation in 1975 he changed his name to Renée Richards and entered the women's singles at the US Open in 1977, but was knocked out in the first round by Virginia Wade. She published her autobiography, *Second Serve: the Renée Richards Story*, in 1983.

General Knowledge Questions

1 Who won the first Wimbledon men's singles championship in which professionals were allowed to compete?
2 Who played the eponymous hero in the 1995 film *Rob Roy*?
3 Which Scottish skier won the bronze medal in the slalom at the Winter Olympics at Salt Lake City in February 2002, only to be stripped of his medal after he tested positive for the banned substance methamphetamine, which he claimed was taken unwittingly through an over-the-counter American nasal inhaler?
4 What was the name of the first British test pilot to fly *Concorde*, in April 1969?
5 Who played the long-suffering husband to Patricia Routledge's Hyacinth Bucket in the BBC TV series *Keeping Up Appearances*?
6 In the language of marketing analysis, for what does the acronym SWOT stand?
7 What garnishing is indicated by the culinary term *à la Véronique*?
8 Which Russian musician composed the *1812 Overture*?
9 Which US President was the immediate predecessor of John F. Kennedy?
10 Who was the Roman emperor at the time of the Crucifixion of Christ?
11 Which word meaning a rod on which wool or flax is wound preparatory to spinning has also come to be applied figuratively and metaphorically to women's work or women considered as a group?
12 What is the motto of the FBI (Federal Bureau of Investigation), which echoes the acronym of its title?
13 In 1986 which English city's cathedral and castle were declared a World Heritage Site?
14 What is the name of the New York cockroach with the soul of a poet, created by Don Marquis, which flings itself at a typewriter in order to hit the keys to write messages to Marquis, but cannot manage punctuation or capital letters?
15 What is the name of the oldest British ship currently still on the naval list, first commissioned in the eighteenth century and now in dry dock in Portsmouth?
16 Which British artist won the 2001 Turner Prize with the entry *Work 227: the lights going on and off* (1995)?
17 Which fictional family lived at The Laurels, Brickfield Terrace?
18 In Old Norse mythology, which two horses were known as 'the horse of the day' and 'the horse of the night'?
19 What is the term for a bird which is 'yoke-toed' – having the first and fourth toes pointing forwards and the second and third pointing backwards?
20 Which French tennis champion of the 1920s was nicknamed 'Le Crocodile' by sportswriters because of his tenacious playing style?

1 **Rod Laver** (b. 1938), in 1968. He had won Wimbledon twice as an amateur (in 1961 and 1962) before turning professional, and was already the holder of the professional world singles title, which he won five times.
2 **Liam Neeson** (b. 1952). The title role in the 1954 film was played by Richard Todd.
3 **Alain Baxter** (b. 1973), from Aviemore, known in the skiing fraternity as 'The Highlander'.
4 **Brian Trubshaw** (1924–2001).
5 **Clive Swift** (b. 1936).
6 **Strengths, Weaknesses, Opportunities, Threats.**
7 **White grapes.**
8 **Pyotr Ilyich Tchaikovsky** (1840–93). It was commissioned for the 1882 Moscow Exhibition, in particular the consecration of the Cathedral of Christ the Saviour, which was built to give thanks for the Russian victory during the Napoleonic Wars.
9 **Dwight D. Eisenhower** ('Ike', 1890–1969). A former general, and Supreme Commander of the Allied forces during the invasion of Europe in 1944, he became the thirty-fourth President and was re-elected in 1956.
10 **Tiberius** (r. 14–37).
11 **Distaff.**
12 **Fidelity, Bravery, Integrity.**
13 **Durham.**
14 **Archy** (in *archy* and *mehitabel*). Archy made his first appearance in *The Coming of Archy*; Mehitabel is his friend, an alley cat whose lineage goes back to Cleopatra. Don Marquis (1878–1937) was a newspaper columnist, poet and writer who wrote regularly for the *New York Sun* and the *Saturday Evening Post*.
15 **HMS *Victory***, Nelson's flagship at the Battle of Trafalgar (21 October 1805) and the only remaining eighteenth-century ship of the line anywhere in the world. It still has its own captain, officers and crew, and flies the flag of the Second Sea Lord, Commander in Chief Naval Home Command.
16 **Martin Creed** (b. 1968).
17 **The Pooter family**, in George and Weedon Grossmith's *The Diary of a Nobody* (1892).
18 **Skinfaxi** (Shining-mane) and **Hrímfaxi** (Frosty-mane). Day rode Skinfaxi, who illuminated the land and sea with light from his mane. Night rode Hrímfaxi, who sprinkled the earth every morning with dew from his bit.
19 **Zygodactyl** (zygodactylous). It applies to many of the woodpeckers, parrots and toucans, for example. Most birds have three toes pointing forwards and one (the hallux) pointing backwards.
20 **René Lacoste** (1904–96). Later Lacoste opened a sportswear company whose logo was a crocodile (which was somehow changed into an alligator).

1 What is the name of the London headquarters of the TUC?
2 Which international organisation was formed at the Paris Peace Conference of 1919?
3 Whose marriage in 1486 united the houses of York and Lancaster?
4 Which group had a hit with *Union City Blue* on their 1979 album *Eat to the Beat*?
5 Who was the first General Secretary of the Transport and General Workers' Union (TGWU), from 1922 to 1940?
6 What was the name of the 1957 treaty which established the European Economic Community (Common Market)?
7 Which Polish labour activist was one of the founders of the trade union Solidarity and went on to become President of Poland (1990–95)?
8 By what name is the European Treaty of Union (December 1991) better known, from the town in the Netherlands where it was signed?
9 The marriage of Ferdinand, son of John II of Aragon, to whom in 1469 brought about the union of Aragon and Castile?
10 What name was given to the treaty of economic union between Belgium, the Netherlands and Luxemburg, signed in February 1958?
11 Who was the first leader of the Christian Democratic Union in West Germany and became the first Chancellor of the Federal Republic of Germany in 1949?
12 Which Norwegian politician was the first Secretary-General of the United Nations?
13 What name was given to the coalition between Germany and Italy, signed in 1936, which opposed the Allies in the Second World War?
14 Which secret police union, formed in 1923 when the USSR was constituted, was absorbed into the NKVD (People's Commissariat for Internal Affairs), which, in turn, became the KGB?
15 Which General Secretary of the Transport and General Workers' Union was elected MP for Nuneaton in 1965 and was Minister of Technology from 1964 to 1966?
16 Of which US labour union was James Hoffa president from 1957 to 1971?
17 Which British Prime Minister was in power at the time of the Act of Union 1801 which united Ireland with England, Scotland and Wales?
18 In 1923 who became the first woman to chair the TUC?
19 Which country's trade union federation is known as RENGO?
20 Which fourteenth-century queen of Denmark engineered the Union of Kalmar which united the kingdoms of Denmark, Norway and Sweden in 1397?

Unions

Answers

1 **Congress House**, Great Russell Street.
2 **The League of Nations.** It was an organisation for international cooperation, established at the initiative of the victorious Allied Powers at the end of the First World War.
3 **Henry VII** (1457–1509, son of Edmund Tudor and Margaret Beaufort), and **Elizabeth of York** (eldest daughter of Edward IV and Elizabeth Woodville).
4 **Blondie.** Union City in Hudson County, New Jersey, was also the setting for the 1980 film *Union City*, in which Debbie Harry, the group's blonde lead singer, made her debut.
5 **Ernest Bevin** (1881–1951). The TGWU was formed in a merger of fourteen unions. Bevin was drafted into the wartime Coalition Government in 1940 as Minister of Labour and National Service, and later became Foreign Secretary in the post-war Attlee administration.
6 **Treaty of Rome.** Britain joined, along with Ireland and Denmark, in 1973.
7 **Lech Walesa** (b. 1943). He was awarded the Nobel Peace Prize in 1983.
8 **Maastricht Treaty.**
9 **Isabella of Castile** (1451–1504). They became joint rulers of Aragon and Castile in Spain on the succession of Ferdinand II (1452–1615) to the throne of Aragon in 1479.
10 **Benelux.** It was designed to create the first completely free international labour market, and to allow the free movement of capital and services.
11 **Konrad Adenauer** (1876–1967).
12 **Trygve Lie** (1896–1968). He was elected Secretary-General in February 1946 but resigned in 1952 over Soviet opposition to his policy of intervention in the Korean War.
13 **Axis.** Later that year Japan joined 'the Axis' as part of the anti-Comintern pact against the Soviet Union.
14 **OGPU** (Unified State Political Administration).
15 **Frank Cousins** (1904–86). He was also chairman of the Community Relations Commission from 1968 to 1970.
16 **Teamsters Union.** James Hoffa (1913–75) helped to make the Teamsters the largest labour union in the USA. He was notorious for his links with the Mafia, and 'disappeared' from a suburban restaurant near Detroit in 1975.
17 **William Pitt the Younger** (1759–1806). The Act remained in force until 1922, after the recognition of the Irish Free State.
18 **Margaret Bondfield** (1873–1953). In 1929 she became Minister of Labour in Ramsey MacDonald's second administration.
19 **Japan.** It was founded in 1989; its full name in Japanese is Nihon Rodo Kumiai Sorengokai.
20 **Queen Margrethe I** (1353–1412, r. 1375–97). As the widow of Håkon VI of Norway, she became Regent of Norway in 1380, and she became Queen of Sweden after invading the country in 1388. She ensured that her sister's grandson, Erik of Pomerania, was crowned king of the three countries as Erik VII in 1397.

General Knowledge Questions

1 Of which trade union are the initials BALPA an acronym?
2 Which actor played the hard-nosed Inspector Jack Regan in the popular ITV series *The Sweeney* (1975–82)?
3 Which British pop singer, who shares her name with a legendary queen of Carthage, won Best Album (for her 1999 album *No Angel*) and Best Female Artist awards in 2002?
4 Which British oarsman won an unprecedented fifth successive Olympic gold medal (in the Coxless Fours) at the Sydney Olympics in 2000?
5 According to the Bible, in whose house in Bethany did a woman anoint Jesus with precious oils on the eve of the Last Supper?
6 In computing, for what does the acronym GIGO stand?
7 What was the original name given to tungsten, commonly used in lamp filaments?
8 Which globe-trotting TV documentary presenter and author, with his trademark spectacles and moustache, started his BBC career on the *Tonight* programme (1957–65)?
9 What is the main ingredient of latkes, the pancakes traditionally eaten at the Jewish festival of Hanukkah?
10 The name of which make of car happens to be a Latin word meaning 'let it be done' and is used for a decree, a formal command or a short order or warrant of a judge?
11 Which phrase from Shakespeare's *Othello* was used by Edward Elgar as the title of a set of five marches for a symphony orchestra?
12 Which sixteenth-century Dutch artist painted the triptych, now in the Prado, Madrid, which features *The Garden of Earthly Delights* with its dreamlike, fantastical people, animals and plants?
13 Which fellow-composer did Rossini dub 'The Mozart of the Champs-Élysées'?
14 Which US cartoonist and film animator was the creator of Bugs Bunny, Daffy Duck, Wile E Coyote, Porky Pig, Road Runner and other anarchic cartoon characters?
15 Which Bristol-born woman became in 1849 the first qualified female physician in the USA?
16 Which grammatical term, derived from a Greek verb meaning 'to yoke together', refers to a phrase in which one word governs or modifies two or more words not connected in meaning: for example, 'Miss Bolo rose from the table considerably agitated and went straight home, in a flood of tears and a sedan chair'?
17 Which Catholic prelate succeeded Cardinal Winning as Archbishop of Glasgow and leader of the Catholic Church in Scotland in 2002?
18 What is the name of the 1700-kilometre dog-sled race run on the first Saturday of March each year in Alaska from Anchorage to Nome?
19 Which US mathematician, despite suffering from severe schizophrenia, was awarded the Nobel Prize for economics in 1994?
20 Which royal wedding in August 1503 was dubbed 'the marriage of the thistle and the rose'?

1 **British Air Line Pilots' Association.**
2 **John Thaw** (1942–2002). He also starred as Inspector Morse in the ITV series of that name, and as the eponymous *Kavanagh QC*.
3 **Dido** (Dido Florio Cloud de Bounivialle Armstrong, b. 1971). She enrolled at the Guildhall School of Music in London at the age of six and learned to play the piano, violin and recorder. After touring with a British classical ensemble, she worked in publishing, singing in her spare time with a series of local groups and, in 1995, joining Faithless, her brother Rollo's group.
4 **Steve Redgrave** (b. 1962). His other gold medals were for Coxed Fours (1984) and Coxless Pairs (1988, 1992 and 1996).
5 **Simon the Leper** (Matthew 26:6–13).
6 **Garbage In, Garbage Out.**
7 **Wolfram.** Tungsten (chemical symbol W) is a hard, malleable grey metal derived from wolframite.
8 **Alan Whicker** (b. 1925), presenter of numerous *Whicker's World* series and associated programmes.
9 **Potatoes.** Grated potatoes and onion are mixed with egg and flour and then fried in olive oil.
10 **Fiat.** Fiat is an acronym for Fabbrica Italiana Automobile Torino.
11 ***Pomp and Circumstance*** (composed between 1901 and 1930). The phrase is spoken by Othello to Iago in Act III, scene iii:
Farewell the neighing steed and the shrill trump,
The spirit-stirring drum, the ear-piercing fife,
The royal banner, and all quality,
Pride, pomp and circumstance of glorious war!
12 **Hieronymus Bosch** (c. 1450–1516). On the left-hand wing of the triptych is *The Garden of Eden with God Creating Eve as a Companion to Adam* and on the right is *Hell*.
13 **Jacques Offenbach** (originally Jacob Eberst, 1819–80), composer of the opera *La Vie Parisienne* (1866).
14 **Chuck Jones** (1912–2002).
15 **Elizabeth Blackwell** (1821–1910). She graduated from Geneva Medical School, New York State.
16 **Zeugma.** Another Greek word for it is 'syllepsis'. The example is from *The Pickwick Papers* by Charles Dickens (chapter 35).
17 **Mario Conti** (former Bishop of Aberdeen).
18 **Iditarod.** The race commemorates the marathon sled run during a diphtheria epidemic in 1925 in which twenty teams relayed vaccine across the 1085 kilometres from Nenana to Nome in 27½ hours. The name comes from Haiditarod ('the distant place'), an old name given by the indigenous Athabascan people to their inland hunting ground.
19 **John Forbes Nash Jr** (b. 1928). He developed the game-theory formulation which became known as the Nash Equilibrium. His story was the subject of the 2002 film *A Beautiful Mind*.
20 **James IV of Scotland and Margaret Tudor** (daughter of Henry VII of England and Elizabeth of York, and sister of the future Henry VIII). The hammer-beam roof of the Great Hall of Edinburgh Castle, completed by James in time for the wedding, rests on a series of stone corbels, one of which depicts a bowl in which a rose nestles between two thistles.

1 Which British artist painted the controversially bleak portrait of the Queen to celebrate the Golden Jubilee of her reign in 2002?
2 What term refers to a painting or sculpture depicting the Virgin Mary holding the dead Christ in her arms or on her lap?
3 Which US artist's work featured tins of Campbell's soup and bottles of Coca-Cola?
4 Which German artist, commissioned by Thomas Cromwell, painted a flattering portrait of Anne of Cleves in 1539 which persuaded Henry VIII to marry her in 1540?
5 What is the name of the award-winning west wing of London's National Gallery, designed by the US architects Venturi, Scott Brown and Associates and opened in 1991?
6 Which Renaissance painter was the subject of the 1961 fictionalised biography *The Agony and the Ecstasy* by Irving Stone?
7 In 1793 the French artist Jacques-Louis David painted the assassinated body of which contemporary politician?
8 Bridget Riley is the leading British exponent of which style of art of the 1960s?
9 Who was the original illustrator of Lewis Carroll's *Alice's Adventures in Wonderland* and *Through the Looking-Glass*?
10 What is the title of the epic-heroic scene painted by the French artist Théodore Géricault between 1818 and 1819 depicting the desperate survivors of a contemporary shipwreck, many of whose companions had died of starvation?
11 Which artist was denounced by John Ruskin as 'flinging a pot of paint in the public's face' with his 1874 painting *Nocturne in Black and Gold: The Falling Rocket*?
12 The chemical barium chromate is often used to make which pigment?
13 Which renowned art collection is held at Hertford House, Manchester Square, in London?
14 Which Turkish-born Canadian photographer, who took a celebrated photograph of Winston Churchill in 1941, published several books, including *Faces of Destiny* (1946) and *Portraits of Greatness* (1959)?
15 In 1632 who painted *The Anatomy Lesson of Dr Nicolaes Tulp*, which depicted the doctor giving a demonstration to Amsterdam's Guild of Surgeons?
16 Which river, immortalised in the paintings of John Constable, forms much of the boundary between Essex and Suffolk?
17 Which Shakespearian figures are represented in the 1931 statue by Eric Gill on the façade of Broadcasting House in London?
18 Which English artist, who died at the age of twenty-five, scandalised Victorian society with his erotic illustrations for Oscar Wilde's play *Salome* (1894)?
19 Which Scottish art gallery houses Dante Gabriel Rossetti's 1880 painting *Dante's Dream*?
20 Which US artist and illustrator painted a portrait of John F. Kennedy in 1960, later used for the cover of the *Saturday Evening Post* after Kennedy's assassination?

1 **Lucian Freud** (b. 1922). Critics described the Queen's unflattering image as 'painful, brave, honest, stoical and, above all, clear sighted' and 'a thought-provoking and psychologically penetrating contribution to royal iconography'.
2 **Pietà**.
3 **Andy Warhol** (c. 1928–87).
4 **Hans Holbein** (the Younger, 1497/8–1543). She was unflatteringly nick-named 'The Flanders Mare', and the marriage was annulled after six months.
5 **Sainsbury Wing**. The awards which it won are: Benjamin Franklin Medal, 1993, Honor Award of American Institute of Architects, 1992, Arts Access Award, 1992, National Drywall Award for New Building, 1992, Queen's Award for Export Achievement, 1991 and Design Award for Natural Stone, 1991. The original building was designed by William Wilkins in 1838.
6 **Michelangelo** (Michelangelo di Lodovico Buonarroti Simoni, 1475–1564). It was filmed in 1965 with Charlton Heston in the title role.
7 **Jean-Paul Marat** (1743–93). *The Death of Marat*: he was assassinated in his bath by Charlotte Corday, a young Girondin conservative.
8 **Op art**. Her work of that era was mainly concerned with geometric abstraction, in which intricate patterns of black and white or alternating colours produce illusions of movement. Examples include *Drift No. 2* (1966) and *Nineteen Greys* (1968).
9 **John Tenniel** (1820–1914).
10 ***The Raft of the Medusa***. Géricault's intention was to provoke public fury at the deliberate casting adrift of the hapless raft people, and a scandal ensued.
11 **James Abbott McNeill Whistler** (1834–1903). He won a farthing in damages after a libel action in 1877.
12 **Lemon yellow**. Barium chromate is also used in safety matches and as a corrosion inhibitor and metal primer.
13 **Wallace Collection**. The collection was built up by Richard Wallace (1818–90), illegitimate son of the 4th Marquess of Hertford, and bequeathed to the nation by his widow in 1897. Its best-known work is Frans Hals' *The Laughing Cavalier* (1624).
14 **Yousuf Karsh** (1908–2002).
15 **Rembrandt** (Rembrandt van Rijn, 1606–69).
16 **Stour**. Constable (1776–1837) was born in the village of East Bergholt, near the River Stour. One of his paintings in which the Stour appears is *The Lock* (Flatford Lock, 1824).
17 **Prospero and Ariel** (from *The Tempest*).
18 **Aubrey Beardsley** (1872–98).
19 **McManus Gallery**, Dundee.
20 **Norman Rockwell** (1894–1978). The portrait was also used on memorial postage stamps issued in 1964.

General Knowledge

Questions

1 In which English city is the Graves Art Gallery?
2 Which actress played the part of Alf Garnett's wife Else in the BBC television comedies *Till Death Us Do Part* and *In Sickness and in Health*?
3 Which country's flag features a cedar tree?
4 Which female singer had No. 1 hits in the 1970s with *Can the Can* and *Devil Gate Drive*?
5 What is the name of the Christian manual containing doctrinal instruction in the form of questions and answers, given to children and adults to study before Confirmation?
6 What is the name given to the glossy black lacquer, produced from the sap of the tree *Rhus vernicifera*, which is used on wood, especially furniture?
7 Who is the only Hollywood star to have won four Academy Awards for acting?
8 Which Canadian-born jazz pianist and composer won the *Downbeat* award for the best jazz pianist of the year twelve times and composed and recorded *Canadiania Suite* (1964)?
9 What is the collective term for a group of nightingales?
10 Which Nobel Prize-winning poet won the 1999 Whitbread Book of the Year award for his translation of *Beowulf*?
11 Which French word for a monk's hood is used in English for a long, lightweight anorak?
12 Which Swiss educationist, a disciple of Jean-Jacques Rousseau, opened his own school for poor children at Berthoud and outlined his theories in *How Gertrude Educates Her Children* (1801)?
13 In which sport are the Thomas Cup and the Über Cup awarded?
14 In Hinduism, what is the name for the festival which takes place in India every three years, when the sun is in the sign of Aquarius, and attracts huge numbers of pilgrims?
15 Which Swiss chemist received the Nobel Prize for physiology or medicine in 1948 for his research into the use of DDT as an insecticide in the 1930s?
16 What is the source of the title *When Love Speaks*, the CD of Shakespearian songs and recitations produced in 2002 in aid of RADA?
17 Which former Olympic hurdler and British Labour statesman was awarded the Nobel Peace Prize in 1959?
18 Which beautiful *femme fatale* in one of Anthony Trollope's novels made a divine impression in a dress of 'white velvet without any other garniture than rich white lace worked with pearls across her bosom'?
19 Which nineteenth-century English astronomer gave his name to the brilliant spots of sunlight ('beads') which appear briefly around the moon just before and after a total eclipse of the sun?
20 In 1963, using the style of comic books, which artist painted *Whaam!*, an image of a jet fighter destroying another aeroplane with a rocket?

1 **Sheffield.** The gallery was established in 1934 with funding from Alderman J.G. Graves (1866–1945), who came to Sheffield as an apprentice watchmaker and later set up a mail-order business.
2 **Dandy Nichols** (1907–86).
3 **Lebanon.** The flag has two horizontal red bands separated by a white band which is twice the width of the red bands and has at its centre a green and brown cedar tree.
4 **Suzi Quatro** (b. 1950).
5 **Catechism.**
6 **Japan.** The tree is indigenous to China and has been cultivated in Japan since about the sixth century.
7 **Katharine Hepburn**, in 1933 (*Morning Glory*), 1967 (*Guess Who's Coming to Dinner*), 1968 (*The Lion in Winter*) and 1981 (*On Golden Pond*).
8 **Oscar Peterson** (b. 1925). He composed many of his own recordings, including *A Royal Wedding Suite* (1981), in honour of the marriage of the Prince and Princess of Wales.
9 **Watch.**
10 **Seamus Heaney** (b. 1939). He was awarded the Nobel Prize for literature in 1995.
11 **Cagoule.**
12 **Johann Heinrich Pestalozzi** (1746–1827). His book is the recognised exposition of the Pestalozzian method.
13 **Badminton.** The Thomas Cup was donated in 1939 by George Thomas (President of the International Badminton Federation) for a series of men's international team competitions. The Über Cup was contributed in 1956 by Mrs H.S. Über, a former English champion, for a series of women's international team competitions. Both tournaments are held every three years.
14 **Khumba-mela.** The venue for the festival rotates between the holy cities of Hardwar, Allahabad (on the site of the old city of Prayaga), Ujjaini and Nasik.
15 **Paul Hermann Müller** (1899–1965). The German chemist Othmar Zeidler had first synthesised DDT (dichlorodiphenyltrichloroethane) in 1874 but had not recognised its potential as an insecticide. In 1939 the Swiss government tested it successfully against the Colorado beetle. It also proved successful in combating typhus (carried by lice) and malaria (carried by various species of mosquito); but it has been banned in the West since 1972, after fears that it had toxic effects on wildlife and humans.
16 ***Love's Labour's Lost***, Act IV, scene iii, spoken by Biron:
And when Love speaks, the voice of all the gods
make heaven drowsy with the harmony.
17 **Philip John Noel-Baker** (1889–1982). He captained the British Olympic team at the Stockholm Games in 1912, and published several books on international problems, including *Disarmament* (1926) and *The Arms Race* (1958).
18 **Signora Madeline Vesey-Neroni**, in *Barchester Towers* (1857). She was the daughter of Dr Stanhope; her romantic escapades in Italy culminated in an unfortunate marriage and her being crippled.
19 **Francis Bailey** (d. 1844) – 'Bailey's Beads'.
20 **Roy Lichtenstein** (1923–97). The painting is now in Tate Modern, London.

Warfare Questions

1 What was the name of the French-produced missile used to dramatic effect by the Argentinian Air Force during the Falklands War in 1982?

2 What did Captain Robert Jenkins exhibit to a committee of the House of Commons in 1738, precipitating the war between Great Britain and Spain which merged into the War of the Austrian Succession?

3 What name did the Romans give to the battle formation in which infantry-men formed a group covered by a protective screen of their overlapping shields held above their heads and around the sides of the group?

4 During which battle of the Crimean War did the 'Charge of the Light Brigade' take place?

5 On the feast day of which two saints did the battle of Agincourt take place in 1415, as recorded in Shakespeare's *Henry V* (Act IV, scene iii) in the king's pre-battle rallying speech to his troops?

6 In the First World War, the slogan 'They shall not pass' symbolised the defence of which French town?

7 Which anti-tank missile of the 1960s has the same name as an old Irish battle club made from hard wood such as blackthorn or oak?

8 From which First World War poem by Laurence Binyon do the following words come?

They went with songs to the battle, they were young,
Straight of limb, true of eye, steady and aglow.
They were staunch to the end against odds uncounted,
They fell with their faces to the foe.

9 Which German aircraft manufacturer produced the Stuka dive-bomber used in the Second World War?

10 How did 'Tommy' come to be a synonym for the ordinary British soldier?

11 Which fifteenth-century Italian artist painted *The Battle of San Romano*, which was fought between Florence and neighbouring Siena in 1432?

12 About which battle in 1745 did the victorious Jacobites ridicule the defeated English commander with a song which opens:

Hey, Johnnie Cope, are ye wakened yet?
Or are your drums a-beating yet?

13 Which British commander surrendered an 8000-strong army to the American commander-in-chief, George Washington, at the siege of Yorktown in 1781, thus ending the American War of Independence?

14 Which ancient siege engine consisted of a sling on a pivoted wooden arm set in motion by the dropping of a large weight?

15 During the South African War, which town in Natal (now KwaZulu/Natal province) was besieged by the Boers for four months in 1899–1900?

16 At which battle in Greece, in 480 BC, did a thousand Spartans led by Leonidas fight to the death against a vast Persian army?

17 Which campaign of the First World War, named after a peninsula in the Dardanelles, hastened Herbert Asquith's resignation in December 1916?

18 By what name is the 'Battle of the Three Emperors' (2 December 1805) better known?

19 In 1993 which artist was commissioned by the Imperial War Museum to record the Bosnian war?

20 Which film-maker produced and directed the controversial nuclear holocaust documentary *The War Game* for the BBC in 1965?

1 **Exocet.** The destroyer HMS *Sheffield* and the container ship *Atlantic Conveyor* were sunk by Exocets.
2 **His amputated ear**, which he alleged had been cut off in April 1731 in the West Indies by Spanish coastguards who had boarded his ship, pillaged it and set it adrift.
3 *Testudo* (tortoise).
4 **Balaclava** (1854). Owing to confusion, the Light Brigade under Lord Cardigan was ordered to charge the Russian guns head-on. About forty per cent of the cavalrymen in the charge were killed.
5 **St Crispin** and **St Crispinian** (25 October).
6 **Verdun** (February 1916). The words are attributed to General, later Marshal, Pétain (*Ils ne passeront pas*); but the first official record of the expression appears in General Nivelle's Order of the Day in June 1916 to his troops at the height of the battle: '*Vous ne les laisserez pas passer*' ('You will not let them pass').
7 **Shillelagh.**
8 *For the Fallen* (1914).
9 **Hugo Junkers** (1859–1935). 'Stuka' was short for *Stürzkampfflugzeug* ('dive-bomber').
10 **'Thomas Atkins'** was the specimen name for a soldier on official documents to be signed.
11 **Paolo (di Dono) Uccello** (1397–1475). The painting (c. 1456) consists of a series of three panels which are now in the National Gallery, London, the Louvre, Paris, and the Uffizi, Florence.
12 **Prestonpans** (21 September 1745) west of Haddington, near Edinburgh. It lasted barely ten minutes. The English, led by General Sir John Cope, were taken by surprise and overwhelmed by a ferocious Highland charge.
13 **Lord Cornwallis** (1738–1805).
14 **Trebuchet.** A mangonel is similar to a trebuchet, but without the falling weight.
15 **Ladysmith**, on the River Klip. It was founded in 1850 after the British annexed the area and named after the wife of Sir Harry Smith (the governor of Cape Colony).
16 **Thermopylae.** After the battle the Persians, under Xerxes I, sacked Athens, but were defeated at the naval Battle of Salamis (also in 480 BC) and withdrew.
17 **Gallipoli** (1915). Asquith was replaced as Prime Minister by Lloyd-George.
18 **Battle of Austerlitz** (in the Napoleonic Wars). It was the first engagement of the War of the Third Coalition and one of Napoleon's greatest victories. The three emperors were Napoleon I of France, Alexander I of Russia and Francis II (the last Holy Roman Emperor, then Francis 1 of Russia).
19 **Peter Howson** (b. 1958).
20 **Peter Watkins** (b. 1935). He resigned from the BBC when the film was banned (even though it won an Academy Award for best Feature Documentary); it was later made available for theatrical release through the British Film Institute. It was eventually screened in 1985 as part of the BBC's coverage of the fortieth anniversary of Hiroshima.

General Knowledge Questions

1 In which country were *The Killing Fields* of Roland Joffé's 1984 film?
2 What colour is produced by mixing red and green light?
3 In which children's book does an evacuee named Peter Prevensie become King?
4 Which was the first garden city in England, founded in Hertfordshire in 1903?
5 Which two singers teamed up to record for Live Aid *Dancing in the Street*, which reached No. 1 in the UK in 1985?
6 The name of which car manufacturer comes from two words meaning 'Japan industry'?
7 What was the name of the spymaster who organised an espionage system for Elizabeth of England which eventually trapped Mary Queen of Scots in the Babington Plot, leading to her execution in 1587?
8 In 1937 which Surrealist artist painted *The Metamorphosis of Narcissus* and wrote a poem to accompany it whose prologue gives the viewer instructions for looking at the painting?
9 Which sport is played under the Cartwright Rules?
10 In the English Civil War, who was the commander-in-chief of the New Model Army when it defeated the royalist army under Prince Rupert at the decisive Battle of Naseby in June 1645?
11 In which BBC1 series were plays such as Mike Leigh's *Abigail's Party* and Jack Rosenthal's *Bar Mitzvah Boy* first shown?
12 Which bridge in Washington State, built in 1940 and known as 'Galloping Gertie', collapsed after only four months?
13 Who became leader of the British Parliamentary Labour Party in 1935 in succession to George Lansbury?
14 What is the main ingredient of *hongshao dan*, which are traditionally eaten at the Chinese Moon Festival in mid-autumn?
15 In classical mythology, which god was the father of the divine winged horse Pegasus?
16 What is the name of the headquarters in Godalming, Surrey, of the World Wide Fund for Nature (WWF)?
17 According to Lewis Carroll's 1876 verses *The Hunting of the Snark*, against what two perils should travellers to Snark Island insure themselves?
18 Who founded the spiritual and metaphysical system, later a church, known as Christian Science?
19 Who was the first winner, in January 2002, of the new BBC *Mastermind* on the Discovery Channel, with Clive Anderson in the inquisitor's seat?
20 What, in medieval warfare, was a destrier?

1 **Cambodia**. The film was based on a Pulitzer Prize-winning article by Sydney Schanberg entitled *The Death and Life of Dith Pran* (1980).
2 **Yellow**.
3 ***The Lion, the Witch and the Wardrobe*** (1950) by C.S. Lewis, the first of the 'Narnia' novels.
4 **Letchworth**, founded by Ebenezer Howard (1850–1928) who put forward his ideas in *Garden Cities of To-Morrow* (1902).
5 **David Bowie and Mick Jagger**. The song was originally recorded by Martha and the Vandellas in the 1960s.
6 **Nissan**, from Nihon Sangyo.
7 **Francis Walsingham** (1532–90), Secretary of State. Anthony Babington (1561–1586) led the plot to assassinate Elizabeth and install her prisoner, Mary Queen of Scots, on the English throne. He wrote to Mary explaining his plans, but his letters and her reply were intercepted by Walsingham's spies.
8 **Salvador Dalí** (1904–89). The viewer is instructed to look at the painting 'from a slight distance' and with a certain 'distant fixedness', focusing first on the large figure of the kneeling Narcissus.
9 **Baseball**. Alexander Cartwright (1820–1892) helped to found the amateur Knickerbocker Baseball Club in New York. He chaired a club committee which prepared the rules, partly from Robin Carter's *Book of Sports* (1834), which were adopted in 1845.
10 **Sir Thomas Fairfax** (1612–71).
11 *Play for Today* (1970–84).
12 **Tacoma Narrows suspension bridge**. It was hailed as the lightest, narrowest and most elegant suspension bridge ever built, but bucked and twisted in a wind like a rodeo horse. No one was on the bridge when it collapsed.
13 **Clement Attlee** (1883–1967), Prime Minister from 1945 to 1951.
14 **Eggs**. Shelled hard-boiled eggs are simmered in a mixture of soy sauce, spices and sugar which flavours them and gives them a deep reddish-brown colour. They are served with rice.
15 **Poseidon**.
16 **Panda House**. WWF (formerly World Wildlife Fund) was founded in the UK in 1961.
17 **Fire** and **Damage from Hail**. They are also advised to take a dagger-proof coat.
18 **Mary Baker Eddy** (1821–1910). She founded the Church of Christ, Scientist, in Boston in 1879.
19 **Michael Penrice**, a primary schoolteacher from Cumbria. Taking 'English History 1603–1714' as his specialised subject, he won by a single point in a cliff-hanging finish.
20 **A knight's charger**. The word derives ultimately from the Latin *dexter* (right-hand); it was a warhorse led by the squire with his right hand.

1 Who wrote the 1848 children's Christmas story of *The Little Match Girl* ?
2 For what did Spike Jones and the City Slickers ask for Christmas 1947 in their popular record?
3 Which fourth-century 'Christmas saint' is the patron saint of pawnbrokers, sailors, scholars, thieves and unmarried girls?
4 In which Cambridge College has the annual Festival of Nine Lessons and Carols been held every Christmas Eve since 1918?
5 What does the Christian festival of Epiphany (6 January) commemorate?
6 In the 1853 Christmas carol by John Neale, for what kind of logs did Good King Wenceslas ask?
7 Which Italian artist painted two versions of a Nativity scene *The Virgin of the Rocks* (now in the Louvre, Paris, and the National Gallery, London)?
8 In which 1932 novel by William Faulkner is Joe Christmas the tragic victim of violent racial prejudice?
9 In the biblical accounts of the Nativity, which pregnant kinswoman did Mary visit soon after the Annunciation?
10 A drinking fountain in Finsbury Square, London, commemorates Tom Smith, who invented which Christmas commodity there in 1847?
11 Which nineteenth- and twentieth-century poet and novelist wrote the following lines?

Christmas Eve, and twelve of the clock.
'Now they are all on their knees,'
An elder said as we sat in a flock
By the embers in hearthside ease.

12 Which four ghosts did Dickens's Scrooge see on Christmas Eve?
13 By what name is the bird *Streptopelia turtur*, which features in *The Twelve Days of Christmas*, better known?
14 With which English city are the words of this Christmas carol associated?

Lullay, thou little tiny Child,
By-bye lully, lullay.
Lullay, thou little tiny Child,
By-bye lully, lullay.

15 In his 1822 poem *A Visit from St Nicholas*, what names did Clement Clarke Moore (1779–1863) give to Santa's eight reindeer?
16 What is the common name of the red-flowered Brazilian plant *Schlumbergera truncata*, which frequently flowers at Christmas?
17 Which Christmas carol was written for guitar music on Christmas Eve, 1818, in Austria by the musician Franz Grüber and the poet-priest Joseph Mohr?
18 Who wrote the rap *Talking Turkeys!!*, which begins with the following lines?

Be nice to yu turkeys dis christmas
Cos turkeys jus wanna hav fun
Turkeys are cool, turkeys are wicked
An every turkey has a Mum.

19 In Italian tradition, what is the name of the woman who fills children's Christmas stockings with gifts on the eve of Epiphany (Twelfth Night)?
20 Which Leith printer produced the first 'Yuletide card', in 1841, five years before the first commercially produced Christmas card?

1 **Hans Christian Andersen** (1805–75).
2 **Their two front teeth.** *All I Want for Christmas is My Two Front Teeth*, written by Don Gardner, also reached No. 1 in the US charts in 1948.
3 **St Nicholas.** In legend he gave gold to three needy girls for their dowries, which led to the custom of exchanging presents on his feast day (6 December).
4 **King's College.** The festival was organised by Eric Milner-White, Dean of King's.
5 **The visit of the wise men to the stable where Christ was born.** The word comes from the Greek word *epiphaneia*, meaning 'an appearing', and refers to the manifestation of Christ to the Magi.
6 **Pine:**
'Bring me flesh, and bring me wine,
Bring me pine logs hither. . .
7 **Leonardo da Vinci** (1452–1519).
8 ***Light in August.***
9 **Elisabeth,** wife of Zechariah, whose unborn son was to be John the Baptist.
10 **Christmas cracker.** On a trip to Paris in 1840 Tom Smith discovered the *bonbon* (a sugared almond in a twist of tissue paper) and began making them, adding a love motto in the wrapping. The crackle of a burning log gave him the idea of adding a cracking sound. By 1847 he had perfected a small chemical explosion to create a 'pop' when the wrapping was broken. He added a small gift and called his invention 'crackers cosaques'.
11 **Thomas Hardy** (1840–1928), in *The Oxen*.
12 **Jacob Marley** (his former partner); **Ghost of Christmas Past; Ghost of Christmas Present;** and **Ghost of Christmas Yet to Come.**
13 **Turtle dove.**
14 **Coventry** (the Coventry Carol), from *Pageant of Shearmen and Tailors*, a fifteenth-century 'miracle play' thought to have been enacted in Coventry on the festival of Corpus Christi.
15 **Blitzen, Comet, Cupid, Dancer, Dasher, Donner, Prancer** and **Vixen.** Rudolph was not one of them. He was created in 1939 by Robert May for the Chicago-based Montgomery Ward chain of stores as a free Christmas story to give to shoppers. *Rudolph the Red-Nosed Reindeer* was made into a cartoon in 1948. May's brother-in-law, Johnny Marks, wrote the song recorded by Gene Autry in 1949, which sold two million copies that year.
16 **Christmas cactus** (also known as crab cactus and Easter cactus).
17 ***Silent Night*** (*Stille Nacht*). The carol was first sung at Midnight Mass in Oberndorf on 24 December 1818.
18 **Benjamin Zephaniah** (b. 1958).
19 **La Befana** ('the giver of gifts'). According to legend, after Herod had killed the baby boys in Bethlehem, a grief-stricken mother believed that her baby was lost. She packed his belongings and set out to find him. She found a baby (Jesus) and, convinced he was the lost child, gave him her son's belongings. He blessed her, saying that on one night a year for eternity all children would be hers: she would bring them gifts.
20 **Charles Drummond.** His card was designed for Hogmanay (which was more important than Christmas in Scotland) and depicted a cheery character proclaiming, 'A gude New year, and mony o' them'.

1 Who had a Christmas hit in 1957 with *Mary's Boy Child*?
2 Which actor portrayed the legendary Muhammad Ali in the 2001 biopic of the great heavyweight boxer's life and career, *Ali*?
3 What is the word for the part of the shore which lies between the high tide and the low tide?
4 Who was the last king of the House of Normandy to rule England?
5 In 1970 who became the first British golfer to win the US Open after the Second World War?
6 Besides Cain and Abel, which other son of Adam and Eve is named in the Bible?
7 Which two actresses played the character Violet Elizabeth in *Just William* in the 1960s BBC TV series and the 1970s LWT series based on the books by Richmal Crompton?
8 Who is the author of the Pulitzer Prize-winning novel *The Shipping News* (1993), set in Newfoundland, which was made into a film in 2001 directed by Lasse Hallström?
9 Which of the Seven Wonders of the Ancient World was destroyed by a series of earthquakes in 1326?
10 For the discovery of which basic ingredient of matter, part of the nucleus of the atom, was James Chadwick awarded the Nobel Prize for physics in 1935?
11 At which Hindu festival do sisters traditionally give their brothers a bracelet made of threads to symbolise love, affection and brotherhood?
12 Which Paris perfume house, founded by the Corsican François Spoturno in 1905, produced Chypre (1917) and L'Aimant (1927)?
13 By what name is *Midsommarvaka for Orchestra Op. 19* (1904), by the Swedish composer Hugo Emil Alfvén, better known?
14 Who was the public relations consultant to John D. Rockefeller during troubles with his mining operations in Colorado in 1914 – one of the first 'spin doctors' in history?
15 What is the term for the specialised mortar used by craftsmen for ornamental plasterwork with incised markings?
16 Which birds are the subject of the 2001 book *The Birds of Heaven* by Peter Matthiessen?
17 What is the name of the harp-shaped bridge across the River Guadalquivir in Seville which was built for Expo '92?
18 What are the nine Orders (divided into three 'circles') in the Christian hierarchy of angels?
19 In 1774 which member of the East India Company became the first Governor General of India?
20 What kind of tree is *Picea abies*, which is traditionally used as a Christmas tree?

1 **Harry Belafonte** (b. 1927). The song had originally been recorded in the same year on the album *An Evening with Belafonte*.
2 **Will Smith** (b. 1968).
3 **Foreshore** or **littoral.**
4 **Stephen** (c. 1097–1154). He was the grandson of William the Conqueror (his mother was William's daughter, Adela). He seized the throne in 1135 on the death of Henry I, precipitating a civil war with a rival claimant, Henry's daughter Matilda, and was captured at the Battle of Lincoln in 1141 and briefly imprisoned. He regained the crown later that year. He was succeeded in 1154 by Matilda's son, Henry II.
5 **Tony Jacklin** (b. 1944). Less than a year earlier he had won the Open. Later he achieved success as non-playing captain of Europe's Ryder Cup team (two wins, one draw, one loss).
6 **Seth** (Genesis 4:26).
7 **Gillian Gostling** and **Bonny Langford.**
8 **E. Annie Proulx** (b. 1935).
9 **The Pharos of Alexandria.** The lighthouse, which stood more than 110 metres high on the island of Pharos in the harbour of Alexandria, was reputed to have been built in about 280 BC for Ptolemy II.
10 **Neutron.** Previously scientists thought that in each atom lightweight negatively charged electrons orbited a tiny, dense nucleus containing more electrons and heavy, positive protons. Chadwick's work showed that the nucleus consisted of protons and neutrons.
11 **Raksha Bandan.** It is celebrated on the fifteenth day of the Hindu month of Shravan (July/August) and commemorates a legend about a war between the gods and the demons. Indrani, the consort of Indra (the King of the Heavens), tied a *rakhi* (a silken amulet) around his wrist; this helped the gods to regain the heavens from the demons which had taken them over.
12 **Coty.**
13 ***Swedish Rhapsody.*** Two versions did well in the UK charts in 1953 – by Mantovani (No. 2) and by Ray Martin (No. 4).
14 **Ivy Ledbetter Lee** (1877–1934). A graduate of Princeton University and former newspaper reporter, he set up his own public relations company in 1903, calling himself a 'physician to corporate bodies'.
15 **Parget** (hence the surname Pargeter), from the Old French *pargeter*, 'to throw over'.
16 **Cranes.** There are fifteen surviving species of crane scattered across the world, most of them under threat. The book is illustrated with paintings by the wildlife artist Robert Bateman.
17 **Alamillo Bridge.** It was designed by the Spanish architect Santiago Calatrava. The footbridge is accompanied by the Cartuja viaduct.
18 **Seraphim, Cherubim** and **Thrones** (who contemplate God and reflect his glory); **Dominions, Virtues** and **Powers** (who regulate the stars and the Universe); and **Principalities, Archangels** and **Angels** (who minister to humanity).
19 **Warren Hastings** (1732–1818). After resigning office in 1784 he was impeached on charges of cruelty and corruption, but was acquitted after a trial which lasted more than seven years.
20 **Norway spruce.**

1 What was the name of the weekly documentary programme first produced by Granada TV in 1960 which showed cinema newsreels from the same week twenty-five years earlier?
2 Which Chancellor of the Exchequer and future Prime Minister introduced Premium Bonds in 1956?
3 What name was given to the crossing point on Friedrichstrasse in the Berlin Wall from 1961 to 1989?
4 Which singing duo represented Britain in the 1959 Eurovision Song Contest with *Sing Little Birdie*?
5 Who was the pilot of the American U2 spy plane who was shot down and sentenced to ten years for espionage by the Russians in 1960?
6 Which former World Champion Formula One racing driver was killed in a crash at the San Marino Grand Prix at Imola in May 1994?
7 In the 1949 Broadway version of which musical did Mary Martin play the part of Nellie Forbush?
8 In the old public telephone boxes, what did one do to get one's money back?
9 For what was 'donkey stone' used?
10 Which estate in Suffolk is famous for the discovery in 1939 of an Anglo-Saxon ship in a burial mound?
11 What is the meaning of the word 'Bolshevik', adopted by a radical faction of the Russian Social Democratic Party after it split in 1903?
12 What was the first British royal occasion to be marked by the issue of a commemorative postage stamp?
13 Which Balkan city was rebuilt after much of its former site was destroyed by an earthquake in 1963?
14 Who returned as President of Uganda after the fall of Idi Amin in 1980?
15 What was the name of the first hovercraft to cross the English Channel, in 1959?
16 Which pioneering French motion-picture executive gave his name to short newsreels which were shown as fillers in music halls and then between the feature films in cinemas?
17 Who, during the Second World War, was the BBC's first 'Radio Doctor', and extolled the virtues of prunes as 'black-coated workers'?
18 What was the name of the English musician who assisted the composer Frederick Delius (1862–1934) as his amanuensis after he went blind?
19 In May 1960 the US Food and Drug Administration licensed norethynodrel under the name of Enovid for use as what?
20 Which Scottish clergyman, minister of the Scots Kirk in Paris, became known as 'the Tartan Pimpernel' for his exploits in helping British servicemen to escape from Occupied France during the Second World War?

1 *All Our Yesterdays*. The programmes later included television news archive footage and studio guests. They were first narrated by James Cameron and later introduced and narrated by Brian Inglis. The programme was revived from 1987 to 1989, hosted by Bernard Braden, using TV footage which was by then available for the period 1962–4.
2 **Harold Macmillan** (1894–1986).
3 **Checkpoint Charlie**. On its site there are remnants of the wall and a small museum dedicated to its history.
4 **Pearl Carr and Teddy Johnson**. They came second.
5 **Gary Powers** (1929–77). His capture led to the cancellation by the Soviet Union of a conference with the USA, Great Britain and France. He was released in 1962 in exchange for the Soviet spy Rudolf Abel.
6 **Ayrton Senna** (1960–94). He won forty-one Grand Prix titles and three circuit world championships (1988, 1990 and 1991).
7 *South Pacific* (Mitzi Gaynor played the part in the 1958 film version).
8 **Press Button B**. For a connection one pressed Button A.
9 **Cleaning stone steps and floors** or, in the textile mills of Yorkshire and Manchester, **for a non-slip surface on greasy stone staircases**. An alternative name was 'hearthstone'. A piece of sandstone could be used but donkey stones were also manufactured from reconstituted stone.
10 **Sutton Hoo**. Its treasures are now held in the British Museum.
11 **Member of the Majority**.
12 **The silver jubilee of King George V**, in 1935. Different versions were produced in the British colonies.
13 **Skopje**, the capital of Macedonia.
14 **Milton Obote** (1924–96). He was forced out of office in 1985 by a military coup after which Basilio Okello briefly ruled Uganda, and eventually settled in Zambia.
15 **SRN1**. The hovercraft was developed from 1953 onwards by Christopher Cockerell (1910–99).
16 **Charles Pathé** (1863–1957). Among the best-known early newsreel series were *Pathé-Journal* (1908) and *Pathé Weekly* (1912).
17 **Charles Hill** (later Baron Hill of Luton, 1904–89). He became a Liberal Conservative MP and Postmaster-General (1955–59), and was appointed chairman of the Independent Television Authority (ITA) in 1963 and chairman of the BBC (1967).
18 **Eric Fenby** (1906–97). His own compositions include the musical score for Alfred Hitchcock's *Jamaica Inn* (1938) but only the three-minute title and opening sequence and the fifteen-second end-title music were used. He also wrote orchestral works such as *Rossini on Ilkla Moor*, an overture for orchestra (1938) and sacred choral music
19 **Oral contraceptive**. Three US biologists – Gregory Pincus (1903–67), Min-Chueh Chang (1908–91) and John Rock (1890–1984) – established that newly synthesised progestogens (synthetic versions of progesterone, extracted from wild yams) could be used to inhibit ovulation.
20 **Donald Caskie** (1902–83). He was captured by the Gestapo in 1942 and sentenced to death, but was reprieved and interned. He published his autobiography *The Tartan Pimpernel* in 1957.

General Knowledge Questions

1 Who is the only Native Australian to have become an international tennis champion and who, at the age of nineteen, beat Margaret Court in the Women's Singles final at Wimbledon in 1971?

2 During the making of which epic film did the actor Oliver Reed die?

3 Which snooker player achieved the first televised maximum score of 147, in 1982?

4 Which singer had a No. 1 hit in the UK in 1954 with *Three Coins in the Fountain*?

5 What was the name of the spacecraft in which Yuri Gagarin, the first cosmonaut, made a single orbit of the Earth in 1961?

6 Who wrote the collection of short stories entitled *The Loneliness of the Long Distance Runner* (1959)?

7 Who became Roman governor of Judaea in AD 26?

8 The name of which infectious disease translates from the Italian for 'bad air'?

9 What is the more common name of the annual herb of the pea family *Trigonella foenum-graecum* (*Fabaceae*), the dried seeds of which are used in food flavourings and, traditionally, as a digestive medicine and a poultice for boils?

10 Which US inventor in his autobiography described genius as 'one percent inspiration and ninety-nine percent perspiration'?

11 In the First World War, what name was given to the final stages of the Third Battle of Ypres, fought between October and November 1917?

12 What was the name of the heroic US captain of the *Flying Enterprise*, which foundered off the Scilly Isles in a fierce storm on 28 December 1951?

13 What is the name of the musical, based on a 1911 play by Edward Knobloch, about a wily Oriental beggar and his devious ways, which included adaptations of music such as *Stranger in Paradise* from Borodin's opera *Prince Igor*?

14 What printer's term means a double or blurred impression caused by shifting paper or type?

15 To which once-abundant North American species of pigeon, which was shot to extinction early in the twentieth century, is there a monument in Wyalusing State Park, Wisconsin, stating, 'This species became extinct through the avarice and thoughtlessness of man'?

16 What is the name of the country house near Burnham, Buckinghamshire, which was presented to the nation by Lord Courtauld-Thomson (1865–1954) as an official residence for the Foreign Secretary or other minister of the Crown?

17 According to Judges 6–8, who was the judge and warrior who delivered the Israelites from the Midianites?

18 To which Poet Laureate are the following lines, written when Edward, Prince of Wales (the future Edward VII), was recovering from a serious attack of typhoid fever in 1871, commonly but wrongly attributed?

Flash'd from his bed the electric message came,
'He is no better; he is much the same.'

19 Whose temple in Ancient Rome was kept open in times of war and closed in times of peace?

20 Which US car manufacturer first introduced a 'hatchback' to the market, in 1949?

1 **Evonne Goolagong** (b. 1951, later Cawley). She was nicknamed 'Sunshine Supergirl' because her graceful movement and gracious manner captivated crowds wherever she played.
2 *Gladiator*. Oliver Reed (1938–99) played the part of Proximo, head of the gladiator school, and Russell Crowe (b. 1964) played the title role, the gladiator Maximus Meridus, for which he won an Academy Award for Best Actor.
3 **Steve Davis** (b. 1957), against John Spencer in the Lada Classic tournament of that year in Oldham, Greater Manchester.
4 **Frank Sinatra** (1915–98).
5 *Vostok 1*. Yuri Gagarin (1934–68) was killed in a plane accident while training.
6 **Alan Sillitoe** (b. 1928). The title story is about a rebellious and anarchic Borstal boy; it was made into a film in 1962, directed by Tony Richardson and starring Tom Courtenay and Michael Redgrave.
7 **Pontius Pilate** (d. c. AD 36). He presided over the trial of Jesus Christ.
8 **Malaria** (*mala aria*). It arose from the belief that the disease was caused by the unwholesome air in swampy districts.
9 **Fenugreek**. It is a characteristic ingredient in some curries and chutneys. Its medicinal use nowadays is mainly for the treatment of cattle and horses.
10 **Thomas Alva Edison** (1847–1931).
11 **Battle of Passchendaele**.
12 **Henrik Kurt Carlsen** (d. 1989). The passengers and crew had to jump into the sea to be rescued but Carlsen stayed put on his ship; he was eventually taken off by the tug *Turmoil* when the ship's list increased to a fatal degree.
13 *Kismet*. Other music by Borodin was included: for example, *And This Is My Beloved* was based on the third movement (*Notturno*) of his String Quartet No. 2.
14 **Mackle** (from the Latin *macula*, spot or stain).
15 **Passenger pigeon** (*Ectopistes migratorius*). It became officially classified as extinct when the last known bird died in 1914 in Cincinnati Zoo, Ohio.
16 **Dorneywood**. It is administered by the National Trust.
17 **Gideon**. Judges gives two separate accounts of the story. In the first, Gideon leads his tribesmen to kill the Midianites and creates an image of the pagan god Baal, which the Israelites worship. In the second, he obeys the command of God to break down the image of Baal and replace it with an altar to God, who inspires the Israelites to destroy the Midianites as a sign of God's supremacy.
18 **Alfred Austin** (1835–1913), Poet Laureate from 1896. Edward's illness was set as a subject for the coveted Newdigate Prize Poem at Oxford, and the couplet was written (anonymously) as a pastiche – long before Austin became Poet Laureate.
19 **Janus**. Janus was one of the oldest gods in the Roman pantheon. He saved the Capitol in Rome from being conquered by the Sabines: hence the decision to leave the door of his temple open in time of war.
20 **Kaiser-Frazer**, founded by Henry J. Kaiser and Joseph W. Frazer. It introduced a 'utility sedan', with a top-hinged tailgate, which would transform the car 'from family sedan to pick-up in ten seconds'.

1 What is the common name of the mammal which has a beak – *Ornithorhynchus anatinus*, one of the primitive order of Monotremata (mammals which lay eggs but suckle their young)?
2 What name is given to the organ between the crop and the intestine of some birds which grinds hard foods such as seeds?
3 Which species of shark 'starred' in the 1975 film *Jaws*?
4 In Kenneth Grahame's *The Wind in the Willows*, Ratty was not a rat – which type of animal was he?
5 Which nocturnal ant-eating mammal's name comes from an Afrikaans word meaning 'earth-pig'?
6 What is the common-or-garden name of the annelid *Lumbricus terrestris*?
7 Who wrote and presented the 1979 television series and book on zoology *Life on Earth*?
8 What is the common name of the shaggy-coated wild ox *Bos grunniens* which inhabits mountain pastures of central Asia?
9 Which arctic animal is sometimes called 'the unicorn of the sea'?
10 Some butterflies can taste sugar solutions – with which part of their bodies?
11 In cattle, what are the rumen, reticulum, omasum and abomasum?
12 The male of which land-dwelling toad forcibly expels the eggs from the female, fertilises them and twists the strings of eggs around his legs, where he carries them until they are ready to hatch?
13 What is the common name of the large North American deer *Cervus canadensis*, which is now also found in South Island, New Zealand?
14 The occasional habit of which marine mammals of the order Sirenia of suckling a young one held vertically by a flipper is thought to have given rise to the folklore about mermaids?
15 Which controversial 'dwarfed' breed of domestic cat was developed from a mutant stray in Louisiana in the 1980s?
16 Of which mammal is the Rambouillet a specialised breed?
17 According to tradition, the behaviour of which 'sacred' wild animal released by Boudica in front of her army inspired them to defeat the Romans?
18 Which creature is the subject of the gigantic steel and marble sculpture entitled *Maman*, by the French artist Louise Bourgeois, at Tate Modern, London?
19 What name is given to the sense organ in the roof of the mouth of a snake which enables it to sense the presence of predators, prey or a mate?
20 What was the name of the nineteenth-century English fossil collector who, when she was about eleven years old, helped others in her family to discover the first specimen of Ichthyosaurus known to the scientific community of London?

1 **Duck-billed platypus.** Like birds, it develops an egg tooth before birth for helping it to break out of the egg. The Monotremata order also includes the echidna (spiny ant-eater).

2 **Gizzard.**

3 **Great white** (*Carcharodon carcharias*), which is considered to be more dangerous to human beings than any other shark.

4 **Water vole** (*Arvicola terrestris*). It is now an endangered species in Britain.

5 **Aardvark** (*Orycteropus afer*). It excavates a burrow in which it rests by day, emerging at night to pillage ant and termite nests, using its long, sticky tongue to lap up the insects.

6 **Earthworm.**

7 **David Attenborough** (b. 1926).

8 **Yak.**

9 **Narwhal** (*Monodon monoceros*), an arctic toothed whale. This small, mottled, grey whale is usually about 3.5–5 metres long. It has no dorsal fin and has only two teeth, both at the tip of the upper jaw. In the male, one of the teeth develops into a long, spiral tusk – hence the reference to the legendary one-horned unicorn.

10 **Feet.**

11 **Stomach chambers.** Food taken into the rumen is later regurgitated into the mouth and completely chewed; it is then swallowed again and passes into the reticulum, the omasum and then the abomasum.

12 **Midwife toad** (*Alytes obstetricans*). When the eggs are due to hatch, the male enters the water and the larvae bite their way through their tough envelope, which is not abandoned by the father until all the young have emerged.

13 **Wapiti.** It is the second largest living deer (exceeded in size only by the moose). The male wapiti can reach a height of more than 1.5 metres at the shoulder.

14 **Dugong** and **manatee.** Sirenians are completely herbivorous; dugong and manatees feed only on green higher plants, and so inhabit shallow waters. The similar, but now extinct, Steller's sea cow fed on marine algae.

15 **Munchkin.** It has very short legs and was named after the tiny characters in *The Wizard of Oz*. It is also known as the Dachshund cat, Weiner cat and Minicat. Other short-legged cats were recorded in the 1940s and 1950s, but they were not systematically bred.

16 **Sheep.** It was developed from the best Merino sheep of Spain between 1786 and 1799 by the French government at its national sheepfold at Rambouillet and exported to the USA from 1840 onwards.

17 **Brown hare** (*Lepus europaeus*). The brown hare has been the subject of many superstitions: it is unlucky if a hare crosses your path (witches were said to turn into hares) and hares were thought to change their sex annually. It is now an endangered species in many parts of Britain.

18 **Spider.** *Maman* (Mother, 1999) depicts the spider carrying her eggs in a steel mesh bag slung between her sinuous legs.

19 **Jacobson's organ** (vomeronasal organ). It is an area of chemically sensitive nerve endings, which is also present in some other animals, including amphibians, lizards, snakes and some mammals. Smells are sampled by flicking out the tongue and retracting it across the organ.

20 **Mary Anning** (1799–1847), of Lyme Regis, Dorset. She also discovered the first plesiosaur in 1821, and the first pterodactyl (*Dimorphodon*) in 1828.

General Knowledge Questions

1 Which former presenter of the children's television programme *Zoo Time* is the author of *The Naked Ape* (1967) and numerous other books on anthropology, including *The Human Zoo* (1969)?
2 What was the stage name of the London-born English actor and comedian Maxwell George Lorimer, the 'man of funny walks', who later specialised in the plays of Samuel Beckett?
3 Which pop group had a hit in 1981 with *Vienna*?
4 Which disease is named after an outbreak of pneumonia which occurred at a convention of the American Legion at Philadelphia in 1976?
5 Which teams were presented with the wrong medals in the 1992 FA Cup Final?
6 Which 1960s TV series, starring Mia Farrow as Allison MacKenzie and Ryan O'Neal as Rodney Harrington, was based on a 1956 novel by Grace Metalious?
7 As what are Zingari better known?
8 Which boxer did Robert de Niro portray in the 1980 film *Raging Bull*, for which he won an Academy Award for Best Actor?
9 Which German-born British astronomer discovered the planet Uranus in 1781?
10 Which religious order runs the boys' public school Stonyhurst?
11 In the USA it is called a 'dishcloth gourd' – what is it called in the UK?
12 In music, the use of which mechanical device is indicated by the instruction *con sordino*?
13 The traditional title page of *Whitaker's Almanack* depicts what looks like a series of medallions linked by a chain. What appear on the medallions?
14 Which US 'beat' poet wrote *Howl*, published in 1956?
15 Which Polish oculist and philologist created the international language of Esperanto ('One Who Hopes') in the 1880s?
16 What is the name of the floating or flying island in Jonathan Swift's novel *Gulliver's Travels*?
17 Which controversial English clergyman wrote the hymn *Rock of Ages* in 1775, allegedly while sheltering from a storm under a rocky overhang near the Cheddar Gorge?
18 What is the familiar name for the series of eight Banavie Locks on the Caledonian Canal near Fort William?
19 Which eighteenth-century English artist, whose early work included many candle-lit scenes, painted *An Experiment on a Bird in the Air Pump*, which shows a travelling scientist giving a demonstration in a private house?
20 What kind of fish is sold in Sainsbury's supermarkets as 'Antarctic icefish'?

General Knowledge Answers

1 **Desmond Morris** (b. 1928).
2 **Max Wall** (1908–90).
3 **Ultravox.**
4 **Legionnaires' disease.** It is caused by the bacterium *Legionella pneumophila*, and is believed to be spread by the inhalation of contaminated water vapour from showers and air-conditioning plants.
5 **Liverpool** and **Sunderland.** Liverpool beat Sunderland 2–0 with goals scored by Ian Rush and Michael Thomas. Sunderland were mistakenly given the winners' medals and Liverpool were given the runners-up medals. The players exchanged medals afterwards.
6 ***Peyton Place.*** It was the first US TV soap to be imported to Britain. There was also a daytime 'revival' series, *Return to Peyton Place* (1972–4), with Kathy Glass as Allison MacKenzie and Lawrence Casey as Rodney Harrington. This was followed by the TV films *Murder in Peyton Place* (1977) and *Peyton Place: The Next Generation* (1985).
7 **Gypsies** (from the Italian *Zingaro*, derived from the Greek *Athigganoi*, an oriental people).
8 **Jake LaMotta** ('the Bronx Bull', b. 1922), who became world middleweight champion in 1949 when he defeated Marcel Cerdan. He held the title until Sugar Ray Robinson beat him in 1951.
9 **William Herschel** (1738–1822). It was the first planet to be discovered using a telescope, which Herschel had made; he named the plant *Georgium sidus* in honour of George III, who appointed him his private astronomer in the following year.
10 **Jesuits.** It originated in a college for English boys founded in 1593 at St Omer in northern France. After moving to Belgium – to Bruges and then Liège – it was established in 1794 at Stonyhurst Hall near Preston, Lancashire.
11 **Loofah** (*Luffa acutangula* and *Luffa aegyptiaca*).
12 **A mute.**
13 **Signs of the zodiac.**
14 **Allen Ginsberg** (1926–97).
15 **Lazarus Ludwig Zamenhof** (1859–1917). He first presented it in 1887.
16 **Laputa.** Laputa hovers over the larger island of Balnibarbi. The bottom of Laputa is shaped like a deep saucer and on its sides are stairways and galleries which make it accessible from below.
17 **Augustus Montague Toplady** (1740–78). The music was composed by Thomas Hastings (1784–1872). He wrote several essays, including *Historic Proof of the Doctrinal Calvinism of the Church of England* (1774).
18 **Neptune's Staircase.** The Caledonian Canal was surveyed in 1801 by the Scottish engineer Thomas Telford (1757–1834). Construction began in 1803.
19 **Joseph Wright of Derby** (1734–97). The painting (1768) is now in the National Gallery, London.
20 **Patagonian toothfish.** Because of its unappetising name, it was originally marketed as 'Antarctic sea bass' in the UK. However, the Ministry of Agriculture, Fisheries and Food ruled that because it was not a member of the sea bass family the name was misleading and it should be renamed.

Advertising Questions

1 Which fizzy drink was launched in 1886 by the Atlanta pharmacist John S. Pemberton (1831–88) as a medicinal drink 'to cure most common ailments'?
2 Which product, in an advertisement devised by Alan Parker, did Leonard Rossiter spill down Joan Collins's cleavage?
3 In January 2002 which girl band was signed up to promote Avon Cosmetics' 'Color Trend' range for the teenage market?
4 In whom were consumers urged to confide about the privatisation of British Gas in 1986?
5 What is the title of the poem by the Welsh poet W.H. Davies (1871–1940), used in Center Parcs holiday advertisements, which begins with the following lines?

What is this life if, full of care,
We have no time to stand and stare.

6 By what name was Angelo Siciliano better known as the figurehead for the 1930s body-building advertising promotion 'I was a seven-stone weakling'?
7 Which film director made his name with a TV commercial for British Railways before making the 1981 film *Chariots of Fire*, which won an Academy Award for Best Picture?
8 Which former disc jockey featured in the 'Clunk, click, *every* trip' road-safety campaign promoting the use of seatbelts in 1971?
9 The role of which 'living logo' in insurance advertisements since 1986 has been played by Debbie Barrymore (daughter of actor Roger Moore) and model Amanda Lamb?
10 Which 2001 novel by Fay Weldon was the subject of controversy because of its sponsorship by a jeweller and perfumer?
11 What was the name of the pirate commercial radio station launched by Ronan O'Rahilly in 1964 which broadcast from a ship off the Isle of Man?
12 Which Canadian writer and media guru wrote, 'Ads are the cave art of the twentieth century'?
13 What was the rhyming slogan of the Campaign for Nuclear Disarmament in the late 1950s?
14 In 1977 which chorus from a Verdi opera was used to advertise Lee jeans and featured the towers of the World Trade Center clothed in a pair of jeans?
15 In a London and North Eastern Railway poster between the wars, which east coast English resort was advertised as a destination with a jolly fisherman symbol and the slogan 'Is so bracing'?
16 Which British writer described advertising as 'the rattling of a stick in a swill-bucket'?
17 Which British industrialist complained, 'Half the money I spend on advertising is wasted; the trouble is, I don't know which half'?
18 Which product, manufactured in the early nineteenth century by Robert Warren, is the subject of many advertisements, recorded in the 1824 book *Warreniana* by William Frederick Deacon?
19 What was the nickname of the 'Fairy baby' which started advertising Thomas Hedley's yellow bars of Fairy soap in a cartoon strip in 1932?
20 In James Joyce's *Ulysses*, for which client was Leopold Bloom (a Jewish advertising canvasser) trying to sell an advertisement in the offices of the *Freeman's Journal and National Press* on 16 June 1904?

1 **Coca-Cola.** The drink was originally based on cocaine from the coca leaf and caffeine-rich extracts of the cola nut. The cocaine was removed from Coca-Cola's formula in 1905. It has been replaced by a synthetic flavouring which resembles that of the cola nut.
2 **Cinzano.**
3 **Atomic Kitten** (Jenny Frost, Liz McClarnon and Natasha Hamilton).
4 **Sid.** The advertising slogan was 'Tell Sid'.
5 ***Leisure.***
6 **Charles Atlas** (1893–1972). He was called 'America's Most Perfectly Developed Man'.
7 **Hugh Hudson** (b. 1936).
8 **Jimmy Savile** (b. 1926).
9 **The Widow in Black,** in the Scottish Widows series of TV and magazine advertisements. The cloak is made of black silk velvet, lined with silk, and weighs about 10 kilograms.
10 ***The Bulgari Connection.***
11 **Radio Caroline.** Ronan O'Rahilly had the ex-ferry *Fredericia* fitted with broadcasting studios and renamed it *Caroline* after a photograph of Caroline Kennedy (daughter of John F. Kennedy) at play in the White House. It closed in 1968 and reopened in 1989, broadcasting from a ship off Gravesend, Kent.
12 **Marshall McLuhan** (1911–80).
13 **'Better red than dead'.**
14 ***Anvil Chorus*** from *Il Trovatore* (1853). The commercial showed workers making the rivets which are used to strengthen joins on the jeans.
15 **Skegness.**
16 **George Orwell** (1903–50), in *Keep the Aspidistra Flying* (1936).
17 **Lord Leverhulme** (1851–1925).
18 **Shoe blacking:** 'Warren's Paste Blacking', which its maker promoted by advertisements paraphrasing the lines of famous writers: for example,

. . . he took up an old newspaper;
The paper was right easy to peruse;
He read an article the king attacking,
And a long eulogy of 'patent blacking'.
(from Canto XVI of Byron's *Don Juan*).

19 **Bizzie.** In the Second World War the company sponsored two Spitfires, *Bizzie 1* and *Bizzie 2*. Fairy soap was launched as a washing-up liquid in 1960 and was an instant success.
20 **Alexander Keyes** (a tea, wine and spirit merchant).

1 Which was the first 'manufactured' musical group, formed by NBC-TV of the USA as the result of an advertisement in the Los Angeles *Daily Vanity* in September 1965?
2 Which rock legend won an Academy Award for Best Song with *The Streets of Philadelphia*, the title track of the 1993 film *Philadelphia*?
3 Which village in Buckinghamshire was the setting for Thomas Gray's poem *Elegy Written in a Country Church-Yard* (1751)?
4 At what London address was Her Majesty the Queen born, on 21 April 1926?
5 What is the literal meaning of the word 'Islam'?
6 Which Pre-Raphaelite artist designed the four stained-glass windows in the Cathedral Church of St Philip in Birmingham?
7 Which wine-growing district of France produces Château d'Yquem?
8 In 1819 who published his *Sketch Book of Geoffrey Crayon, Gent*, in which he recounted tales of Rip Van Winkle?
9 In the late nineteenth century the Portland Club in London published the first official rules of which game, introduced to its members by Lord Brougham in 1894?
10 The common name of which tropical evergreen tree of the myrtle family comes from the flavour of its aromatic dried berries, which resembles a combination of cloves, cinnamon and nutmeg?
11 In which English city did the BBC open its first local radio station?
12 In the First World War, which was the only full-scale naval battle to be fought between the British Grand Fleet and the German High Sea fleet?
13 In 1665 which English scientist, also known for his law of elasticity, observed the microscopic honeycomb-like formation of cavities in cork and introduced the term 'cell'?
14 In 1995 who was the first athlete to run a 3000-metre steeplechase in less than eight minutes?
15 Which species of birds are known as 'chickadees' in North America?
16 What is the literal meaning of the word 'anthology' for a collection of poems?
17 In 1989 who was elected the first woman president of the Royal College of Physicians?
18 The Bronze Age timber circle known as 'Seahenge' stands on Holme Beach off the coast of which English county?
19 Which First World War soldier and writer lived at a cottage called Clouds Hill in Dorset which is now maintained by the National Trust?
20 The 'muse' in the advertisements for which perfume, launched in 1995 by Lancôme, was Juliette Binoche?

1 **The Monkees** (Davy Jones, Mickey Dolenz, Mike Nesmith and Peter Tork). Their first record, *Last Train to Clarksville*, reached No. 1 in the US charts and their second, *I'm a Believer*, was a transatlantic No. 1.
2 **Bruce Springsteen** (b. 1949).
3 **Stoke Poges**. The poet is buried in the churchyard.
4 **17 Bruton Street, Mayfair.**
5 **Submission** (to the will of Allah).
6 **Edward Burne-Jones** (1833–98). The subjects of the windows are the *Ascension* (1885), the *Nativity* (1887), the *Crucifixion* (1887) and the *Last Judgement* (1897).
7 **Sauternes**. The grapes are picked one by one at exactly the right moment – when they have a sugar content which could, in theory, produce wine of an alcohol content of 19–20 degrees. Fermentation stops naturally at 13–14 degrees of alcohol and the unconverted sugar remains.
8 **Washington Irving** (1783–1859). His source was purportedly the papers of a Dutch antiquary in New York. 'Rip Van Winkle' was an easy-going farmer in the Catskills who escaped from his nagging wife to the mountains, where he met a ghostly crew playing bowls. After partaking of their 'old Hollands' (gin) he slept for twenty years, missing the Revolutionary War.
9 **Bridge**. The Portland Club is still one of the approving bodies of the World Bridge Federation (WBF), along with the WBF Laws Committee, the European Bridge League and the American Contract Bridge League.
10 **Allspice** (*Pimenta diocia,* formerly *P. officinalis*). It is used in baking, mincemeat and pickling spice. Early Spanish explorers mistook it for a type of pepper and called it 'pimenta'.
11 **Leicester** (1967).
12 **Battle of Jutland** (May–June 1916). The commander-in-chief of the British fleet was Admiral John Jellicoe (1859–1935). The battle was inconclusive: the smaller German fleet escaped under cover of darkness, having inflicted more damage than it suffered.
13 **Robert Hooke** (1635–1703). The German botanist Matthias Schleiden (in 1838) and the German biologist Theodor Schwann (in 1839) were among the first to state that cells are the fundamental particles of plants and animals.
14 **Moses Kiptanui** (b. 1970) of Kenya. His time was 7 minutes 59.18 seconds. He was world steeplechase champion in 1991, 1993 and 1995, and winner of the silver medal at the 1996 Atlanta Olympics.
15 **Tits** (of the genus *Parus*).
16 **'Discourse about flowers'**, from Greek *anthos* (flower) and *-logy* (discourse).
17 **Margaret Turner-Warwick** (b. 1924), a specialist in lung disease.
18 **Norfolk**. It was discovered by a local man, John Lorimer, in 1998. The site was excavated by archaeologist Francis Pryor, who described it in his 2001 book *Seahenge*. The timbers have been precisely dated to the spring of 2049 BC.
19 **T.E. Lawrence** (Lawrence of Arabia, 1888–1935). He rented it as a retreat from nearby Bovington Camp, where he had enlisted in the Royal Tank Corps under the pseudonym of 'Shaw'. His account of the Arab Revolt and his part in it (*The Seven Pillars of Wisdom*) was privately printed in 1926.
20 ***Poême***. Its ingredients include Himalayan blue poppy, datura, mimosa, jonquil, daffodil, jasmin, freesia and vanilla.

1 Which ballet by Tchaikovsky features the dance of the Sugar Plum Fairy?
2 Which Polish-born dancer and choreographer gave her name to Britain's oldest ballet company in 1935, based on the Ballet Club she had formed in 1931?
3 Which ballet, first performed in 1841, was inspired by a story by Heinrich Heine about a peasant girl who kills herself when she discovers that Albrecht, the man she loves, is betrothed to another woman?
4 Which cat did the dancer Wayne Sleep portray in the long-running London production of Andrew Lloyd Webber's musical *Cats*?
5 The centenary of the birth of which artist was commemorated by the award-winning 1987 ballet *A Simple Man*?
6 In 1911 which Russian dancer, famous for his ability to perform spectacular leaps, danced the part of the Rose in the premiere, in Paris, of Michel Fokine's *Le Spectre de la Rose*?
7 Which dance, from a ballet by Tchaikovsky, was performed by animated characters in a 1989 advertisement for Batchelors Slim-a-Soup?
8 Who played the part of the ballet dancer Isadora Duncan in the 1969 film *Isadora*?
9 For which Russian ballerina did the Indian dancer and choreographer Uday Shankar create *Hindu Wedding* and the duet *Radha and Krishna*, for inclusion in her programme *Oriental Impressions*?
10 What is the name, from the French word for 'throw', for a ballet leap in which the weight of the dancer is transferred from one foot to the other?
11 Which Italian ballerina, in her father's ballet *La Sylphide* (1832), created a new style marked by floating leaps and balanced poses such as the arabesque and was one of the first to use the *pointe*?
12 Who was the first US-born and US-trained ballerina to make her mark on the world stage, and founded the Chicago City Ballet in 1980?
13 Who succeeded Anthony Dowell as director of the Royal Ballet in 2001?
14 Which South African-born choreographer wrote the musical revue *Cranks* (1955) and created the ballets *Romeo and Juliet* (1958), *Onegin* (1965) and *Carmen* (1971) for the Stuttgart Ballet?
15 The 3rd Duke of Dorset commissioned Gainsborough to paint a portrait of which ballerina dancing in 1782 in the ballet *Les Amants Surpris*?
16 Which Latvian-born 'bravura' dancer of the New York City Ballet, who had defected to the west in 1974, appeared in the films *The Turning Point* (1977) and *Dancers* (1987)?
17 Which French-born ballet master of the Imperial Ballet in St Petersburg (now the Kirov Ballet) from 1869 to 1903 is considered 'the father of classical ballet'?
18 Which seventeenth-century Italian composer at the court of Louis XIV is credited with the first ballet starring a female dancer?
19 Which sixteenth-century production at the court of Catherine de Médicis, queen regent of France, combined dance, music, decor and special effects and launched the genre known as *ballet de cour* (court ballet)?
20 In 1995 which US modern dancer and choreographer, and winner of the American Dance Festival's 1997 Lifetime Achievement Award, created *Embracing Earth: Dances with Nature*?

Answers

1 *The Nutcracker* (1892).

2 **Marie Rambert** (1888–1982). She founded Ballet Rambert, which was renamed Rambert Dance Company in 1987 to reflect its emphasis on contemporary dance.

3 *Giselle*. Her ghost joins the spirits of women who seek vengeance upon men who betrayed them, but when Albrecht visits Giselle's grave in remorse she cannot bring herself to take revenge, and saves his life by watching over him and warding off phantoms until dawn.

4 **Mr Mistoffelees** ('The Original Conjuring Cat' of T.S. Eliot's 1939 series of poems *Old Possum's Book of Practical Cats*). The show opened on 11 May 1981 and closed exactly twenty-one years later – on 11 May 2002 – making it Britain's longest-running musical ever.

5 **L.S. (Lawrence Stephen) Lowry** (1887–1976). Salford City Council commissioned Gillian Lynne to create the ballet for Northern Ballet. Carl Davies composed the music and, after an absence of twenty years from the stage, Christopher Gable danced the title role in the first production.

6 **Vaslav Nijinsky** (1890–1950). The music was by Carl Maria von Weber, with an orchestration by Berlioz of the piece known as *Invitation to the Waltz*.

7 **Dance of the Little Swans** from *Swan Lake*. The music was played by the Chicago Symphony Orchestra conducted by Georg Solti.

8 **Vanessa Redgrave** (b. 1937).

9 **Anna Pavlova** (1881–1931).

10 *Jeté*. The dancer throws one leg to the front, side, or back and holds the other leg in any desired position upon landing.

11 **Marie Taglioni** (1804–84). Her father was the Italian dancer and choreographer Filippo Taglioni (1777–1871).

12 **Maria Tallchief** (b. 1925 in Fairfax, Oklahoma). Her father was an Osage Native American and her mother's family were Scottish, Irish and Dutch. She danced in many roles in the ballets of her husband (George Balanchine), which established her international reputation.

13 **Ross Stretton** (b. 1952), previously Director of the Australian Ballet.

14 **John Cranko** (1927–73).

15 **Giovanna Baccelli** (d. 1801). The painting is in Tate Britain.

16 **Mikhail Baryshnikov** (b. 1948). He was director of the American Ballet Theatre from 1980 to 1989.

17 **Marius Petipa** (1818–1910). He created forty-six original ballets, including *The Sleeping Beauty* (1890) and *Swan Lake* (1895).

18 **Jean Baptiste Lully** (1632–87). The ballet, *Le Triomphe de l'Amour* (1681), was choreographed by Pierre Beauchamp, and Mlle Lafontaine (1665–1738) became the first *première danseuse* of the Paris Opéra.

19 ***Circé ou le Balet comique de la Royne*** (1581). It was staged by Catherine's chief musician, Balthasar de Beaujoyeux. A grand spectacle lasting five anda half hours, it told the story of the legendary Circe who turned men into swine.

20 **Anna Halprin** (b. 1920). She founded the San Francisco Dancers' Workshop in 1955, established the Marin County-based Tamalpa Institute in 1978 and has published six volumes about her work on movement and healing, including *Movement Ritual* and *Circle the Earth Manual*.

1 By what name is the dancer Margaret Hookham, famous for her partnership with Rudolf Nureyev in ballets such as *Swan Lake* and *Le Corsaire*, better known?
2 Which Edinburgh-based tartan-wearing pop group, initially named the Saxons, had their first No. 1 hit with *Bye Bye Baby* in 1975?
3 Which publication used the slogan 'Let your fingers do the walking' in its 1960s television advertisements?
4 In 1998 which astronaut, the first American to orbit the earth, in 1962, became the oldest man to fly in space, at the age of seventy-seven?
5 What was the name of the Russian submarine which sank to the bottom of the Barents Sea in August 2000 after explosions in its torpedo compartments?
6 Which Dutch actress-model appeared as Xenia Onatopp in the 1995 James Bond movie *Goldeneye*, as the femme fatale who crushed men to death between her thighs?
7 Of what fossilised material does the semi-precious gem amber consist?
8 What is the title of the theme music which introduces BBC Radio's long-running quiz programme, *Brain of Britain*?
9 What is the common name of plants of the genus *Antirrhinum*?
10 What is the name of the doctor who became the first British woman athlete to win a gold medal in the Modern Pentathlon (the first in which women's and men's competitions were the same), at the Sydney Olympics in 2000?
11 Which eminent nineteenth-century French writer spent fifteen years in exile on the island of Guernsey, where his statue stands above the town of St Peter Port?
12 What is the more familiar name for the goatfish (*Mullus barbatus* and *Mullus surmuletus*)?
13 On which Cheshire town did Mrs Gaskell base her 1853 novel *Cranford*?
14 Who defeated Gary Kasparov to become world champion in the fourteenth World Chess Championship in November 2000?
15 Two London hospitals were founded in the nineteenth century by William Marsden. One is the Royal Marsden (1851), the first hospital in the world to be dedicated wholly to the study and treatment of cancer – which is the other?
16 Who in the book of Genesis is described as 'a mighty hunter before the Lord'?
17 In 1947 who developed the technique of radiocarbon dating, for which he received the Nobel Prize for chemistry in 1960?
18 Which word for illicitly produced alcoholic drinks comes from the name of the small tribe on Admiralty Island, Alaska, who distilled molasses, yeast, berries and sugar to produce their favourite beverage?
19 Which Victorian artist painted the scene of Bonnie Prince Charlie saying farewell to Flora Macdonald, which has adorned countless tins of Walkers Shortbread?
20 Which twentieth-century Spanish artists designed the scenery for the 1919 Ballets Russes and the 1949 Ballet Español productions of *The Three-Cornered Hat*?

1 **Margot Fonteyn** (1919–91).
2 **Bay City Rollers** (at the time of the recording: Derek Longmuir, Alan Longmuir, Stuart Wood, Eric Faulkner and Les McKeown). 'Rollermania' was all the teen rage in the 1970s, but this original 'boy band' had only one other No. 1 hit – *Give A Little Love* (also 1975).
3 ***Yellow Pages***.
4 **John Glenn** (b. 1921).
5 ***Kursk***. The team of divers who first entered the wreck found that all of the 118 crew members had died.
6 **Famke Janssen** (b. 1964).
7 **Resin** from coniferous trees. The main deposits of amber are found along the shores of the Baltic Sea in sands which are 40–60 million years old.
8 ***Eine Kleine Nachtmusik*** (1787), by Mozart.
9 **Snapdragon**.
10 **Stephanie Cook** (b. 1972). She won the World Championship the following year. The Modern Pentathlon consists of five events: horse riding over jumps, fencing with electric épée, freestyle swimming, pistol shooting and cross-country running. Before 2000 the Women's Pentathlon, which Mary Peters won in 1972, consisted of shot put, 100 metres hurdles, high jump, long jump, and 200 metres sprint.
11 **Victor Hugo** (1802–85). He first established himself on Jersey in 1852 and stayed until 1855, when he was expelled and moved to Guernsey. He lived in Hauteville House, St Peter Port, from 1855 to 1870, where he completed the final draft of *Les Misérables* (1862).
12 **Red mullet**.
13 **Knutsford**. The novel was first published serially in the weekly periodical produced by Charles Dickens, *Household Words*.
14 **Vladimir Kramnik** (b. 1975).
15 **The Royal Free Hospital** (1828). William Marsden (1796–1867), a young surgeon, opened the London General Institution for the Gratuitous Cure of Malignant Diseases. By 1844 his dispensary had become the Royal Free Hospital and was treating 30,000 patients a year. The hospital moved to its present site in Hampstead in the mid-1970s.
16 **Nimrod**, son of Cush, a king of Mesopotamia, and grandson of Noah. He ruled a large kingdom in what is now Iraq. The ninth of Elgar's *Enigma Variations*, a portrait of his friend A.J. Jaeger (German for 'hunter') was named after Nimrod.
17 **Willard Frank Libby** (1908–80). The technique is used for dating material from former living organisms by measuring minute amounts of radioactivity from carbon-14. The older the materials, the less radioactivity they have.
18 **Hooch** (from Hoochinoo).
19 **George William Joy** (1844–1925). He is now best known for *The Bayswater Omnibus* (1895), in the Museum of London.
20 **Pablo Picasso** (1881–1973) designed the scenery and costumes for the 1919 production and **Salvador Dalí** (1904–1989) designed the scenery for the 1949 production. The music was by Manuel de Falla (1876–1946) and the choreographer was Léonide Massine (1896–1979). The ballet was based on the novel *El Sombrero de Tres Picos* (1874) by the Spanish writer Pedro Antonio de Alarcón y Ariza (1833–91).

1 Which 2001 film musical, starring Nicole Kidman and Ewan McGregor, features a penniless writer in 1899 Paris coming up with the idea for *The Sound of Music* more than fifty years before Rodgers and Hammerstein?
2 In the 2001 film *Harry Potter and the Philosopher's Stone* directed by Chris Columbus, who played the part of Hagrid?
3 Which British-made 1962 film epic was described by the critic of the *New York Times* as 'just a huge thundering camel-opera'?
4 In which 1933 film did Fred Astaire first partner Ginger Rogers?
5 Which 1915 epic silent film about the American Civil War, directed by D.W. Griffith, was based on Thomas Dixon's book *The Clansman* and includes the assassination of President Lincoln, the surrender of General Lee and the rise of the Ku Klux Klan?
6 Which John Ford film ends with the newspaper editor saying, 'When the legend becomes fact, print the legend'?
7 In films about which true-life Wild West incident were the parts of Wyatt Earp and Doc Holliday played by Henry Fonda and Victor Mature, Burt Lancaster and Kirk Douglas, and Kevin Costner and Dennis Quaid?
8 Which family drama of 1980, starring Donald Sutherland and Mary Tyler Moore, won an Academy Award for Best Director for Robert Redford on his debut as a director?
9 Which cosmetic item was invented by film director D.W. Griffith to enhance the appearance of actress Seena Owen, playing Princess Beloved in the 1916 film *Intolerance*?
10 Which 1966 Richard Fleischer film features a team of miniaturised medical and scientific personnel travelling in a submarine through the bloodstream of a scientist whose life they are trying to save?
11 Which British film star of aquiline appearance was described by Dorothy Parker as 'two profiles pasted together'?
12 Which Hollywood movie mogul is alleged to have said to Albert Einstein, 'I have a theory of relatives, too – don't hire 'em'?
13 Who played the pair of cricket-loving, stiff-upper-lipped Englishmen, Charters and Caldicott, in Hitchcock's 1938 film *The Lady Vanishes*?
14 What is the name of the Indian 'arthouse' film director who first 'broke through' in 1955 with *Pather Panchali (Song of the Road)* based on the novel of the same title by Bibhutibhushan Banerjee?
15 Which US author starred as his own tough-guy creation in the 1963 film *The Girl Hunters*?
16 Which leading composer of film music was Alfred Hitchcock's collaborator on several films, including *Vertigo* (1958) and *Psycho* (1960)?
17 Which French-born inventor was granted US and British patents for a motion-picture camera in Leeds as early as 1888, but disappeared in 1890 on a journey from Dijon to Paris, where he was to give a demonstration?
18 The 1998 film *Solomon and Gaenor* has the unique distinction of being made in three different languages – which ones?
19 What was the name of the British film production company set up in 1942 by Michael Powell and Emeric Pressburger?
20 Which Hollywood superstar makes a cameo appearance at the end of the 1997 film *Fairytale: A True Story* as a soldier returning from the First World War?

1 *Moulin Rouge*.
2 **Robbie Coltrane** (b. 1950). His real name is Anthony McMillan; his stage name was devised in honour of the US jazz saxophonist and composer John Coltrane (1926–67).
3 *Lawrence of Arabia*, directed by David Lean and starring Peter O'Toole.
4 ***Flying Down to Rio***. They were not billed as the stars of the film (Dolores Del Rio and Gene Raymond were), but their appearance led to a string of major successes – ten films in all, ending with *The Barkleys of Broadway* (1948).
5 ***The Birth of a Nation***. It is now considered irredeemably racist in content, but its scope and editing techniques meant the demise of the old two-reeler.
6 ***The Man Who Shot Liberty Valance*** (1962), starring James Stewart and John Wayne. The words were written by James Warner Bellah (1899–1976) and Willis Goldbeck (1899–1979).
7 **The Gunfight at the OK Corral**. The films were *My Darling Clementine* (1946), *Gunfight at the OK Corral* (1957) and *Wyatt Earp* (1994). Other versions have also been made.
8 ***Ordinary People***. It also won Academy Awards for Best Picture and Best Supporting Actor (Timothy Hutton).
9 **False eyelashes**. A wigmaker wove human hair through fine gauze, which was then gummed to her eyelids.
10 ***Fantastic Voyage***. The film won Academy Awards for Best Colour Art Direction and Special Visual Effects.
11 **Basil Rathbone** (1892–1967). He is best known for portraying Sherlock Holmes.
12 **Jack L. Warner** (1892–1978). He was the youngest of the four brothers who established the Warner Brother Studios in the 1920s. The others were Harry, Albert and Sam.
13 **Basil Radford** (1897–1952) and **Naunton Wayne** (1901–70). Their parts were played in a 1979 remake of *The Lady Vanishes* by Arthur Lowe (1915–82) and Ian Carmichael (b. 1920).
14 **Satyajit Ray** (1921–92). It was the first film in the Apu trilogy.
15 **Mickey Spillane** (b. 1918). He played Mike Hammer.
16 **Bernard Herrmann** (1911–75). They eventually split after a disagreement over the proposals for *Torn Curtain* (1966).
17 **Louis le Prince** (1842–90). He devised the camera to take sequences of pictures on film with a paper base which George Eastman introduced in 1885.
18 **English, Welsh** and **Yiddish**. It is a tale of tragic romance between a Jewish salesman and a girl from a chapel-going Welsh family, set in the Welsh valleys in 1911.
19 **The Archers**. It lasted until 1956, having produced some of the most distinctive and idiosyncratic films in British cinema, including *A Matter of Life and Death* (1946), *Black Narcissus* (1947) and *The Red Shoes* (1948).
20 **Mel Gibson** (b. 1956). He plays the father of one of the two young girls at the centre of the 'Cottingley Fairies' story – they claimed to have photographed fairies at the bottom of their garden.

General Knowledge

1 Which 1965 film, directed by David Lean, produced by Carlo Ponti and starring Omar Sharif and Julie Christie, was based on a novel by Boris Pasternak set in Russia at the time of the Bolshevik Revolution?
2 What name is given to a female swan?
3 Which clarinet-playing musician had a hit in 1962 with *Stranger on the Shore*, which was in the UK charts for fifty-five weeks and reached No. 1 in the USA?
4 Who is to the cult figure Ali G what Barry Humphries is to Dame Edna Everage?
5 Who wrote the poem *She Walks in Beauty*?
6 According to the gospels of Mark and Luke, what was the name of the president of the synagogues who asked Jesus to save his dying daughter, saying, 'Come and lay your hands on her, so that she may be made well and live'?
7 Which series of six paintings by Hogarth depicts the loveless marriage of Viscount Squanderfield, his wife and her lover Silvertongue?
8 What is the name given to the financial crash which occurred in 1720 after a private company, which had been set up to trade (mainly in slaves) with Spanish America, took over the British National Debt in return for a trade monopoly?
9 From a speech on the Abyssinian crisis in December 1935 by which politician are the words 'My lips are sealed' popularly, but wrongly, quoted?
10 Who is the patron saint of accountants, bookkeepers and tax collectors, whose feast day is 21 September (West) or 16 November (East)?
11 Training days for members of which profession are sometimes known as 'Baker Days'?
12 Which musical instrument is known in French as *musette*, in Italian as *zampogna* and in German as *Dudelsack*?
13 What was the name of the warship in which Lord Kitchener, the Secretary for War, was drowned in June 1916 when it struck a German mine off Orkney?
14 Which unit of measurement, equal to twenty pennyweights, derives its name from a town in north-eastern France and is still legally authorised in the UK for weighing precious metals such as gold and silver?
15 *Inter Arma Caritas* ('Charity in the midst of weapons') is one of the mottoes of which international organisation?
16 The name of which medicinal and food plant comes from the ancient use of its rhizomes in the West Indies to absorb poison from wounds caused by poisoned arrows?
17 Who was the first Sikh Guru and the founder of the faith?
18 Which scientist put forward the Gaia hypothesis in 1972, which proposes that terrestrial biological and physical processes work together to produce and regulate conditions conducive to the continued existence of life?
19 Which veteran French photojournalist, a contemporary of Henri Cartier-Bresson, took the celebrated nude photograph of his wife, Anne-Marie, at a wash basin in *Le Nu Provençal Gordes*, (1949) and in 2002 published *Derrière l'objectif* (*Behind The Lens*)?
20 In which 1937 spoof western did Laurel and Hardy sing the duet *The Trail of the Lonesome Pine*, which became a No. 2 hit in the UK in 1975?

General Knowledge Answers

1 *Doctor Zhivago*. When Pasternak (1890–1960) submitted the novel to a Moscow monthly magazine in 1956, it was rejected because 'it represented in a libelous manner the October Revolution, the people who made it, and social construction in the Soviet Union'. It reached the West in 1957, but was not published in Russia until 1988.

2 **Pen.**

3 **Acker Bilk** (Bernard Stanley Bilk, b. 1929).

4 **Sacha Baron Cohen** (b. 1972). Cohen, an observant Jew, emerged from the Cambridge Footlights as a talented comedian and has made Ali G the epitome of falsely naïve interviewers.

5 **Lord Byron** (1788–1824). The first lines are:

She walks in beauty, like the night
Of cloudless climes and starry skies;
And all that's best of dark and bright
Meet in her aspect and her eyes . . .

6 **Jairus.**

7 ***Marriage à la Mode*** (1743), which is in the National Gallery, London having been part of its founding collection.

8 **South Sea Bubble.** The South Sea Company was granted a monopoly of trade with the South Seas, causing a feverish rise and subsequent collapse in the value of its shares when they were offered (at an ever-increasing premium) in exchange for government stocks.

9 **Stanley Baldwin** (1867–1947). What he actually said was, 'I shall be but a short time tonight. I have seldom spoken with greater regret, for my lips are not yet unsealed.' The cartoonist David Low portrayed him for weeks in the *Evening Standard* with sticking plaster over his mouth.

10 **St Matthew.** He was a tax collector before he became one of Jesus's disciples.

11 **Teaching.** These training days were introduced to implement the Education Reform Act 1986 by Kenneth Baker (b. 1934) when he was Secretary of State for Education.

12 **Bagpipes.**

13 **HMS *Hampshire*.**

14 **Troy (ounce).** The word comes from the town of Troyes, where the unit of weight was first used.

15 **ICRC (International Committee of the Red Cross).** It also acknowledges the motto *Per humanitatem ad pacem* ('Peace through humanity').

16 **Arrowroot** (*Maranta arundinacea*). The rhizomes consist almost entirely of pure, edible starch.

17 **Guru Nanak** (1469–1539). He was a Hindu who, according to Sikh writings, disappeared in a river for three days and had a vision in which he was given the message that life based on knowledge of God was more important than the name or outward practice of religion. The faith he taught became known as Sikhism (the word 'Sikh' means 'one who learns').

18 **James Lovelock** (b. 1919). He supported his theory with *Daisyworld* (1981), a computer simulation of a world populated by white or black daisies which either reflect or absorb solar radiation.

19 **Willy Ronis** (b. 1910).

20 ***Way Out West.***

Dublin Questions

1 What is the name of the ferry port on Dublin Bay which houses the National Maritime Museum?
2 Which library holds the magnificent illuminated manuscript known as *The Book of Kells* (c. 800)?
3 Which fabled Dublin street seller is commemorated by a life-sized bronze statue across the road from Trinity College?
4 Which poet commemorated the 1916 Easter Rising in Dublin with the elegiac epitaph 'A terrible beauty is born'?
5 Who was the lead singer of the Dublin-based pop group, formed in 1975, whose other members were Gary Roberts and Gerry Cott (guitars), Johnnie 'Fingers' Maylett (keyboard), Pete Briquette (Pat Cusack, bass) and Simon Crowe (drums)?
6 The career of which charismatic nineteenth-century politician, who died in Brighton and is buried in Glasnevin cemetery in Dublin, was ruined because of his affair with a married woman, Katherine O'Shea?
7 What are the main ingredients of 'Dublin coddle'?
8 What is the name of the building in Dublin which houses the Irish Parliament, the Dáil?
9 Where is the source of the River Liffey?
10 What is the meaning of the Irish name for Dublin, Baile Átha Cliath?
11 Which High King of Ireland defeated a viking army at the Battle of Clontarf, just outside Dublin, on Good Friday in 1014, but was killed in the aftermath of the battle?
12 What is the name given to the area of Dublin between the Guinness brewery and St Patrick's Cathedral?
13 Which fervently Nationalist eighteenth-century politician, whose statue stands in the centre of College Green, led the abortive parliamentary opposition to domination by Westminster and the eventual Act of Union of 1801?
14 What is the name of the Viking Age archaeological site between Christ Church Cathedral and the River Liffey which provoked huge public demonstrations in the 1970s?
15 Which twentieth-century poet and novelist is commemorated by a bench near Baggot Street Bridge, where he often sat composing his poems?
16 What was the original name (from the Old Norse *haugr*, a burial mound) of College Green, the broad street leading west from Trinity College?
17 What was the real name of 'Strongbow', the leader of the Anglo-Norman force who was invited to invade Ireland in 1170 and who became ruler of Dublin?
18 Which religious group was founded in Dublin in 1831 by Catherine McAuley?
19 Who were the two victims of the Phoenix Park Murders on 6 May 1882?
20 Which two Dublin theatres are known jocularly as 'Sodom and Begorrah'?

Dublin

1 **Dún Laoghaire.**
2 **Trinity College,** Dublin
3 **Molly Malone.** Molly was an eighteenth-century fishwife who is thought to have died in a cholera epidemic. The statue is familiarly known as 'The Tart with the Cart'. The ballad about her has become Dublin's unofficial anthem:

In Dublin's fair city, where the girls are so pretty,
I first set my eyes on sweet Molly Malone. . .

4 **W.B. Yeats** (1865–1939), in his poem *Easter 1916* (Canto 1):

All changed, changed utterly:
A terrible beauty is born.

5 **Bob Geldof** (Boomtown Rats).
6 **Charles Parnell** (1846–91).
7 **Chopped sausages and ham or bacon,** cooked in a stock with potatoes and onions; it is a traditional Saturday-night supper.
8 **Leinster House.** It was built in 1745 for the Earl of Kildare and was known as Kildare House until he became Duke of Leinster.
9 **Lackan Reservoir** (in a gorge cut into the Slievethoul Ridge), south-west of Dublin.
10 **Town of the Ford of the Hurdle.**
11 **Brian Boru** (Brian Bóraime, 926–1014).
12 **The Liberties** (formerly outside the jurisdiction of the city and under the sole jurisdiction of the bishop).
13 **Henry Grattan** (1746–1820). The bronze statue, by John Henry Foley, was unveiled in 1876.
14 **Wood Quay.** Excavations in the 1970s demonstrated that it was the Viking Age embankment to create a waterfront for the Liffey (which was much broader than it is now). Some 200,000 people marched through the city in 1987 to protest against a decision by Dublin Corporation to build civic offices on the site.
15 **Patrick Kavanagh** (1905–67). His best-known poem is *The Great Hunger* (1942).
16 **Hoggen Green.** It was formerly dominated by an artificial earthen mound named 'Thingmote' ('Parliament meeting-place') built by the Norsemen around 1000. It was levelled in 1881–2.
17 **Richard de Clare** (also called Richard FitzGilbert, Earl of Pembroke, c. 1130–76). In 1172 he commissioned the building of Christ Church Cathedral, where his remains are interred.
18 **Sisters of Mercy.** Catherine McAuley (1787–1841) used a legacy to commission the building in Dublin which she opened in 1827 as the House of Mercy, educating poor children. She and two companions took their vows in 1831 and officially formed the Sisters of Mercy, with Catherine as superior.
19 **Lord Frederick Cavendish** (Chief Secretary for Ireland) and **T.H. Burke,** his Under-Secretary. They were stabbed by four members of a secret society, 'The Invincibles'.
20 **The Gate** (founded in 1928 by Micheál MacLiammóir the actor and Hilton Edwards, who were gay) and **The Abbey** (founded in 1904 by W.B. Yeats, J.M. Synge and Lady Isabella Augusta Gregory to foster local playwrights. Synge was its first Director).

General Knowledge Questions

1 Which Irish writer and poet published *Dubliners*, a collection of short stories, in 1914?
2 Which 1950s radio comedy show used the catchphrase 'If you haven't been to Manchester, you haven't lived'?
3 Which singer had a No. 1 hit in 1979 with *Bright Eyes*, the theme tune of the animated film *Watership Down*?
4 Which former international gymnast, a law graduate from Durham University and pioneering TV football presenter, is the daughter of a Welsh football international and the wife of a Scottish rugby union international?
5 In the 1934 film *Belle of the Nineties*, who spoke the words 'A man in the house is worth two in the street'?
6 In which sport are there moves called barani, miller and triffus?
7 What was the name of Alexander the Great's horse?
8 In the Second World War, for what were Gold, Juno, Omaha, Sword and Utah code names?
9 *Papavar* is the Latin name for which flowering plant?
10 By which two Latin words was nitric acid known to early alchemists?
11 Which R&B singer, who was killed in a plane crash in August 2001 at the age of twenty-two, played the role of the vampire Queen Akasha in the film *Queen of the Damned*, which was released in February 2002?
12 For which occasion did William Walton compose the *Crown Imperial* march?
13 What is the name of the annual sculling race on the Thames from London Bridge to Chelsea, which began in 1715, originally between skiffs once used as ferries?
14 What are the next two lines of the following clerihew by Edmund Clerihew Bentley?
The Art of Biography
Is different from Geography . . .
15 Which tiny island in the middle of the South Atlantic, now a dependency of St Helena, was named after the day on which it was 'discovered' in 1503?
16 What is the word for a hollow fossil or nodule of clay ironstone with a small piece of debris trapped inside, which produces a rattling sound when shaken?
17 What is the name of Europe's giant 'green eye' satellite, launched from the European spaceport in Kourou, French Guiana, in March 2002 to record observations of the Earth?
18 Which real-life village church and churchyard in Kent was the setting for the opening of Dickens's *Great Expectations*?
19 Who wrote the classic book on cuckoos, *The Cuckoo's Secret* (1922)?
20 By what name is the Norway lobster or langoustine (*Nephrops norvegicus*) more usually known in the UK?

General Knowledge Answers

1 **James Joyce** (1882–1941). He began writing them in response to George Russell's offer of £1 each for some simple short stories with an Irish background to appear in *The Irish Homestead*, of which he was the editor. Russell decided that the stories were not suitable for his readers and some of them were lost.

2 ***Ray's A Laugh*** (1949–61 on the Light Programme). It starred Ted Ray (Charlie Olden, 1905–77) with Kitty Bluett, Ted Yule, Patricia Hayes, Kenneth Connor and Peter Sellers.

3 **Art Garfunkel.** The song was composed by Mike Batt, who collaborated with Andrew Lloyd Webber on *The Phantom of the Opera* (1986) and wrote the theme tune for the Conservative Party's election campaign in 2001.

4 **Gabby Logan.** Her father is Terry Yorath, Leeds United and Wales soccer star; her husband, whom she married in 2001, is Kenny Logan, the Scottish rugby cap who plays for Wasps.

5 **Mae West.**

6 **Trampolining.** A barani is a front somersault with half twist; a miller is a triple-twisting double back somersault; and a triffus is any triple somersault with a twist.

7 **Bucephalus** (Ox-head), who died in 326 BC at Alexander's last great battle on the left bank of the River Hydaspes (now Jhelum) in the Punjab, and whose name Alexander gave to the city of Bucephala which he founded there.

8 **Beaches on which the Normandy landings were made in 1944.**

9 **Poppy.**

10 ***Aqua fortis*** (strong water).

11 **Aaliyah** (Aaliyah Haughton, 1979–2001). Her single *More Than A Woman* reached No. 1 in the UK in January 2002.

12 **The coronation of George VI** in 1937. The score is headed by a line from the poem *In Honour of the City* by William Dunbar (c. 1465–c. 1520): 'In beautie beryng the crone imperialle.'

13 **Doggett's Coat and Badge.** Thomas Doggett (1670–1721), a comedy actor, bequeathed the prize and the livery and badge.

14 ***Geography is about Maps/Biography is about Chaps.***

15 **Ascension Island.** It was first discovered by the Spanish navigator Juan de Nova Castella (d. 1509) returning from a voyage to India in 1501 (although this visit apparently went unrecorded) and found again two years later on Ascension Day by Alphonse d'Albuquerque (Governor and 2nd Viceroy of Portuguese India, 1453–1515), who gave the island its name.

16 **Eagle-stone** (*aetites*, from the Greek *aetos*, eagle). The term derives from the ancient belief, because they were often found in eagles' nests, that eagles were unable to hatch healthy chicks without them.

17 **Envisat.** Launched at a cost of £1.4 billion by an Ariane 5 rocket, it is designed to monitor the seas, lands, atmosphere and ice caps for five years.

18 **St James, Cooling.**

19 **Edgar Chance** (1881–1955). The book was accompanied by a groundbreaking film recording of a cuckoo laying an egg in a host nest.

20 **Dublin Bay prawn.** It is a burrow-dwelling marine crustacean closely related to the lobster and is the only Nephrops ('kidney eye') species found in European waters.

Engineering

Questions

1 Which Renaissance artist designed the first battle tank between 1482 and 1499 while he was in the service of Ludovico Sforza, Duke of Milan?
2 Which US railway engineer, who died with one hand on the brake and the other on the whistle of the engine '382', was popularised in several ballads (some telling erroneous versions of his story), including a 1909 vaudeville song by Lawrence Siebert and Eddie Newton?
3 What was the name of the first steamship (a paddle steamer) to provide a regular service across the Atlantic, designed by Isambard Kingdom Brunel?
4 In the 1980s which Detroit car manufacturer opened the factory in Belfast which produced the futuristic DCM 12 with its gull-wing doors and the first catalytic converter?
5 Which Scots-born locomotive engineer designed the A4 class Pacific 4–6–2 *Mallard*, which achieved the world record speed for a steam locomotive of 126 miles (201.5 kilometres) per hour in July 1938?
6 Which German car manufacturer also developed the first motorcycle, in 1885?
7 Which US-born engineer and inventor (later a British citizen), whose first patent, in 1866, had been for a hair-curling iron, produced the first fully automatic machine-gun in 1884?
8 In May 1904 a historic meeting took place in the Midland Hotel (now the Crowne Plaza), Manchester, between a designer and a financier to set up which world-famous car company?
9 Which was the first canal engineered in Britain, by the Romans in about AD 120?
10 Which Devon engineer took out the first patent for a practical steam engine in 1698, which was described in *The Miner's Friend* (1702) as a device for pumping out mines and was also sold for supplying water to large buildings?
11 Which engineer, Hitler's Inspector of Roads, was responsible in the 1930s for the construction of the Siegfried Line system of pillboxes and strong-points along the German western frontier and, in 1937, for the development of the German autobahn system?
12 What was the name of the first practical steamboat to be built, in 1802, in Britain?
13 In 1901 which British engineer invented a horse-drawn vacuum cleaner – the first automatic cleaner to suck up debris instead of blowing it away?
14 Which Irish engineer developed the high-speed steam turbine (patented in 1884) and built the first turbine-driven steamship, the *Turbinia*, in 1897?
15 Which two engineers designed the Forth Railway Bridge, opened in 1890?
16 Which was the first lighthouse to be built by the Northern Lighthouse Board in Scotland, in 1787, and the only one to be built on top of a fortified castle?
17 Which Lancashire-born engineer settled in Fiume (now Rijeka, Croatia) in 1856 and there invented the world's first self-propelling torpedo in 1866?
18 Which Liverpool-born electrical engineer and inventor developed the concept of high-voltage AC generation which laid the foundations for the National Grid?
19 Who designed the Golden Gate Bridge in San Francisco, which was opened in 1937, having built more than four hundred bridges in the USA?
20 Which English civil engineer, a former apprentice of George Stephenson, designed the Grand Junction Railway and the Paris–Rouen railway?

1 **Leonardo da Vinci** (1452–1519). The tank was roughly circular with a broad, conical top made from thick planks of wood bolted on to a frame, bristling with guns and designed to move in any direction.
2 **Casey Jones** (John Luther Jones, 1864–1900, named 'Casey' after his home town, Cayce, Kentucky).
3 *Great Western*. It left Bristol on its maiden voyage on 8 April 1838 and arrived in New York fifteen days later (half the time normally taken by sailing ships). It was broken up at Vauxhall, London, in 1856.
4 **John De Lorean** (b. 1924). The car was featured in the *Back to the Future* films. The company went into receivership in 1982.
5 **Nigel Gresley** (1876–1941). *Mallard* is now in the National Railway Museum in York.
6 **Gottlieb Daimler** (1834–1900). His partner was Wilhelm Maybach (1846–1929).
7 **Hiram Stevens Maxim** (1840–1916). His Maxim machine-gun harnessed the energy of the recoil of a gun to reload and fire the gun automatically.
8 **Rolls-Royce.** The designer was Frederick Henry Royce (1863–1933) and the financier was Charles Stewart Rolls (1877–1910).
9 **Fosdyke**, linking Lincoln with the River Trent.
10 **Thomas Savery** (1650–1715). He based his machine on principles set out by the French physicist Denis Papin and others.
11 **Fritz Todt** (1891–1942). The first autobahn, the 10-kilometre Avus Autobahn in Berlin, had been built in 1921 by Karl Fritsch, with a loop at each end so that it could double as a racetrack.
12 *Charlotte Dundas*, designed by Lanarkshire-born William Symington (1763–1831) and intended as a tug for use on the Forth & Clyde Canal.
13 **Hubert Cecil Booth** (1871–1955, founder of the British Vacuum Cleaner Company). The vacuum cleaner was so big that it had to be left outside the building and only the hose brought in. In 1907 a US school janitor, James Murray Spangler, patented an 'electric suction sweeper', which he sold to the industrialist William Henry Hoover (1849–1932).
14 **Charles Algernon Parsons** (1854–1931). The *Turbinia*, with a top speed of 35 knots, was much faster than any other ship of its time. It was built at Parsons works, Newcastle upon Tyne, and is now in the city's Discovery Museum.
15 **Benjamin Baker** (1840–1907) and **John Fowler** (1817–98). Thomas Bouch had designed a suspension bridge for the Forth in 1873 but, after the collapse in 1879 of his Tay Railway Bridge, his plans were scrapped in favour of a cantilever bridge.
16 **Kinnaird Head**, Fraserburgh. The lighthouse was reconstructed inside Kinnaird Castle by Robert Stevenson. It was decommissioned in 1991, and is part of the Museum of Scottish Lighthouses at Kinnaird Head.
17 **Robert Whitehead** (1823–1905).
18 **Sebastian de Ferranti** (1864–1930). In 1887 he designed Deptford Power Station (the largest of its time, producing 10,000 volts) and founded Ferranti Ltd in 1905.
19 **Joseph Baermann Strauss** (1870–1938).
20 **Joseph Locke** (1805–60). He was appointed with Stephenson as joint chief engineer on the Grand Junction Railway but Stephenson withdrew.

General Knowledge Questions

1 What spectacular fairground attraction is named after the Pittsburgh engineer who invented it for the World's Columbian Exposition in Chicago in 1893?
2 Which singer was known as 'the Forces' sweetheart' during the Second World War?
3 Which tough grass is widely used to stabilise sand dunes?
4 The name of which meat product comes from a Romanian word for highly spiced smoked meat?
5 Which US writer was the author of the Mafia novel *The Godfather* (1969)?
6 Which king of Wessex defeated an invading Danish army at the Battle of Edington, Wiltshire, in May 878?
7 Which punk group released an anarchic version of *God Save the Queen* for the Queen's Silver Jubilee in 1977?
8 Which British politician published a book on international affairs entitled *State Craft* in March 2002?
9 In which castle on the Isle of Wight was Charles I imprisoned for a time between 1647 and 1648?
10 In which trade or craft are majuscules, uncials and versals used?
11 Which ribbed or corded ribbon used in hatbands and for stiffening skirt waistbands is named after a nineteenth-century British aristocrat and soldier?
12 Of what is palynology the study?
13 In Greek mythology, which Thessalonian king tried to rape Hera, the wife of Zeus, and was punished by being fastened to a burning wheel which rotated for all eternity?
14 Who is the oldest monarch to have ascended the British throne?
15 To which two animals during their second year is the term 'teg' applied?
16 Which British author wrote under the pseudonym of 'Saki', which he took from the *Rubaiyat* of Omar Khayyam?
17 Of which mineral are sapphires and rubies formed?
18 Which sixteenth-century artist painted *The Massacre of the Innocents*, which is in the Royal Collection?
19 Who was the leader of the Nore naval mutiny in 1797, who was later hanged on board HMS *Sandwich*?
20 What was the name of the world's first steam warship, launched for the US Navy in 1814 to protect New York Harbour during the war of 1812–14 against Britain known as the Second War of American Independence?

General Knowledge Answers

1 **Ferris wheel**. The inventor was George W.G. Ferris (1859–96).
2 **Vera Lynn** (Vera Welch, b. 1917).
3 **Marram grass** (*Ammophila arenaria*).
4 **Pastrami**.
5 **Mario Puzo** (1920–99). The film, starring Marlon Brando as Mafia leader Vito Corleone, was released in 1972 and won Academy Awards for Best Picture, Best Actor (Marlon Brando) and Best Adapted Screenplay.
6 **Alfred the Great** (849–99). The Danes surrendered, and their king, Guthrum, was baptised, with Alfred as sponsor; in the following year the Danes settled in East Anglia.
7 **The Sex Pistols**. It reached No. 2 in the UK charts and was re-released to coincide with the Golden Jubilee in 2002.
8 **Margaret Thatcher** (b. 1925), Prime Minister from 1979 to 1990.
9 **Carisbrooke Castle**. He surrendered to the Scots at Newark in 1646, was handed over to Parliament and held at Holmby House near Northampton, from where he negotiated a treaty with the Scots. He escaped to the Isle of Wight in November 1647, but he and his family were soon captured.
10 **Calligraphy** (and **printing**). A majuscule is a capital letter; an uncial is a letter having the large, round, unjoined form characteristic of Greek and Latin manuscripts; and a versal is an ornate style of capital letter used at the beginning of a verse or paragraph.
11 **Petersham**. Viscount Petersham (Charles Stanhope, 4th Earl of Harrington, 1790–1851) also gave his name to a type of overcoat.
12 **Living and fossil pollen grains and plant spores.**
13 **Ixion**.
14 **William IV**, in 1830. He was sixty-four years old when he succeeded his elder brother George IV.
15 **Sheep** and **deer**. The term applies to any sheep from the time when it is weaned until its first shearing.
16 **Hector Hugh Munro** (1870–1916).
17 **Corundum** (aluminium oxide).
18 **Pieter Bruegel the Elder** (c. 1525–69). The painting records the slaughter of male babies by Herod after the birth of Christ, on Childermas (now Holy Innocents Day, 28 December). During the seventeenth century almost all of the slaughtered babies were painted over with less disquieting objects such as poultry, cattle and bundles, and flames (removed in 1942) were added to make it look like the sack of a village. Another version (in Vienna), by Pieter Bruegel the Younger, shows the whole horrific scene.
19 **Richard Parker**. The Nore is a sandbank in the Thames Estuary, extending between Shoeburyness and Sheerness. Its name was used for a naval command for the eastern area of England until 1961.
20 ***Demologos***. It was renamed ***Fulton*** after its designer, Robert Fulton (1765–1815). It was destroyed by an accidental explosion in 1829.

Flowers Questions

1 By what name is the 'Lenten lily' better known?
2 What is the more common term for a garland of *Bellis perennis*, which children like to make?
3 Which former solo oboist with the CBS Symphony Orchestra had a UK No. 2 hit in 1955 with *The Yellow Rose of Texas*?
4 The name of which popular garden flower means, literally, 'many flowers'?
5 A variety of which flower bulb, introduced into Europe from Turkey in about 1551, was valuable enough to be exchanged for a flourishing brewery in France in the early seventeenth century?
6 What term is used for the part of a flower which consists of the petals?
7 According to the opening lines of T.S. Eliot's poem *The Burial of the Dead* (Part 1 of *The Waste Land*), which flowers does April ('the cruellest month') breed out of the dead land?
8 A spray of which flowers, made of gold, does the Pope bless on Laetare Sunday (also called Golden Sunday), the fourth Sunday in Lent – Mothering Sunday?
9 The name of which flower means, literally, 'rock-breaker'?
10 In Stella Gibbons's 1932 novel *Cold Comfort Farm*, what was the plant whose blossoming 'in the fullness o' summer' was regarded by the Starkadder family as a baleful aphrodisiac?
11 Which pink flowering plant was given the nickname 'fireweed' because it flourished so luxuriantly on bomb sites after the Blitz?
12 In honour of which flowering plant did the ancient Romans hold annual festivals, naming it '*herba sacra*' (sacred herb) because they believed it could heal the bites of rabid animals, cure the plague, avert sorcery and reconcile enemies?
13 Which flowers are featured in the title of John Singer Sargent's 1885–6 painting of two little girls in a garden lighting Japanese lanterns?
14 Plants growing in what type of place are described as 'ruderal'?
15 Which flower follows 'I am the rose of Sharon' in the first line of the *Song of Solomon*, Chapter 2?
16 Which common flower is sometimes known as 'Jack-go-to-bed-at-noon' because its flowers usually open in the morning sunshine and close at about midday?
17 Which flower did Apollo cause to spring from the blood of a beautiful youth he accidentally killed?
18 In 1653 who wrote his *Complete Herbal*, which he dedicated to his wife, Alice, with the words: 'These are my choicest secrets, which I have had many years locked up in my own breast'?
19 Which French navigator and soldier gave his name to a genus of flowering shrub which includes more than a dozen species in the 'four-o'clock' family (*Nyctaginaceae*), and to the largest of the Solomon Islands?
20 Which German botanist and physician was the first to demonstrate, in 1694, evidence of the sexual reproduction of flowering plants?

1 **Daffodil** (*Narcissus pseudonarcissus*), which blooms in Lent. It is not a lily (which belongs to the genus *Lilium*).
2 **Daisy chain.**
3 **Mitch Miller** (b. 1911).
4 **Polyanthus.**
5 **Tulip** (*Tulipe brasserie*), which appears to be extinct. The demand for rare tulips exceeded the supply, and prices for individual bulbs increased dramatically in northern Europe. By the early seventeenth century a single bulb of a new variety was valuable enough for a bride's dowry.
6 **Corolla.**
7 **Lilacs.**
8 **Rose.** One of the roses of the 'The Golden Rose' is a receptacle for balsam and musk. The Golden Rose award is occasionally conferred on sovereigns or cities distinguished for their services to the Roman Catholic Church. '*Laetare*' ('to rejoice') is the first word of the introit of the liturgy.
9 **Saxifrage** (from the Latin *saxum*, rock, and *frangere*, to break).
10 **Sukebind.** Unwanted pregnancies were blamed on 'the disastrous effect of too much sukebind and too many long summer evenings upon the female system'.
11 **Rosebay willow herb** (*Epilobium angustifolium*), also called great willow herb. Its seeds can lie dormant for many years, and then germinate in warm conditions.
12 **Vervain** (verbena). Verbenalia were the festivals in its honour. Heralds wore wreaths of vervain when they announced wars.
13 **Carnation, lily** and **rose** (*Carnation, Lily, Lily, Rose*, in Tate Britain).
14 **Waste ground** (from the Latin *rudus*, 'rubble').
15 **Lily of the valley** (which, like the rose of Sharon, might not have been the same flower known by that name today):
I am the rose of Sharon and the lily of the valleys.
As the lily among thorns, so is my love among the daughters.
16 **Goat's-beard** (*Tragopogon pratensis*).
17 **Hyacinth** (*Hyacinthus orientalis*). In Greek mythology, Hyacinthus was killed when a discus thrown by his lover, Apollo, was caught by a gust of wind and struck him on the head; the wind was the personification of a jealous rival for the youth's affections, Zephyrus.
18 **Nicholas Culpeper** (d. 1654). The book contained advice such as 'Of the leaves of Primroses is made as fine a salve to heal wounds as any that I know; you shall be taught to make salves of any herb at the latter end of the book: make this as you are taught there, and do not (you that have any ingenuity in you) see your poor neighbours go with wounded limbs when an halfpenny coat will heal them.'
19 **Louis Antoine de Bougainville** (1729–1811). He was the first Frenchman to circumnavigate the globe (1766–69); the plant bougainvillaea, and Bougainville Island, are named after him.
20 **Rudolf Jakob Camerarius** or **Camerer** (1665–1721), professor of botany at Tübingen. His surgical experiments on flowers proved that a deposit of pollen on stigmas was necessary for a plant to set seed. He first recounted his findings in 1694 in a letter to a colleague entitled *De sexu plantarum (On the sex of plants)*, and later in *Opuscula botanica* (1697, Botanical Works).

1 Which purple-flowering plant is commonly known as the 'butterfly bush' because of its attraction for butterflies?

2 Who directed the 1980 horror film *The Shining*, starring Jack Nicholson and Shelley Duvall and based on the book of the same title by Stephen King?

3 Who wrote and presented BBC Radio 4's 2002 series *In the Footsteps of St Paul*, in which he followed the journeys made by St Paul to Damascus, Jerusalem, Philippi, Corinth, Ephesus and Rome?

4 Which veteran Labour politician famously said that he was retiring from the House of Commons in 2001 in order to have more time for politics?

5 Which controversial Indian author wrote the 1997 Booker Prize-winning novel *The God of Small Things*, and in March 2002 served a symbolic one-day prison term and was fined two thousand rupees for contempt of court?

6 Which US jockey, who retired in 1989, saddled a record 8833 winners in a career spanning forty-two years?

7 In Roman Catholic and Anglican churches, which term refers to the four weeks set apart for special prayer and the ordination of the clergy?

8 Who was the first Prime Minister (later first President) of the independent republic of Ghana (formerly the Gold Coast) in 1957?

9 Which major department store, founded in 1875 in London's Regent Street, reopened in March 2002 after a £10 million refurbishment?

10 Which long war ended with the minor battle of Castillon in 1453?

11 Whose love poem opens with the following lines?

How do I love thee? Let me count the ways.
I love thee to the depth and breadth and height
My soul can reach . . .

12 Which part of the British Isles is divided into six areas called 'sheadings'?

13 Which subtropical island group in the West Atlantic was for a time given the name Somers Islands after the first settler, who was shipwrecked there in 1609?

14 What is the derivation of the word 'mystery' when applied to medieval Mystery Plays?

15 By what name was the sixteenth-century nun Elizabeth Barton better known, who was recognised by the Archbishop of Canterbury as a case of 'religious ecstasy' but who was later arrested as a fraud and hanged after her erroneous prophecy of the death of Henry VIII within six months if he married Anne Boleyn?

16 Who was the Liverpool philanthropist who provided work for men returning from the Napoleonic Wars in 1816 by creating a labyrinth of brick-lined tunnels under Liverpool, which were opened as a tourist attraction in 2002 as the Mersey Tunnels?

17 Which town in the USA is the only place in the world to have built a full-scale replica of the Parthenon in Athens, for its Centennial in 1897?

18 Who was the creator of Bob the Builder, who first appeared on television in April 1999?

19 Which item of office stationery was developed by Spencer Silver and Arthur Fry and first marketed in 1981 by 3M?

20 Where is Scotland's National Heather Collection housed – the largest collection of heathers in the UK, containing nearly a thousand cultivars of heather (*Calluna*) and heath (*Erica*)?

1 **Buddleia.** It was named by the Swedish botanist Carolus Linnaeus (Carl von Linné, 1707–78) in honour of the English botanist Adam Buddle (1665–1715).
2 **Stanley Kubrick** (b. 1928).
3 **Edward Stourton.**
4 **Tony Benn** (Anthony Wedgwood Benn, b. 1925), who entered the House of Commons as MP for Bristol South East in December 1950.
5 **Arundhati Roy** (b. 1961). The Supreme Court of India made the judgement following Roy's remarks about a legal decision to allow work on the controversial Narmada Dam project.
6 **Willie Shoemaker** (b. 1931). His record stood until Laffit Pincay Jr broke it in 1999.
7 **Ember Weeks**: the complete weeks following Holy Cross Day (14 September), the Feast of St Lucy (13 December), the first Sunday in Lent and Pentecost (Whit Sunday).
8 **Kwame Nkrumah** (1909–72).
9 **Liberty.** It was founded by Arthur Lasenby Liberty (1843–1917), who had been managing an Oriental warehouse.
10 **Hundred Years' War.** It lasted for longer than a hundred years; by convention it is said to have started in 1337 and ended in 1453.
11 **Elizabeth Barrett Browning** (1806–61), *Sonnets from the Portuguese*, No. 43.
12 **The Isle of Man.** The sheadings are split into two divisions: the North Side (Glenfaba, Michael and Ayre) and the South Side (Garff, Middle and Rushen).
13 **The Bermudas.** 'Bermudas' was marked on a 1511 Spanish map. The Spanish navigator Fernández de Oviedo, who sailed close to the islands in 1515, attributed their discovery to his countryman Juan Bermúdez in 1503. Sir George Somers (1554–1610), commander of a shipwrecked fleet of settlers bound for Virginia, claimed the islands for England. The wreck of the *Sea Venture* inspired Shakespeare's *The Tempest* (1611/12): Ariel refers to 'the still-vex'd Bermoothes'.
14 **Trade,** from the medieval French *mestier, métier* (occupation, guild). The performers were amateurs; the genre took its name from their occupations.
15 **Nun of Kent** or **Holy Maid of Kent** (1506–1534).
16 **Joseph Williamson** (1769–1840), who styled himself 'King of Edge Hill'.
17 **Nashville, Tennessee.** The 'Parthenon' was made permanent because it became so popular and has undergone a complete restoration.
18 **Keith Chapman.** The TV series was developed by Peter Orton and Rob Lawes, of Hit Entertainment.
19 **Post-It notes.** In 1970 Spencer Silver, a research chemist at 3M, came up with a glue which would not stick to anything for long, having been asked to produce the strongest glue on the market. He noticed that the glue could be reused and left no residue, but could think of no use for it. In 1980 his colleague Arthur Fry used the 'useless glue' to stop the papers with which he marked the pages of his hymn-book from falling out, and the Post-It was born.
20 **Bell's Cherrybank Centre, Perth,** now owned by Scotland's Garden Trust. It was established in 1984.

Gods and Goddesses Questions

1 In classical mythology, what became of the hundred eyes of Argus the herdsman when he was killed by Zeus?
2 In the Greek pantheon, who was the goddess of health?
3 What was the name of the feathered serpent, one of the major deities of the ancient Mexican pantheon?
4 In the Old Testament, who was the Canaanite warrior god and god of fertility?
5 Which twentieth-century English poet wrote the following lines?

Blonde Aphrodite rose up excited,
Moved to delight by the melody,
White as an orchid she rode quite naked
In an oyster shell on top of the sea.

6 In classical mythology, who was the Greek equivalent of Pax, the Roman goddess of peace?
7 In Ancient Egyptian mythology, who was the mother of the deity Osiris, the god of the dead?
8 Which Hindu god, in the form of king of the Monkeys, led the rescue of Sita, the beautiful wife of Rama, from the clutches of Ravana, the demon king of Lanka?
9 In Greek mythology, which goddess became associated with witchcraft and black magic?
10 Which Hindu goddess is usually depicted riding a lion (or a tiger) and carrying a weapon in each of her eight or ten hands?
11 Who was the chief god of the Aztec city of Tenochtitlán?
12 What is the name of the dancing three-eyed Hindu god, worshipped in the form of the *lingam* (phallus), who is associated with both destruction and restoration?
13 In the Old Norse pantheon, who was the god of poetry?
14 Who is the Hindu goddess of art, music and literature and is usually depicted riding on a swan (or goose) and playing a *veena* (a stringed instrument similar to a lute)?
15 In 1530 which German artist painted *The Judgement of Paris*, with Venus, Minerva and Juno naked (apart from golden necklaces and Juno's fashionable red hat), Paris as a bearded knight wearing golden armour and Mercury as an old man wearing contemporary clothing and a peacock-feathered headdress?
16 What was the name of the Sumerian sky god, the highest of the gods in the Mesopotamian pantheon?
17 Which god of the spring sun was the head of the Babylonian pantheon?
18 In West African tradition, what are the names of the twin daughter and son of Nana-Buluku (the 'one god', who is neither male nor female), who shaped the world and continue to control it with their fourteen children, the Vodou, or lesser gods?
19 Who was the abstract, invisible chief god of the Maya?
20 In classical mythology, who was the god of ridicule, the son of Nox, who was driven from Olympus for his constant criticism of the gods?

Gods and Goddesses Answers

1 **They were placed by Hera in the tail of her peacock.**

2 **Hygeia**, the daughter of Aesculapius, the god of medicine and healing. Her symbol was a serpent drinking from a cup in her hand.

3 **Quetzalcóatl**. As the morning and evening star, Quetzalcóatl symbolised death and resurrection. He was said to have descended to the underworld, Mictlan, with Xolotl, a dog-headed god, to gather the bones of the ancient dead. He anointed the bones with his own blood, and thus created the ancestors of modern people.

4 **Baal.**

5 **W.H. Auden** (1907–73), in *Anthem for St Cecilia's Day* (1941); it was set to music by Benjamin Britten as *Hymn to St Cecilia* (1942).

6 **Irene.**

7 **Nut**, the mother goddess of Egypt. She was also the mother of Horus, Seth, Isis and Nephthys.

8 **Hanuman**. The story is told in the *Ramayana*.

9 **Hecate**. In the earliest myths, however, she was the friend of all mankind, granting prosperity, farming fertility and fishing success in response to prayers.

10 **Durga**. To help her to slay the buffalo-demon Mahisasura, the other gods lent her their weapons. Durga is worshipped at the nine-day festival of Navaratri.

11 **Huitzilopochtli** (from *huitzilin*, 'hummingbird', and *opochtli*, 'on the left'). The Aztecs believed that the dead became hummingbirds and went to the left (the South), which was the home of the dead. Huitzilopochtli was the god of war and of the sun; human victims (usually war captives) were sacrificed to him by ripping out their hearts while they were still alive. It is thought that the purpose of these sacrifices was to give strength to the sun, whose light is very weak when it rises.

12 **Shiva**. He is usually depicted with the bull Nandi, a snake around his neck and the River Ganges flowing from his topknot.

13 **Bragi.**

14 **Sarasvati**. Giant images of her are carried in processions at the beginning of spring.

15 **Lucas Cranach the Elder** (1472–1553).

16 **Anu** (or An).

17 **Bel (Marduk)**. A poem entitled *Enuma elish*, from the reign of Nebuchadrezzar I (r. 1124–3 BC), relates his rise to eminence as the god of fifty names – each a name of a deity or a divine attribute. According to the poem, he vanquished Tiamat, the monster of primeval chaos, and became supreme god of heaven and earth.

18 **Mawu** and **Lisa**. Some people regard them as one deity who is both female (Mawu) and male (Lisa).

19 **Hunabku**

20 **Momus** – hence the term 'momus' for a carping critic.

General Knowledge

Questions

1 In Greek mythology, what was the fluid which flowed like blood through the veins of the gods?
2 Who was shot by Mark David Chapman on 8 December 1980?
3 Which Hollywood heartthrob, the star of the 1980 film *American Gigolo*, converted to Buddhism and founded the Tibet House to promote Tibetan culture?
4 By what name is the fragrant, white-flowering garden shrub *Philadelphus* commonly known?
5 Which New York R&B singer won five of the top 2002 Grammies, including Best Newcomer, Song of the Year (*Fallin'*) and Best R&B album (*Songs in A Minor*)?
6 Which renowned tragic actress, painted by Joshua Reynolds in 1784 as *The Tragic Muse*, was the sister of the theatrical Kemble brothers (Charles, John Philip and Stephen)?
7 Which term for structures such as telephone boxes, newsstands and information booths was originally used in Islamic architecture for an open circular pavilion?
8 In 1876 which US librarian originated the system of decimal book classification which bears his name?
9 Which Scottish estate is the real-life setting of Glenbogle in the BBC TV series *Monarch of the Glen*?
10 After the dough for a bagel is made into its familiar ring shape, what process – unique in bread-making – does it undergo before it is browned in an oven?
11 The invention of which electronic component in the USA in 1947 replaced the vacuum tube in radios and made feasible the miniaturisation of complex circuitry as used in computers?
12 Which early bicycle was originally known as an 'Ordinary'?
13 Who was the designer of the gold-plated figurine which became known as an Oscar, awarded annually by the American Academy of Motion Picture Arts from 1929?
14 In which English county has the old coast-to-coast Mineral Railway between Portreath and Devoran been reopened as a cycle way?
15 In a square in the centre of which English city is the huge cast-iron statue of a mummified *Iron Man*, by Antony Gormley?
16 Which twelfth-century English saint (once a Cistercian monk)is associated with the ruined Rievaulx Abbey in Yorkshire?
17 Of what is the word 'toady', meaning a sycophant, an abbreviation?
18 Which caricaturist illustrated life in eighteenth-century England, creating comic stock characters such as the blowsy barmaid, the antiquarian, the old maid and the Grub Street hack, and engraved the illustrations for *The Tour of Dr Syntax in Search of the Picturesque* (1813) and its two sequels?
19 Which US writer, who won the 1992 Hans Christian Andersen Medal for children's literature, was the author of books specifically designed for Black American children, including *Zeely* (1967) and the best-selling *MC Higgins, the Great* (1974), for which she was awarded the Newbery Medal?
20 Which Hindu goddess is depicted as black-faced, smeared with blood, with bared teeth and protruding tongue, wearing a garland of skulls and a girdle of severed hands?

General Knowledge Answers

1 **Ichor.**
2 **John Lennon** (1940–80).
3 **Richard Gere** (b. 1949).
4 **Mock orange.**
5 **Alicia Keys** (b. 1981). In March 2002 she was the first singer to perform at the House of Commons, from a makeshift stage in the Portcullis Rooms accompanied by a portable piano. She was introduced by the youngest MP, David Lammy (Tottenham), who had invited twenty-five of his young constituents to ask Alicia questions and watch her perform because he thinks that 'politicians need to bridge the gap between politics and music and appeal to young people'.
6 **Sarah Siddons** (1755–1831). Born in Brecon, Wales, she was the eldest child of Roger and Sarah Kemble, who ran a troupe of travelling actors.
7 **Kiosk.** It had a roof supported by pillars. Examples include the summer palaces of the sultans of Turkey.
8 **Melvil Dewey** (1851–1931). He designed the system for the Amherst College Library; he later became chief librarian and professor of library economy at Columbia University, New York, and founder and director of the New York State Library School.
9 **Ardverikie estate**, on the shores of Loch Laggan, owned by Patrick and Phillida Gordon-Duff-Pennington.
10 **It is immersed in boiling water for a few seconds.**
11 **Transistor.** It was developed by three US physicists at the Bell Telephone Laboratories: John Bardeen (1908–91), Walter H. Brattain (1902–87) and William B. Shockley (1910–89).
12 **Penny-farthing**, which was first produced in Coventry in 1871. The name arose because of the relative sizes of the wheels to the old penny and farthing coins.
13 **Cedric Gibbons** (1893–1960), art director of Metro-Goldwyn-Mayer (MGM). The sculptor George Stanley was commissioned to make the original statuette from Gibbons's design. There are several versions of the source of the name 'Oscar'.
14 **Cornwall.** The cycle way runs alongside the River Camel.
15 **Birmingham.** The statue, made from four pieces of cast iron just over 3 centimetres thick and set into the paving at an angle, was a gift from the Trustee Savings Bank (TSB) to mark its relocation in the city in 1993.
16 **St Ailred** (c. 1110–67). He became abbot of Rievaulx in 1147.
17 **Toad-eater.** A 'toad-eater' was the assistant of a medical mountebank and was required to pretend to eat toads (which were considered poisonous) and then be 'cured' by his master: hence the meaning of 'stooge' or a fawning flatterer.
18 **Thomas Rowlandson** (1756–1827). The attitudes and pretensions of his larger-than-life characters were conveyed through details such as enormous bosoms and bottoms, elaborate coiffures, uniforms, and trailing handkerchiefs to express dejection.
19 **Virginia Hamilton** (1936–2002).
20 **Kali** (Sanskrit for 'black'). Her most renowned worshippers were the professional robbers and assassins known as 'Thugs'; their practice, known as ritual thuggee, was suppressed by William Bentinck, Governor General of India from 1833 to 1835.

Heraldry

1 Which institution in London is the official repository of the coats of arms and pedigrees of English, Welsh, Northern Irish and Commonwealth families and their descendants?
2 What is the name of the medieval uniform worn by royal heralds – the coat embroidered on its front, back and sides with the Royal Arms?
3 What is the heraldic term for black?
4 Which two creatures support the Royal Arms of the United Kingdom?
5 Which heraldic beast is described as a winged monster with the head, wings and talons of an eagle and the body, rear legs and ears of a lion?
6 Which Scottish king first adopted the red lion on his standard?
7 Which heraldic emblem is featured on the badge worn by the Yeomen of the Guard?
8 What is the heraldic term for a protective cloth attached to the helmet and, on a coat of arms, flowing from beneath the crest?
9 Which single item is depicted on a green background on the arms of Leinster?
10 Which university has as its arms a shield with a circle at the top left as you view it?
11 If a horse on a coat of arms is described as '*forcené*', what is it doing?
12 The arms of which English king were '*azure* (blue), a cross *flory* (with fleurs-de-lis decorated points), five doves *or* (gold)', and have been incorporated into the heraldry of Westminster Abbey, Westminster School, Westminster Hospital and the City of Westminster?
13 In heraldry, a stylised pattern of blue and silver skins of which animals joined head to tail is referred to as '*vair*'?
14 The heraldry of which early twentieth-century author's ancestral home inspired her to write the following lines?

Leopards on the gable-ends
Leopards on the stair,
Stiff the blazoned shield they bear,
Or and Gules, a blend of Vair,
Leopards on the gable-ends,
Leopards everywhere.

15 What are represented by the eight points on the crosses of the Knights Templars and the Knights Hospitallers?
16 What are *seaxes*, which are found on the coats of arms of many counties and boroughs of south-east England (for example, Essex and the former county of Middlesex)?
17 Which fifteenth- and sixteenth-century German father-and-son artists used the family coat of arms (a winged serpent) in place of a signature, giving rise to many problems of attribution?
18 In English heraldic cadency, what is the charge which indicates a second son?
19 What are the titles of the four Kings of Arms of the English Officers of Arms Ordinary, who are the only people with authority to grant armorial bearings?
20 With what heraldic device did Henry VII commemorate his victory over Richard III at the Battle of Bosworth in 1485?

Heraldry

Answers

1 **College of Arms** (also known as Heralds' College). It is headed by the Earl Marshal; the office is hereditary in the family of the Duke of Norfolk. In Scotland the equivalent institution is the Lyon Court, presided over by the Lord Lyon King of Arms, at New Register House in Edinburgh.
2 **Tabard.**
3 **Sable.**
4 **Lion and Unicorn.**
5 **Griffin** (griffon, gryphon).
6 **William I** ('The Lion', r. 1165–1214). During the reign of his son Alexander II (r. 1214–49) it appeared within a border of fleurs-de-lis.
7 **The crowned Tudor Rose.** It dates back to the days of Henry VII, who united the red and white roses of Lancashire and Yorkshire by marrying Elizabeth of York, eldest daughter of Edward IV.
8 **Mantling** (or **lambrequin**).
9 **A gold harp** (from the legendary harp of Tara): '*vert*, a harp *or*'.
10 **Open University.** The shield is shown either blue with a yellow circle or yellow with a blue circle.
11 **Rearing.**
12 **Edward the Confessor** (c. 1003–1066), the founder of Westminster Abbey. The arms originated on the silver coins of his reign.
13 **Squirrel.**
14 **Vita (Victoria) Sackville-West** (1892–1962) in *Leopards at Knole* – about Knole Park, Kent.
15 **The eight Beatitudes of Christ.**
16 **Short, curved, notched swords.**
17 **Lucas Cranach the Elder** (1472–1553) and **Lucas Cranach the Younger** (1515–86). Before 1515 Lucas Cranach the Elder used his initials alone or with the coat of arms, but his later work carried the coat of arms alone. The lack of dates on most of the paintings and the similarity of style and subject matter between father and son add to the difficulties of attribution.
18 **Crescent.** It is usually placed centrally or at the top of the shield.
19 **Garter, Clarenceaux, Norroy and Ulster.** They are heraldic and genealogical consultants and members of the Royal Household.
20 **A crowned hawthorn.**

General Knowledge Questions

1 Which heraldic beast is a two-legged winged dragon?
2 In the BBC television series *Only Fools and Horses*, what are the make and model of Del Boy's van?
3 Which English singer-songwriter's debut album, in 1977, was named *My Aim Is True*?
4 Which species of plant, whose name is also an alternative for the silica mineral bloodstone, is named from the way its flower turns to follow the movement of the sun?
5 In which 1992 and 1994 films did Harrison Ford play the CIA agent Jack Ryan in the second and third of a series of spy stories by Tom Clancy?
6 What is the name of the remodelled children's playground in London's Kensington Gardens created in memory of Diana, Princess of Wales?
7 Who played the role of Gary in the 1990s BBC hit TV series *Men Behaving Badly*?
8 The Free Trade Hall in Manchester was built on the site of which 1819 event?
9 Which English composer wrote the church-pageant children's opera *Noyes Fludde* (1958), based on one of the medieval Chester miracle plays?
10 In railway parlance, for what does the acronym SPAD stand?
11 What is the meaning of the nineteenth-century slang term 'to hornswoggle'?
12 Who painted the great triptych altarpiece in Antwerp Cathedral whose centre panel is entitled *The Descent from the Cross* (1611–14)?
13 Which twentieth-century General Election, prompted by Joseph Chamberlain, was known as 'the Khaki Election'?
14 Which ecclesiastical term refers to the system of dedicating children to the church to become monks?
15 Which English mathematician worked on the design of the Automatic Computing Engine (ACE) and in 1950 devised a test (the 'imitation game') for determining whether a computer can be said to 'think'?
16 Which Middle Eastern city was transformed by Sheikh Rashid bin Saeed al Maktoum in the 1960s from a small township into a vibrant commercial centre, with the help of wealth created by the discovery of oil?
17 Which jazz ensemble recorded the world's first jazz record to be released, in 1917?
18 What is the common name of the silver-legged arachnid *Dicranopalpus ramosus*, which was first identified in Britain near Bournemouth in 1957 and has now colonised hedges and trees all over England and Wales?
19 What is the name, deriving from a Czech word meaning 'catapult', of a short-range cannon with a steep angle of fire, related to the mortar?
20 In heraldry, what is the term for a broad, horizontal stripe across the middle of the field of a shield?

1 **Wyvern** (from the Latin *vipera*, viper).
2 **Reliant Regal.**
3 **Elvis Costello** (Declan Patrick McManus, b. 1955).
4 **Heliotrope.**
5 ***Patriot Games*** (1992) and ***Clear and Present Danger*** (1994). The first of the series was *The Hunt for Red October* (filmed in 1990 with Alec Baldwin as Jack Ryan).
6 **Peter Pan Playground.** It was officially opened by Gordon Brown, the Chancellor of the Exchequer, in June 2000. It was so named because the original playground, created in 1906, was funded by J.M. Barrie (1860–1937), the author of *Peter Pan, the Boy Who Wouldn't Grow Up* (1904).
7 **Martin Clunes** (b. 1961).
8 **Peterloo Massacre.** A radical political demonstration on St Peter's Fields, 60,000 strong, demanding Parliamentary reform, was ruthlessly dispersed by cavalry: some five hundred demonstrators were injured and eleven people were killed.
9 **Benjamin Britten** (1913–76). It is intended for adults' and children's voices, chamber ensemble and children's chorus and orchestra, and was first performed in Orford Church as part of the 1958 Aldeburgh Festival.
10 **Signal Passed At Danger.** It was a SPAD which caused the rail crash at Ladbroke Grove, London, in October 1999 which cost thirty-one lives.
11 **To cheat.**
12 **Peter Paul Rubens** (1577–1640). The left-hand panel depicts the *Visitation* and the right shows the *Presentation in the Temple*. When the panels are closed the reverse sides of the wings show *St Christopher Carrying the Infant Jesus*.
13 **1900, after the Boer War.**
14 **Oblation,** from the Latin *oblatus*, one offered up.
15 **Alan Turing** (1912–54). It has come to be known as the Turing Test: a remote human interrogator, within a set time, has to distinguish between a computer and a human subject from the replies they give to various questions. In a series of tests a computer's success at 'thinking' can be quantified by its probability of being misidentified as the human subject.
16 **Dubai.** It is now the chief seaport and largest town in the Emirate of Dubai.
17 **Original Dixieland Jazz Band.** They were not the first band to *play* jazz (Buddy Bolden beat them by twenty-two years); after playing at Resenweber's restaurant in Chicago they were signed up first by Columbia (which was afraid to release *Darktown Strutters Ball* and *Indiana*) and then by Victor, which released *Livery Stable Blues* and *The Dixie Jazz Band One-Step* in 1917.
18 **Harvestman.** It is a relative of the spider (having eight legs), but not a true spider, having no silk glands and an oval body in which the front and back ends form one piece – unlike spiders, in which the front and back end are separated by a pedicel (stalk).
19 **Howitzer.** Big Bertha guns, used by advancing German forces against the Belgian forts at Liège and Namur at the start of the First World War, were 420-millimetre howitzers.
20 **Fess** (from the Latin *fascia*, fillet).

1 What is the salivary secretion produced by worker honeybees with which they feed young larvae in order to produce queen bees?
2 Which red dye is made from the dried, pulverised bodies of some female scale insects of the Coccidae family?
3 In the nursery rhyme, which insect is told to fly away home because 'your house is on fire and your children all gone'?
4 In which 1915 short story by Franz Kafka does the hero, Gregor Samsa, find himself transformed into a human-sized beetle?
5 By what name are the elaborately patterned migratory butterflies of the genus *Vanessa* better known?
6 To which of the three sections of an insect's body are the legs attached?
7 Which insect has the species name *religiosa*, from the name 'diviner' or 'soothsayer', given to it by the ancient Greeks because they believed it had supernatural powers?
8 What name is given to an abnormal growth of plant tissue caused by insects laying their eggs in it and by the activities of the hatching young?
9 To which order of insects does the European glow-worm (*Lampyris noctiluca*) belong?
10 What is the name of the tubular sucking organ of an insect?
11 What is the common name of the huge scarab beetle with black, leathery wings larger than those of a sparrow?
12 Where do ichneumon wasps lay their eggs?
13 Which order of insects are the true flies?
14 How do orchids of the genus *Ophrys* attract pollinating bees and wasps?
15 What name is given to the layer of inert material which covers the body of an insect and is the skeleton to which the muscles are attached?
16 Parasol ants of South America grow what kind of food for their own consumption?
17 What substance is produced in the cells of 'cold hardy' insects (those which survive in very cold conditions) which helps to stop their cell contents from freezing?
18 What is the source of the biblical food manna, which sustained the Israelites in the Sinai desert on their journey to the Promised Land?
19 What is the name for the openings on the abdomen and thorax of an insect through which oxygen passes in and carbon dioxide passes out?
20 Which nineteenth-century French entomologist wrote the ten-volume *Souvenirs entomologiques* (1879–1907) and earned himself the title of 'the Insect Man'?

1 **Royal jelly**. The single queen in the hive secretes a pheromone known as 'queen substance', which the workers circulate among the colony by food sharing, to inform the colony of the presence of a queen.
2 **Cochineal**. It originally came from Mexico, where it had been used long before the coming of the Spaniards. It has been largely superseded by synthetic dyes, but is still used as a colouring agent in cosmetics and beverages.
3 **Ladybird**.
4 ***Metamorphosis***.
5 **Painted lady**.
6 **Thorax**. The other sections are the head and the abdomen.
7 **Praying mantis** (*Mantis religiosa*).
8 **Gall**. The young usually live and feed inside the gall and develop fully before emerging.
9 **Beetles** (Coleoptera). The luminescence is caused by substances known as luciferins (organic compounds which oxidise in the presence of an enzyme known as a luciferase).
10 **Proboscis**.
11 **Goliath beetle** (*Goliathus giganteus*). It can be more than 10 centimetres long, and is the largest known beetle.
12 **In the larvae or pupae of other insects**, especially moths and butterflies. The ichneumon larva feeds on the fats and body fluids of the host until fully grown, and then usually spins a silken cocoon.
13 ***Diptera*** ('two-winged').
14 **By imitation**. The structure of parts of the flower resembles a female insect so closely that males try to copulate with it.
15 **Cuticle**. It is made up mainly of a carbohydrate called chitin and a hard protein called sclerotin. The surface of the cuticle is covered with a waterproofing wax which prevents loss of water through evaporation.
16 **Fungi**. Above their heads they carry leaves (hence the name 'parasol ants'), which they store in huge underground chambers; the fungi grow on the leaves.
17 **Glycerol**. It was formerly used in antifreeze; methanol and ethylene glycol are now used instead.
18 **The excreta of insects**. Certain insects of the coccid family deposit their dry, scaly excreta mainly on tamarisk and larch trees.
19 **Spiracles**. The spiracles have muscular valves which are closed most of the time and open only to allow gases to pass in and out.
20 **Jean Henri Fabre** (1823–1915).

General Knowledge Questions

1 Which insect is associated with sericulture?
2 In children's literature, who lived in the Outer Circle of Regent's Park?
3 Which British comedian starred in the 1960 film satirising Bohemian art, *The Rebel*?
4 Which Scottish golf course features a road called 'Granny Clark's Wynd', which runs across the fairways of the first and eighteenth holes?
5 By what name is the eleventh-century Spanish warrior hero Rodrigo Díaz de Vivar better known?
6 In the Bible, which archangel is the leader of the army of angels which fights the 'great dragon', Satan?
7 Which Russian composer turned Tolstoy's novel *War and Peace* into an epic opera in 1942–3?
8 At which naval battle in 1571 did allied Christian forces defeat the Ottoman Turks to acquire the Venetian island of Cyprus, only to see Venice surrender it to the Turks in 1573?
9 A deficiency of which vitamin causes the failure of blood to clot?
10 Where was the body of Oliver Cromwell finally buried?
11 Which guitar-playing Tory politician's 'signature tune' is *Streets of London*, which was a huge hit for left-wing folk icon Ralph McTell in 1974?
12 A film of the life of which surrealist artist, starring Ewen Bremner, was produced for the opening night of BBC4, the new arts and culture digital channel, in March 2002?
13 What was the original meaning of the word 'lackey'?
14 What is the name of the 'virtual' TV presenter who joined the BBC's *Tomorrow's World* team in March 2002 and, it is claimed, can converse in twenty languages?
15 Which entirely mythical saint, whose feast day is 12 February, is regarded as the patron saint of innkeepers, boatmen and travellers at river crossings?
16 Which Croatian-born US physicist and electrical engineer discovered, in 1881, the principle of the rotating magnetic field, the basis of all AC (alternating current) machinery?
17 Which English choreographer created, for the American Ballet Theatre, the ballet *Pillar of Fire* (1942) to music by Arnold Schoenberg?
18 What is the name of the small container fixed to doorposts of Jewish homes and which contains the most important prayer of Judaism – the Shema?
19 What was the name of the world's first jet-powered flying boat, built in Britain, which first flew in July 1947 but never entered service because of the high drag of its fuselage?
20 Where on its body are the hearing organs of a cricket?

1 **Silkworm** (*Bombyx mori*).
2 **Mr and Mrs Dearly, Pongo and Missus** in *The One Hundred and One Dalmatians* (1956) by Dodie Smith (1896–1990).
3 **Tony Hancock** (1924–68).
4 **The Old Course at St Andrews.** The course is open to the public and the road, which was once used for pushing the lifeboat from the lifeboat shed to the coast, was given a tarmac surface in 1923.
5 **El Cid** (c. 1043–99); his name is also spelt de Bivar.
6 **Michael.**
7 **Sergei Prokofiev** (1891–1953).
8 **Battle of Lepanto.**
9 **Vitamin K.**
10 **Newburgh Priory**, near Coxwold, North Yorkshire. He was originally buried in Westminster Abbey, but at the Restoration his body was dug up, tried and hanged before being finally laid to rest. His head was buried in the antechamber of the chapel of Sidney Sussex College, Cambridge.
11 **Michael Ancram** (b. 1945), MP for Devizes and former chairman of the Conservative Party (1998–2001).
12 **Salvador Dalí** (1904–89).
13 **A liveried male servant** (in the sixteenth century, from the French *laquais*).
14 **Maddy**. She is a 'cyberbabe' (described as an 'avatar') created by the Glasgow company Digital Animations Group. She has an artificial chat engine program which enables her to learn about science and respond to questions; she is driven by a real-time animation program which gives her human mannerisms and movements.
15 **St Julian the Hospitaller**. According to legend, a stag he was hunting predicted he would kill his own parents. Julian moved far away to prevent this, but his parents tracked him down and made a surprise visit to his home while he was away. His wife gave them her and Julian's bed; when Julian returned he killed them, thinking they were his wife and another man. In penance, he built a hospice beside a river, cared for the poor and sick, and rowed travellers across the river free of charge.
16 **Nikola Tesla** (1856–1943). He invented the Tesla coil (1891) and designed the AC lighting for the World's Columbian Exposition in Chicago in 1893.
17 **Anthony Tudor** (1908–87).
18 **Mezuzah.** If the mezuzah has a window the parchment on which the Shema (Deuteronomy 6:4–9, 11:13–21) is written is folded so that the first letter of Shaddai (Almighty) (ש – *shin*) shows. Otherwise the letter is inscribed on the outside of the mezuzah.
19 **Saunders Roe SR A1**. A US jet-powered flying boat (the P6M *Seamaster*) first flew in 1955 but was dropped after two prototypes crashed. The only jet-powered flying boat to enter service was the Russian Beriev Be–12, which first flew in August 1961 and is still in service.
20 **On its forelegs.**

1 Which editor of the *New Statesman* presented BBC TV's *Face to Face* interviews from 1958 to 1960?
2 In which daily newspaper did two fictional old men ('the Old Codgers') answer readers' letters from 1936 to 1990?
3 Which magazine, founded by Gordon Roddick of the Body Shop and A. John Bird, was launched in 1991 to be sold by homeless vendors?
4 Which Scottish poet gave the following warning?
A chiel's amang you taking notes,
And, faith, he'll print it.
5 By what name is Tony Blair known in *Private Eye*?
6 In which Shakespeare play are the words 'What news on the Rialto?' spoken?
7 What is the name of the editor of the *Matlock Mercury* in Derbyshire whose campaigning led in 2002 to the quashing of the conviction of Stephen Downing for the murder of Wendy Sewell in 1973?
8 Which renowned English editor wrote in a leading article, 'Comment is free but facts are sacred'?
9 Which eighteenth-century parliamentarian is said to have been the first to call the Press 'the Fourth Estate'?
10 Which US statesman said, 'An editor is one who separates the wheat from the chaff and prints the chaff'?
11 What is the title of the 2001 book featuring contributions from journalists and subtitled *Understanding September 11th*?
12 What was the name of the official government daily newspaper, edited by Winston Churchill, published during the 1926 General Strike?
13 Which British writer and journalist claimed to have won a competition at *The Times* for the dullest headline with 'Small earthquake in Chile. Not many dead'?
14 Which English poet wrote the following lines?
You cannot hope to bribe or twist,
thank God! the British journalist.
But, seeing what the man will do
unbribed, there's no occasion to.
15 From which writer did Stanley Baldwin borrow his celebrated denunciation of popular press barons, that their aim was 'power without responsibility – the prerogative of the harlot throughout the ages'?
16 Which Ancient Egyptian moon deity was the scribe of the gods, and patron of all scribes?
17 In which London journal did the 'Letters of Junius', savagely criticising George III's ministers and the king himself, appear from November 1768 to January 1772?
18 *Sing Tao* and *Wen Wei Po* are Chinese daily newspapers available in major cities in the UK; where are they printed and published?
19 Which nineteenth-century Liberal MP and exponent of the Victorian 'New Journalism' founded several successful periodicals, including *Tit-Bits* (1881), the *Strand Magazine* (1891), the *Westminster Gazette* (1873) and *Country Life* (1897)?
20 What was the name of the first British daily newspaper, which was published from 11 March 1702 until 1735?

Journalism

Answers

1 **John Freeman** (b. 1915). His penetrating interviews were unprecedented at the time; on one occasion he caused Gilbert Harding to break down and weep. Freeman was a politician who became British ambassador in Washington (1969–71).

2 ***Daily Mirror.***

3 ***The Big Issue.*** Gordon Roddick was inspired to create the magazine on a visit to the USA when he saw *Street News*, a newspaper sold by homeless people in New York.

4 **Robert Burns** (1759–96), in *Hear, Land o' Cakes, and brither Scots.*

5 **The Vicar of St Albions.**

6 ***The Merchant of Venice*** (Act I, scene iii, spoken by Shylock).

7 **Don Hale** (b. 1952). Hale was editor of the *Matlock Mercury* from 1985 to 2001. He was voted *What the Papers Say* Journalist of the Year for 2001 and won thirteen other awards. His book about the case, *The Scapegoat*, was published in 2002.

8 **C.P. Scott** (1846–1932), in an editorial in the *Manchester Guardian* (6 May 1927).

9 **Edmund Burke** (1729–97). According to William Hazlitt's *Table Talk* (1821), he looked at the Reporters' Gallery in the House of Commons and said, 'Yonder sits the fourth estate, more important than them all'.

10 **Adlai Stevenson** (1900–65). He twice stood unsuccessfully for the Presidency as the Democratic candidate (1952 and 1956).

11 ***The Day that Shook the World***, edited by Jenny Baxter and Malcolm Downing, published by BBC News.

12 ***British Gazette.*** It was printed on the commandeered presses of the *Morning Post*, for which Churchill had reported on the Boer War.

13 **Claud Cockburn** (1904–81), in *In Time of Trouble* (1956).

14 **Humbert Wolfe** (1886–1940), in *The Uncelestial City*, Book I, ii, *Over the Fire* (1930).

15 **Rudyard Kipling** (1865–1936). Kipling said it to Max Aitken (Lord Beaverbrook), according to the *Kipling Journal* (1940). Baldwin used it (without attribution) at a by-election meeting in 1931; upon which the Duke of Devonshire is alleged to have commented, 'Good God, that's done it. He's lost us the tarts' vote!'

16 **Thoth.**

17 ***Public Advertiser.*** The identity of the author has never been established, although scholars now think it was probably Sir Philip Francis (1740–1818).

18 ***Sing Tao*** in London; ***Wen Wei Po*** is now printed in Hong Kong and flown to the UK for distribution the following day.

19 **George Newnes** (1851–1910). He was Liberal MP for Newmarket (1885–1895).

20 ***Daily Courant.*** It was printed on one side of the page only, and cost a penny. There were two columns with 104 lines in ten paragraphs, presenting extracts from three European newspapers, with reports from Rome, Vienna, Liège, Paris and Naples (there was no British news). The first provincial newspaper is thought to have been the *Norwich Post* (first published on 6 September 1701).

1 The newspaper of which organisation, first published in 1879, is *The War Cry*?
2 Who played the role of Inspector Barlow in the BBC1 police series *Z-Cars*, which went out live, fifty minutes a week, from 1962 to 1978?
3 Which pop band, which was named Best Band in Britain at the 2002 Brit Awards, had a hit in 1999 with *Why Does It Always Rain on Me*?
4 Which film director made the 1994 film *Pulp Fiction*, an episodic black comedy about philosophical hit men, junkies, boxers and gangsters?
5 By what name is the world's largest herb, *Musa sapientum*, better known?
6 Which blonde model was hanged in Britain in 1955 for the murder of her lover, David Blakely?
7 Which nuts are used in making the sauce pesto?
8 Which climbing garden plant is known as Traveller's Joy and Old Man's Beard?
9 Which Scottish-born dancer and choreographer became principal choreographer of the Royal Ballet in 1977?
10 The meaning of the name of which type of religious building is 'place of prostration'?
11 Which seventeenth-century adventuress and author wrote fifteen racy and popular Restoration plays, including *The Forced Marriage* (1670) and *The Rover* (in two parts, 1677–81)?
12 What was the original form and meaning of the word 'umpire'?
13 Which US artist and pioneer of kinetic art is credited with the invention of the 'mobile' in the 1930s?
14 Which contemporary British novelist appeared as a youngster as one of the children kidnapped by pirates in the film *A High Wind in Jamaica* (1965), based on the 1929 novel by Richard Hughes?
15 Which nineteenth-century Irish artist painted the frescos in the House of Lords entitled *The Death of Nelson* and *The Meeting of Wellington and Blücher*?
16 Which English alchemist, geographer and mathematician was astrologer to Mary Tudor, and was imprisoned but acquitted on charges of plotting her death by magic?
17 On which version of the Bible was J.R.R. Tolkien one of the major collaborators and translators, working mainly on the book of Job?
18 What are the only three ferromagnetic elements (those which can be permanently magnetised)?
19 In the Second World War, from which seventeenth-century manor house in the northern mainland of Shetland did the Norwegian Resistance movement run the 'Shetland Bus' to ferry agents on fishing boats to and from Norway?
20 Which veteran journalist and presenter of Radio 4's *Today* programme published her memoirs *Woman of Today* when she retired in February 2002?

General Knowledge

1 **Salvation Army**, founded in 1865 by William Booth (1829–1912).
2 **(Alan) Stratford Johns** (1925–2002). He went on to play Detective Chief Superintendent Barlow in *Softly Softly*.
3 **Travis** (Andy Dunlop, Francis Healey, Douglas Payne and Neil Primrose).
4 **Quentin Tarantino** (b. 1963).
5 **Banana.** It is not a tree, but a gigantic herb springing from an underground stem, or rhizome, and forming a false trunk 3–6 metres high.
6 **Ruth Ellis** (1927–55). She was the last woman to be executed in Britain, after killing David Blakely outside a pub in Hampstead, north London.
7 **Pine nuts.** Pesto (from the Italian *pestato*, crushed) is a sauce for pasta made from pounded pine nuts, basil leaves, garlic and Parmesan cheese, bound with olive oil.
8 **Clematis** (*Clematis virginiana* – Traveller's Joy; *Clematis vitalba* – Old Man's Beard).
9 **Kenneth Macmillan** (1929–92). His works included *Romeo and Juliet* (1965), *The Seven Deadly Sins* (1973), *Isadora* (1981) and *The Judas Tree* (1992).
10 **Mosque** (from the Arabic *masjid*).
11 **Aphra Behn** (1640–89). She has been called 'England's first professional woman author'.
12 **Numpire**, from the French *non per*, 'not equal'). The word, meaning a third person called in to arbitrate between two others, arose from a mistaken division between the words 'a numpire', as in 'a nadder' (adder) and 'an ewt' (newt).
13 **Alexander Calder** (1898–1976). The term 'mobile' was coined for Calder's works by Marcel Duchamp after he saw them in a Paris exhibition in 1932.
14 **Martin Amis** (b. 1949), playing John Thornton.
15 **Daniel Maclise** (1806–70).
16 **John Dee** (1527–1608). He sought 'the treasure of heavenly wisdom and knowledge', made significant contributions to navigational and geographical knowledge, and was the model for Prospero in Shakespeare's *The Tempest*.
17 **Jerusalem Bible** (1966).
18 **Iron, nickel** and **cobalt.**
19 **Lunna House.**
20 **Sue MacGregor** (b. 1941). After presenting *Woman's Hour*, she was a presenter on *Today* from 1984.

Knaves

Questions

1 What was the name of the investment officer of Barings Bank, working in its Singapore office, who was given a jail sentence of six and a half years in Singapore in 1995 for forgery and cheating?
2 Under what nickname did the murderer Albert DeSalvo become infamous?
3 Who is Superman's arch-enemy, who uses kryptonite (the radioactive remains of Krypton, Superman's home planet) to weaken him?
4 What is the name of the family doctor in Hyde, Greater Manchester, who was sentenced to life imprisonment in January 2000 for the murder of fifteen of his women patients?
5 Which apparently respectable Edinburgh businessman and councillor, said to have been the model for Robert Louis Stevenson's *Dr Jekyll and Mr Hyde*, was hanged for robbery in 1788?
6 What do the French call the knave, or jack, in a pack of cards?
7 What was the name of the US figure skater who was involved in a plot leading to an assault in which her teammate Nancy Kerrigan was clubbed on the knee seven weeks before the 1994 Winter Olympics in Norway?
8 Which 1971 film was based on Ted Lewis's novel *Jack's Return Home*, inspired by the so-called 'One-Armed Bandit Murder' of money collector Angus Sibbett in 1967 in South Hetton, County Durham?
9 What was the name of the 'Oklahoma City Bomber' of April 1995, who was executed in 2001?
10 Who were the two ringleaders of the abortive raid to snatch £200 million worth of diamonds from the Millennium Dome in November 2000?
11 Which US murderer was the focus of Norman Mailer's Pulitzer Prize-winning study *The Executioner's Song* (1979)?
12 Which English journalist, financier and MP was jailed for fraudulent conversion in 1922?
13 Who painted the seventeenth-century picture *Cheat with the Ace of Clubs*, which shows a table of card players, one of whom is hiding the ace of clubs behind his back?
14 What was the nickname earned by the contagious Mary Mallon in the USA?
15 What nickname was given to the French multi-murderer Henri-Désiré Landru, who was guillotined in 1922, having been convicted, on circumstantial evidence, of murdering ten women and a boy, although their bodies were never found?
16 By what name was the flamboyant Essex highwayman John Rann, who was hanged at Tyburn on 30 November 1774, better known?
17 What is the name of the Libyan terrorist who, in March 2002, was sentenced to life imprisonment in Scotland for blowing up Pan Am flight 103 in the skies above Lockerbie in December 1988?
18 Where did the Australian itinerant fruit picker Robert Paul Long kill fifteen people when he set fire, in June 2000, to a 100-year-old timber hostel?
19 Who massacred the King and Queen of Nepal and seven other royals with a machine-gun in the Narayanhiti Palace in Kathmandu on 2 June 2001?
20 Which seventeenth-century Polish multi-murderer, a niece of Stephen Bathori, king of Poland, was known as the 'Blood Countess' because she murdered 650 young girls so that she could keep her youth by bathing in their warm blood?

1 **Nick Leeson**. He was accused of losing $1.3 billion in a risky investment. The result was the financial collapse of the bank, which was bought for £1 by the Dutch banking and insurance group ING. His book *Rogue Trader* (1997) was filmed in 1998 starring Ewan McGregor as Nick Leeson.
2 **The Boston Strangler** (1931–73). He strangled thirteen women in Boston, Massachusetts, in the early 1960s. He was jailed for life, but was stabbed to death by a fellow prisoner in Walpole Prison, Massachusetts.
3 **Lex Luthor**. He had a ring with a gemstone made from a piece of kryptonite, to use against Superman, but eventually the radiation affected him too, leading to the loss of his hand and terminal illness.
4 **Harold Shipman** (b. 1946).
5 **William Brodie** (Deacon Brodie, 1741–88). He started leading a double life as a burglar in 1787. After an abortive raid on the Excise Office he fled to Amsterdam, where he was arrested on the eve of his departure for America.
6 **Valet**.
7 **Tonya Harding**. At the Olympics, Nancy Kerrigan won a silver medal. Tonya Harding was placed tenth.
8 ***Get Carter***. Michael Luvaglio and Dennis Stafford were convicted for the murder, given life sentences and served twelve years before being released on licence.
9 **Timothy McVeigh**. He left the bomb in a truck outside the Alfred P. Murrah government building in Oklahoma City.
10 **Raymond Betson** and **William Cockram**.
11 **Gary Gilmore**. He murdered two men in robberies on consecutive evenings in 1976 while on parole from a twelve-year sentence for armed robbery. In 1977 he became the first man to be executed in the USA after the death penalty was reinstated in 1976.
12 **Horatio Bottomley** (1860–1933). He founded the weekly *John Bull* in 1906 and became MP for South Hackney (1906–12), but went bankrupt. During the First World War he raised subscriptions worth nearly £900,000 for financial enterprises. He became an MP again (1918–22), until his financial misdemeanours caught up with him.
13 **Georges de La Tour** (1593–1652). The painting is now in the Kimbell Art Museum, Fort Worth.
14 **Typhoid Mary** (c. 1870–1938). She was the first carrier of typhoid to be identified in the USA, although she was immune to it.
15 **The Modern Bluebeard** (1869–1922). Claude Chabrol directed a 1962 film about him called *Landru* (*Bluebeard* in the English version).
16 **Sixteen-String Jack** (from the sixteen coloured ribbons which fluttered from the knees of his breeches). He wore top boots, ruffled shirts, natty crimson waistcoats and a hat covered with buttons and bound with silver strings.
17 **Abdel Baset al-Megrahi**. He was found guilty by a special Scottish court built for the purpose at Camp Zeist, near Utrecht, in the Netherlands.
18 **The Palace Backpackers Hostel**, in Childers, Queensland.
19 **Crown Prince Dipendra**. He killed them after his parents refused to allow him to marry Devyani Rana (because her great-grandmother had been a court mistress).
20 **Elizabeth Bathori-Nádasdy**. Her crimes were discovered in 1610 and she was imprisoned in her fortress of Csej until her death in 1614.

General Knowledge Questions

1 In the nursery rhyme, who stole the queen's tarts and was beaten 'full sore' by the king?

2 Which singer had a hit in 1971 with *Sweet Caroline*, which stayed in the UK charts for eleven weeks?

3 Which British director made the 1968 film *If . . .*, starring Malcolm McDowell as Mick Travis, the nonchalantly savage ringleader of a rebellion in a public school?

4 What is the name of the Tudor warship, built between 1509 and 1511, which was swamped and sank in the Solent in 1545 but was raised from the seabed in 1982 and is now on display in the Historic Dockyard at Portsmouth?

5 A 'comedo' is a skin blemish more familiarly known as what?

6 Which actor starred as Ralph Ernest Gorse in the TV mini series *The Charmer*, for which he won the TV Times Actor of the Year award in 1987?

7 Which nineteenth-century tsar of Russia, known as 'the Liberator', emancipated the serfs in 1861?

8 Which island on the south-east of the Thames Estuary is separated from the mainland by a channel called the Swale?

9 In early monasteries, what was the 'calefactory'?

10 Who was the only bachelor President of the USA?

11 What is the brand name of the coffee produced by Fair Trade?

12 The scheming Dorothy Hardcastle, second wife of Squire Richard Hardcastle, and her son Tony Lumpkin, are central characters in which 1773 play?

13 Which historic burgh was designated as the sixth Scottish city in March 2002?

14 Which Japanese species of tree, the sole survivor of the nuclear attack on Nagasaki, has become a symbol of world peace, with seedlings being planted by children all over the world?

15 What is the stage name of Geoffrey Durham, the magician husband of comedienne Victoria Wood?

16 What name was given to the trial in 1925, in the Rhea County Courthouse in Dayton, Tennessee, of John T. Scopes, a biology teacher, who was found guilty of teaching evolution?

17 What title is given to the minister who presides over the annual General Assembly of the Church of Scotland?

18 The literal meaning of the French word *bergère* is 'shepherdess' – but what does it mean in the name 'Folies Bergère'?

19 What is the title of the 2002 book by Stephanie Theobald, described in the *Good Book Guide* as 'an emotional and gastronomic roller-coaster', in which the streetwise Cornish schoolgirl Rosa Barge strikes up a friendship with the well-to-do Jack Flowers?

20 Which Shakespearian character fraudulently claimed to have been set upon and robbed by several rogues in buckram suits, reinforced by 'three misbegotten knaves in Kendal Green'?

General Knowledge Answers

1 **The Knave of Hearts.** 'He brought back the tarts/And vowed he'd steal no more.'
2 **Neil Diamond** (b. 1943).
3 **Lindsay Anderson** (1923–94).
4 ***Mary Rose.***
5 **Blackhead.** It is a black-tipped plug of debris and fatty matter clogging a pore of the skin.
6 **Nigel Havers** (b. 1949). He has appeared in several films, including *Chariots of Fire* (1981), *A Passage to India* (1985) and *Empire of the Sun* (1987).
7 **Alexander II** (1818–81). After unsuccessful attempts to shoot him, derail his train and even blow him up in the Winter Palace in St Petersburg, he was eventually killed by bombs thrown by the revolutionary group 'The People's Will'.
8 **Isle of Sheppey.** The Kingsferry Bridge links the island to the mainland. The eastern end of the Swale joins the Thames Estuary at Harty Ferry to the west of Whitstable and its western end flows into the River Medway at Sheerness.
9 **Common Room** (literally, warming room).
10 **James Buchanan** (1791–1868), the fifteenth President (1857–61)
11 **Cafédirect.** Fair Trade is an association of fair-trade wholesalers, retailers and producers whose members are committed to providing fair wages and good employment opportunities to economically disadvantaged artisans and farmers.
12 ***She Stoops to Conquer***, by Oliver Goldsmith.
13 **Stirling.**
14 **Kaki** (Oriental persimmon, *Diospyros kaki*).
15 **The Great Soprendo.**
16 **Monkey Trial.**
17 **Moderator.**
18 **A sofa or armchair** (first made in the 1720s).
19 ***Sucking Shrimp.***
20 **Falstaff**, in *Henry IV Part 1* (Act II, scene iv).

1 In classical legend, which sculptor and king of Cyprus fell in love with the ivory statue he made of the ideal woman, who was then given life by the goddess Aphrodite?
2 In Germanic legend, what was the name of the dwarf who spun straw into gold for a miller's daughter, on condition that she give him her first child, unless she could guess his name?
3 In English folklore, which tree is credited with magical protective powers against witchcraft?
4 The colossal wooden effigies of which two legendary gatekeepers stand in London's Guildhall and are carried in the annual Lord Mayor's procession?
5 Which fairytale was included in Charles Perrault's seventeenth-century collection of stories and inspired a ballet by Tchaikovsky which was first performed in St Petersburg in 1890?
6 According to legend, which plant, attributed with quasi-human properties, could be safely uprooted only on a moonlit night with a cord pulled by a black dog, which would later die?
7 In late-medieval and Tudor times what was the name of the mischievous shape-changer who played tricks on people and whose 'Mad Prankes and Merry Jests' were described in a 1628 pamphlet?
8 In Greek legend, who was the mother of Castor and Pollux, the twins who were finally placed as Gemini, a constellation in the zodiac?
9 In the legendary Germanic *Nibelungenlied* (which Wagner used as the basis for part of *The Ring of the Nibelungs*), which hero married Kriemhild?
10 A museum dedicated to which fabled local resident is to be found at Drumnadrochit in Scotland?
11 Which warrior in Greek legend was the son of Peleus (king of the Myrmidons) and the sea nymph Thetis?
12 Which fabled lost land between Land's End and the Scilly Isles features in the Arthurian legend cycle as the place where King Arthur was born and died?
13 In classical legend, which beast with a goat's fire-breathing head, the forequarters of a lion and the hindquarters of a dragon was slain by the Corinthian hero Bellerophon?
14 According to Hindu legend, which god was raised by the leader of the cowherds, Nanda, and his wife, Yashoda?
15 Which of Jason's Argonauts was so keen-sighted that he could see right through the earth, and distinguish objects from many miles away?
16 Which opera by Wagner, named after a ghost ship whose appearance to sailors is believed to be a portent of disaster, is based on the legend of a sea captain named Vanderdecken who gambled his salvation on a rash pledge to sail around the Cape of Good Hope in a storm and so was condemned to sail that course for eternity?
17 In Greek legend, what was the name of the race of man-eating giants in Sicily who attacked Odysseus and his men in Homer's *Odyssey* (Book 10)?
18 Which Sumerian hero, two-thirds god and one-third man, is the subject of an ancient Babylonian epic cycle of legends?
19 In Indian legend, the world rests on the head of which animal?
20 Which *fée* of French romance was condemned to change into a serpent from the waist down every Saturday, and disappeared from mortal sight when her husband broke his vow never to visit her on that day?

1 **Pygmalion.** The flesh-and-blood statue, whom he married, was named Galatea. The musical *My Fair Lady* was based on George Bernard Shaw's 1913 play on the theme.

2 **Rumpelstiltskin.** There are several versions of the legend, the best known of which was retold by the brothers Grimm in *Children's and Household Tales* (1812).

3 **Rowan** (mountain ash).

4 **Gog and Magog.** They were the sole survivors of the monstrous brood of the thirty-three infamous daughters of the Emperor Diocletian. Captured by King Brut, the legendary first king of Britain, they were taken to his capital, Troia Nova (London), and made to serve as palace gatekeepers. The figures have been replaced several times, the first ones having been destroyed in the Great Fire of 1666. The present figures were carved by David Evans in 1953 as a gift to the City by Alderman Sir George Wilkinson (Lord Mayor in 1940, when the previous ones were destroyed).

5 ***The Sleeping Beauty.***

6 **Mandrake.** The shriek of the mandrake as it was pulled was thought to kill or drive mad anyone who heard it.

7 **Robin Goodfellow.** The name became a generic term for mischievous fairies.

8 **Leda.** She was seduced by Zeus in the guise of a swan while she was bathing, and in due course she brought forth two eggs.

9 **Siegfried.**

10 **Loch Ness Monster.**

11 **Achilles.**

12 **Lyonesse.**

13 **Chimaera.** The beast had been laying waste to the country when Bellerophon killed it from the winged horse Pegasus.

14 **Krishna.** He had been smuggled across the River Yamuna as a baby to save him from the wicked king Kamsa.

15 **Lynceus.**

16 ***The Flying Dutchman*** (*Der Fliegende Holländer*, 1843). Wagner moved the setting to the seas off Norway. In another version of the legend the captain, named Falkenberg, sailed for eternity in the North Sea, playing at dice with the devil for his soul. This is echoed in Samuel Taylor Coleridge's *Rime of the Ancient Mariner* (1798), where the mariner sees a ghost ship on which Death and Life in Death play at dice to win him.

17 **Lestrigons.**

18 **Gilgamesh,** King of Erech. Portions of the epic were found inscribed on clay tablets in the library of Assurbanipal, King of Assyria (668–26 BC), in Nineveh.

19 **Muha-Pudma,** a giant elephant which, in some versions of the legend, stands on the back of a tortoise called Chukwa. When the beast becomes stiff from prolonged inactivity, it moves its head and thus causes an earthquake.

20 **Mélisande** (Melusina). The story goes that Mélisande was punished for immuring her father in a mountain for offending her mother. Her husband (Raymond, Comte de Lusignan) secretly spied on her during one of the forbidden days, and she was destined to wander about as a spectre until doomsday.

1 In Arthurian legend, who was the father of King Arthur?
2 Who is the principal patron of the Liverpool Institute of Performing Arts?
3 Which Polish concert pianist and composer became Prime Minister of his country in 1919 and President of Poland's provisional parliament in Paris in 1940?
4 Who, in the words of the song, was the Grand Old Duke of York, who 'marched his men to the top of the hill, and marched them down again'?
5 What is the yellow-flowering herb, of the mustard family (Brassicaceae), *Isatis tinctoria*, which was once grown as a source of the blue dye indigo?
6 What is the term for the 'dimples' on voting papers which played a controversial part in the election of President George W. Bush in 2001?
7 Who built Glyndebourne Opera House in the grounds of his country estate near Lewes, East Sussex, and opened it to the public in 1934?
8 Which member of a Hollywood dynasty plays the part of Etheline, the mother of a charismatic but dysfunctional family, in the 2002 film *The Royal Tenenbaums*?
9 In mobile telephony, for what do the letters 'SMS' stand?
10 Who wrote the poem which begins with the following words?

I'm the dolly on the dustcart,
I can see you're not impressed,
I'm fixed above the driver's cab,
With wire across me chest.

11 Which everyday commodity is produced from the bark of the tree *Quercus suber*?
12 In December 2001 which Americas Cup-winning yachtsman was murdered by armed bandits on his yacht *Seamaster* near Macapa on the Amazon?
13 What name, derived from that of a tower in Corsica, is given to the small, circular brick forts built to defend England's south coast against invasion in the Napoleonic Wars?
14 Which subtropical woodland gardens on the west coast of Scotland were reopened in 2002 after a successful £1.5 million appeal by the National Trust for Scotland?
15 Which founder member of the Royal Academy of Arts painted, in 1771–2, the celebrated picture of its selection committee entitled *The Academicians of the Royal Academy*?
16 Which eighteenth-century English physician and botanist introduced the idea of using digitalis, extracted from the leaves of the common foxglove, as a drug for the treatment of congestive heart failure?
17 Who wrote the epistolary novel *Evelina*, published anonymously in 1778, in which the beautiful eponymous heroine, after a fraught introduction to London society, is ultimately recognised as an heiress?
18 What is the more common term for the phenomenon of bioluminescence?
19 Who, in fifteenth-century chivalric literature, was the original 'White Knight'?
20 Which German composer wrote an opera (1893) about Hänsel and Gretel, the children in the brothers Grimm's fairytale?

1 **Uther Pendragon.** Uther was King of England, but had no heir. He coveted Igraine, the wife of the Duke of Cornwall, who hid her away in a castle at Tintagel. Merlin the magician transformed Uther into the resemblance of the Duke of Cornwall, so that he could enjoy a night of passion with Igraine; Arthur was the result.

2 **Paul McCartney.** LIPA is housed in the building of his old school, the Liverpool Institute.

3 **Ignacy Jan Paderewski** (1860–1941).

4 **Frederick Augustus, Duke of York and Albany** (1763–1827), second son of George III and Queen Charlotte. He has been described as 'brave but incapable' and the popular rhyme is said to have referred to his ineffective marching and counter-marching.

5 **Woad.**

6 **Chads.** It is a term used for the pre-punched holes on 'Vote-O-Matic' cards. Each square chad is held in place by a small wad of paper fibres at each corner. The voter makes a hole by pushing the chad out with a round stylus.

7 **John Christie** (1882–1962). His wife was the soprano Audrey Mildmay.

8 **Anjelica Huston**, daughter of John Huston, who directed her in her cinematic debut in a small role at the age of eighteen in the 1969 film *Sinful Davey*; this was followed by a starring role (also in 1969) in the medieval romance *A Walk with Love and Death* and, in 1985, her Academy Award-winning performance in *Prizzi's Honor*.

9 **Short Message Service.**

10 **Pam Ayres** (*The Dolly on the Dustcart*).

11 **Cork.**

12 **Peter Blake.** He won several trophies, including the Americas Cup (twice) with Team New Zealand.

13 **Martello Towers.** In February 1794 the original tower (now demolished), at Cape Mortella, frustrated a British squadron commanded by David Dundas. The British were so impressed that between 1805 and 1812 they built seventy-four similar towers, twenty-four of which still stand, along the south coast from Folkestone to Seaford.

14 **Crarae Gardens**, near Inverary on Loch Fyne. They were created by Sir George Campbell of Succoth, who turned Crarae Glen into a magnificent evocation of a Himalayan gorge.

15 **Johann Zoffany** (1733–1810). The Royal Academy of Arts was founded in 1768 and Zoffany's painting of the academicians is now in the Royal Collection.

16 **William Withering** (1741–99). He was chief physician of Birmingham General Hospital. In 1785 he published *An Account of the Foxglove and Some of Its Medical Uses*.

17 **Fanny Burney** (1752–1840). It was her first and most successful novel.

18 **Foxfire** (from French *faux feu*, false fire). It is the faint luminescent glow emitted by certain fungi on rotting wood.

19 **Tirant lo Blanc.** He was the eponymous hero of a Catalan romance of c. 1460 by Joanot Martorell.

20 **Engelbert Humperdinck** (1854–1921).

Monuments

1 What was the name of the beloved wife of Shah Jehan in whose memory he built the Taj Mahal beside the River Jamuna in Agra?
2 In 1986 which natural 'monument' was declared the first World Heritage Site in Northern Ireland?
3 Whose inscription in St Paul's Cathedral reads '*Lector, si monumentum requiris, circumspice*'?
4 On which Hebridean island are the Standing Stones of Calanais?
5 Which nineteenth-century artist designed the four bronze lions, unveiled in 1867, at the foot of Nelson's Column in London's Trafalgar Square?
6 What is the modern name of the great Roman fortress of Isca which was built during the course of the conquest of the Silures in mid-Wales?
7 To which Greek goddess was the Parthenon on the Acropolis of Athens dedicated?
8 To which religious leader are 'stupas' (also known as 'chortens') dedicated?
9 Which eighteenth-century event is commemorated by the Glenfinnan Monument at the head of Loch Shiel on the west coast of Scotland?
10 There are two obelisks known as 'Cleopatra's Needle'; one is on the Thames Embankment in London – where in the USA is the other?
11 Which Roman emperor commissioned the building of the Colosseum in Rome?
12 Where is the so-called 'Rufus Stone' to be found?
13 Who was the designer of the Cenotaph in London's Whitehall, completed in 1920 and inscribed with the words 'To the Glorious Dead'?
14 What is the popular name given to the prehistoric circle of standing stones near Little Salkeld in the Vale of Eden, Cumbria?
15 To which Northumberland-born statesman is the Monument in Newcastle dedicated, which was built in 1838 to commemorate the Great Reform Act of 1832?
16 Which prehistoric mound in Wiltshire has been dubbed 'the Hill with the Hole'?
17 What is the name of the government agency responsible for maintaining ancient monuments in Wales?
18 What is the name of the huge Buddhist temple complex in central Java, constructed between about 778 and 850, which was buried under volcanic ash from about 1000 and overgrown with vegetation until rediscovered by Thomas Stamford Raffles in 1814?
19 In which Indian city is the triumphal arch called the Gateway of India?
20 What were the original Seven Wonders of the Ancient World?

1 **Mumtaz Mahal** (d. 1631). Her name means 'Chosen One of the Palace'. The buildings were completed in 1643, although work on the decoration continued for a few more years.
2 **The Giant's Causeway**, County Antrim. It is formed from vertical hexagonal columns made from molten basalt as it cooled after volcanic activity during the Tertiary Period some 50–60 million years ago.
3 **Christopher Wren** (1632–1723), the architect of St Paul's. It means 'Reader, if you seek a monument, look around.'
4 **Lewis**. Calanais (formerly called Callanish) is a huge Megalithic stone circle not far from Stornaway.
5 **Edwin Landseer** (1802–73).
6 **Caerleon**.
7 **Athena**. The interior was dominated by a huge gold and ivory statue of her by the sculptor Phidias, who also supervised the construction of the Parthenon (designed by Ictinus and Callicrates).
8 **The Buddha**. They are stone- or brick-built monuments, usually housing a relic of the Buddha.
9 **The Raising of the Standard by Bonnie Prince Charlie** in August 1745 at the start of the Jacobite Rising. The monument was erected in 1815 – a 20-metre tower topped by the statue of a Highlander.
10 **Central Park**, New York. The pair (which have no historical connection with Cleopatra) were donated by the Egyptian government in the late nineteenth century. They had been erected in Heliopolis by Thutmose III (d. 1426 BC), and have inscriptions to him and to Ramses II (d. 1237 BC).
11 **Vespasian** (AD 9–79).
12 **New Forest**, in Hampshire. It marks the spot where William II (William Rufus, r. 1087–1100), successor to William the Conqueror, was killed by an arrow (believed to have been shot by Sir William Tirel) during a hunting expedition in 1100.
13 **Edwin Lutyens** (1869–1944).
14 **Long Meg and Her Daughters**. Twenty-seven of the original sixty stones are still upright. According to legend, they are witches turned into stone.
15 **Earl Charles Grey** (1764–1845), Prime Minister from 1830 to 1834 as Whig head of a coalition cabinet committed to Parliamentary reform. 'Earl Grey tea' is said to derive from a special mixture which he received as a gift from a grateful mandarin in China.
16 **Silbury Hill**. The huge, 4500-year-old earthwork at Silbury has been explored by adventurers and archaeologists since the eighteenth century, and is now as riddled with tunnels and shafts and voids as a Gruyère cheese. It is in the care of English Heritage, which is responsible for stabilising it.
17 **Cadw** (Welsh 'to keep', Welsh Historic Monuments). Equivalent agencies in Britain are English Heritage, Historic Scotland, and the Environment and Heritage Service Northern Ireland.
18 **Borobudur**.
19 **Mumbai** (Bombay). The arch was built in 1924 by George Willet to commemorate the visit of George V and Queen Mary in 1911.
20 **Colossus of Rhodes, Hanging Gardens of Babylon, Pharos of Alexandria, Pyramids of Egypt, Statue of Olympian Zeus, Temple of Diana at Ephesus and Tomb of Mausolus** (Mausoleum) at Helicarnassus (now Bodrum).

General Knowledge Questions

1 In the statue in the Albert Memorial in London's Kensington Gardens, what is Prince Albert holding?
2 What was Elvis Presley's occupation before he was 'discovered' as a singer by Sun Records in 1953?
3 What was the title of the final film made by Hollywood's legendary tough-guy character, John Wayne (1907–79)?
4 Which Offenbach opera on a classical theme features the cancan?
5 Which two Flemish painters who worked in England were knighted by Charles I?
6 The 2002 ITV dramatisation of John Galsworthy's *The Forsyte Saga* starred Damian Lewis and Gina McKee as Soames Forsyte and his wife Irene; but who played those parts in the original 1967 dramatisation on BBC2?
7 In October 2000 which television presenter was sent an Enigma machine, the decoding device stolen from Bletchley Park Museum in April that year?
8 Which Scottish village claims to have been the birthplace of Pontius Pilate?
9 Which Canadian-born Nobel Prize-winner wrote the 1953 novel *The Adventures of Augie March*?
10 Which Shakespearian character says the following lines?

Then must you speak
Of one that loved not wisely, but too well.

11 Which English clergyman and economist published anonymously in 1798 his *Essay on the Principle of Population*, propounding the theory that population growth would always tend to outrun the food supply unless checked by birth control or sexual abstinence?
12 Where in London is the home base of the London Symphony Orchestra and the London base of the Royal Shakespeare Company?
13 What is the word, taken from the name of a nineteenth-century British soldier in India, for a flap of cloth hanging from the back of a service cap (especially a French Foreign Legionnaire's cap) to protect the wearer's neck from the sun?
14 To which United Nations post was Mary Robinson appointed when she retired as President of Ireland in 1997?
15 In which religion is the main prayer the Japji?
16 What name was given to the rapidly spinning magnetic neutron stars discovered in 1967 by Jocelyn Bell and Antony Hewish?
17 Which bird of prey is sometimes known as 'St Martin's bird'?
18 Which annual sporting event is held each March on a frozen fjord off the coast of Greenland at Uummannaq?
19 The year 2002 was the centenary of the death of William McGonagall (1830–1902), the Scottish versifier who has been dubbed 'the world's worst poet'; but which US frontierswoman poet, known as the 'Sweet Singer of Michigan', rivalled him with lines such as the following?

And now kind friends, what I have wrote,
I hope you will pass o'er,
And not criticise, as some have done,
Hitherto herebefore.

20 Which monument in O'Connell Street Upper, Dublin, was blown up by an IRA bomb in 1966?

1 **A catalogue of the Great Exhibition,** which he had planned and promoted in Hyde Park in 1851. The sculptor was John Foley (1818–74) and the Memorial was designed by George Gilbert Scott (1811–78).
2 **Truck driver.**
3 ***The Shootist*** (1976), co-starring Lauren Bacall and James Stewart.
4 ***Orpheus in the Underworld*** (*Orphée aux enfers*, 1858). The French word '*can-can*' originally meant gossip or tittle-tattle, particularly of a scandalous nature.
5 **Anthony Van Dyck** or **Vandyke** (1599–1641) and **Peter Paul Rubens** (1577–1640).
6 **Eric Porter** and **Nyree Dawn Porter.**
7 **Jeremy Paxman.** Bletchley Park was the home of British military intelligence staff during the Second World War who interpreted messages encoded by the Nazis on Enigma machines.
8 **Fortingall,** Perthshire. The claim is associated with an ancient yew tree in the local churchyard.
9 **Saul Bellow** (b. 1915). Bellow, a naturalised American, was awarded the Nobel Prize for literature in 1976.
10 **Othello** (Act V, scene ii).
11 **Thomas Robert Malthus** (1766–1834).
12 **The Barbican Centre.** Designed by Peter Chamberlin, Geoffry Powell and Christof Bon, it was completed in 1982 on a Blitz site north of St Paul's.
13 **Havelock,** named after General Sir Henry Havelock (1795–1857). He had a vivid career as a soldier in India: during the Indian Mutiny (1857–8) he relieved Cawnpore and Lucknow, but died of dysentery soon afterwards.
14 **High Commissioner for Human Rights.** Mary Robinson (b. 1944), a lawyer, was President of Ireland from 1990 to 1997.
15 **Sikhism.** It is a morning prayer and declaration of faith.
16 **Pulsars** (pulsating radio stars). They emit extremely regular pulses of radio waves.
17 **Hen harrier** (*Circus cyaneus*). It is known in France as *l'oiseau de Saint Martin*, because it migrates across France around 11 November (St Martin's Day).
18 **Drambuie World Ice Golf Championship.** Ice golf (originally known as 'kolven') dates back to the seventeenth century. Uummannaq is an inlet in Baffin Bay 600 kilometres north of the Arctic Circle.
19 **Julia Moore** (1847–1820), in *The Sentimental Song Book* (1878).
20 **Nelson's Pillar.** The monument was erected in 1815. It was so badly damaged by the explosion that it had to be demolished. The head is now in the Dublin Civic Museum.

1 What is the most abundant mineral in the human body?
2 The lack of which fat-soluble vitamin over a long period of time causes rickets in children and contributes to osteomalacia in adults?
3 From which type of acids is a molecule of protein composed?
4 According to the early advertisements, what 'fortifies the over forties'?
5 Which Swiss nutritionist invented muesli?
6 What is the sugar found in milk?
7 Which 'tonic wine' was originally produced by monks at a monastery in south Devon?
8 What was the name of the Minister of Food during the Second World War who had a vegetable and cheese pie (topped with potato pastry) named after him?
9 Which nineteenth-century folk remedy for several wasting diseases became established by 1922 as a food supplement containing vitamins A and D and was supplied free to children in Britain by the Welfare Food Service?
10 What is the name of the professional qualifying body for food scientists and technologists?
11 Which slimming diet, named after the US doctor who promoted it, is based on food combining?
12 What is the name of the B vitamin which helps the body to make nucleic acids (RNA and DNA), amino acids and red blood cells?
13 In which European city are the headquarters of the World Food Council, which coordinates information and suggests strategies for food policy to assist developing countries?
14 Which delicacy, prepared from the flesh of the pufferfish (blowfish) is the principal cause of food poisoning in Japan?
15 Which is the simplest amino acid?
16 Which Polish-born biochemist, working at the Lister Institute in London in 1912, coined the word 'vitamine' (later changed to 'vitamin') for accessory food factors in his work to isolate vitamin B as a cure for the dietary disease beriberi?
17 Which vitamin is also known as pyridoxine?
18 A deficiency of which vitamin causes xerophthalmia, an eye disease of children in whose early stages the conjunctiva becomes dry, wrinkled and thickened?
19 The proverbial saying 'You are what you eat' is based on which nineteenth-century German philosopher's words '*Der Mensch ist, was er isst*' ('Man is what he eats')?
20 To which protein complexes must cholesterol be attached in order to be transported through the bloodstream?

Nutrition

Answers

1 **Calcium.** It is the main structural element in bones and teeth.
2 **Vitamin D.** The natural source of vitamin D is from the action on the skin of short-wave ultraviolet light from the sun.
3 **Amino acids.** More than a hundred amino acids occur naturally, but only twenty of them are commonly found in the make-up of proteins.
4 **Sanatogen.**
5 **Max Otto Bircher-Benner** (1867–1939). It used to be called 'Bircher muesli' (from the Swiss-German *muesli*, mix) and the original recipe contained raw grains (mainly rolled oats), with nuts and fresh and dried fruits. Dr Bircher-Benner set up a sanatorium in Zurich in 1897 promoting a regime of exercise and raw foods.
6 **Lactose.** It is the only common sugar of animal origin.
7 **Buckfast.** The recipe, consisting of macerated maté tea, coca leaves and vanilla added to a fortified Spanish wine, was sent to one of the original French monks at Buckfast in 1897 by his nephew. By the 1920s 1400 bottles were sold annually as medicinal wine, labelled with the dosage 'Three small glasses per day', but in 1927 local magistrates withdrew the Abbey's licence to sell the wine and production was taken over by J. Chandler & Co, who still make it.
8 **Lord Woolton** (1883–1964). His task at the Ministry was to ensure that the nation was well nourished despite wartime food shortages, and his name became a household word.
9 **Cod liver oil.**
10 **Institute of Food Science and Technology** (IFST).
11 **Hay Diet.** Dr William Hay (1866–1940), having been seriously ill owing to overweight, and having recovered, developed the diet, based on combining proteins and vegetables or carbohydrates and vegetables, but never proteins and carbohydrates.
12 **Folic acid** (folate, pteroylglutamic acid).
13 **Rome.** It was set up by the UN General Assembly in 1974 to increase food production, increase and improve the efficiency of food-aid systems, improve international nutritional conditions, build up an international grain reserve as part of a global food security system and reduce food-trade barriers between developing and developed countries.
14 ***Fugu.*** The ovaries, roes and liver of the fish contain the deadly poison tetraodontoxin; if they are cut during preparation, the poison seeps into the flesh, causing paralysis and death to anyone who eats it. Chefs entrusted with preparation of *fugu* have to train for seven years, but despite this dozens of people die from *fugu* poisoning every year.
15 **Glycine.** It was one of the first amino acids to be isolated, in 1820, from gelatin.
16 **Casimir Funk** (1884–1967). He demonstrated that beriberi in pigeons could be cured by feeding them a concentrate made from rice polishings. He used the term 'vitamine' because he believed that these substances were amines (chemicals derived from ammonia).
17 **Vitamin B6.** It was first isolated in 1938 and synthesised in 1939.
18 **Vitamin A.**
19 **Ludwig Feuerbach** (1804–72).
20 **Lipoproteins.** Cholesterol is insoluble.

General Knowledge Questions

1 In the field of nutrition, what term is popularly used as a measure of the amount of energy provided by food?
2 Which English actor, who died in December 2001, played the part of the suave and conniving senior civil servant Sir Humphrey Appleby in the TV series *Yes Minister* and *Yes, Prime Minister*?
3 Which pop group had No. 1 hits between 1961 and 1963 with *Kon Tiki, Wonderful Land, Dance On* and *Foot Tapper*?
4 By what name are flowering plants of the genus *Lonicera* better known?
5 What is the new name of the refurbished Liverpool Airport?
6 Which Hollywood actress played the part of Cora Munro opposite Daniel Day-Lewis in the 1992 film *Last of the Mohicans*?
7 Who lost to Jimmy Connors in both the US and Wimbledon men's singles finals in 1974 at the age of thirty-nine?
8 Which Lerner and Lowe musical was based on T.H. White's 1958 tetralogy of novels known collectively as *The Once and Future King*?
9 The Clore Gallery at the Tate Gallery (now Tate Britain) in London was opened in 1987 specifically to house the works of which painter?
10 Who is the last of the story-tellers in Chaucer's *The Canterbury Tales*?
11 Which eighteenth-century poet wrote the following lines?

Ill fares the land, to hast'ning ills a prey,
Where wealth accumulates, and men decay.

12 What is the name of the new 'Bridge across the Baltic' linking Denmark and Sweden?
13 After which character in Dickens's *Barnaby Rudge* is a style of large picture hat named?
14 Which US economist, one of President Kennedy's closest advisers, won the Nobel Prize for economics in 1981 for his 'portfolio' selection theory of investment, which he summed up as 'Don't put your eggs in one basket'?
15 The Burj al Arab (literally, 'Arabian Tower') in Dubai is the tallest structure of its kind in the world – what kind?
16 What is the name of the *Wall Street Journal*'s South Asia bureau chief who was kidnapped in Pakistan and executed by Islamic extremists on video in February 2002?
17 Which nineteenth-century Hungarian obstetrician discovered the cause of puerperal fever and was responsible for reducing the mortality rate in maternity hospitals throughout Europe?
18 In Judaism, what is the name (meaning 'hand') of the pointer used to follow the print on the Torah scroll?
19 Who, in the ancient world, were the Diadochi?
20 Casein is a soluble calcium salt which is converted by enzymes into insoluble paracasein in the production of which foodstuff?

General Knowledge Answers

1 **Calorie.** Dieticians prefer to use the more accurate terms kilocalorie (1000 calories) and joule (1 kilocalorie equals 4.184 kilojoules).

2 **Nigel Hawthorne** (1929–2001). His major film role was as George III in *The Madness of King George* (1994), which earned him a nomination for an Academy Award for Best Actor.

3 **The Shadows.**

4 **Honeysuckle.**

5 **Liverpool International John Lennon Airport.** It was officially renamed in March 2002 when Lennon's widow, Yoko Ono (accompanied by Cherie Blair) unveiled there a 2.13-metre-high bronze statue by the sculptor Tom Murphy.

6 **Madeleine Stowe.**

7 **Ken Rosewall** (b. 1934). It was his fourth Wimbledon final defeat.

8 *Camelot* (1960). T.H. White (1906–64) based the novels on the legends about King Arthur. The four books are *The Sword in the Stone, The Queen of Air and Darkness* (first published as *The Witch in the Wood*), *The Ill-Made Knight* and *The Candle in the Wind.*

9 **J.M.W. Turner** (1775–1851).

10 **The Parson.** He gives a long prose treatise on penitence, dealing at length with the Seven Deadly Sins.

11 **Oliver Goldsmith** (1730–74), in *The Deserted Village* (1770).

12 **Öresund Bridge.** Designed by Georg Rothne, it opened in 2000 and cost £3.3 billion.

13 **Dolly Varden.** She was the coquettish daughter of the locksmith Gabriel Varden, and ultimately married the gallant Joe Willett, host of the Maypole inn.

14 **James Tobin** (1918–2002).

15 **A hotel.** Built in the shape of an Arab dhow, it stands on an artificial off-shore island.

16 **Daniel Pearl** (b. 1963).

17 **Ignaz Philipp Semmelweiss** (1818–65). He initiated a strict regime of washing hands and instruments in chlorinated lime solution between autopsy work and the examination of living patients.

18 **Yad.** It is usually made of silver and has a hand with a pointing finger at its tip.

19 **The six Macedonian generals** who fought for control of the empire of Alexander the Great after his death, in the 'Wars of the Diadochi' (321–281 BC). The Greek word '*diadochi*' means 'successors'.

20 **Cheese.** Casein is also used in the production of thermoplastic materials and for priming artists' canvases.

Oceans and Seas

1 What was the title of the major 2001 BBC1 series, narrated by David Attenborough, on the natural history of the oceans?
2 What is the name of the twenty-four-year-old British solo sailor who came second in the Vendée Globe round-the-world race in February 2001 in her boat *Kingfisher*?
3 Which fictional character was forced to carry the Old Man of the Sea on his shoulders for many days and nights before managing to get him drunk and kill him?
4 In 2002, to avoid confusion with a smaller area known by the same name in Spain, what new name was given to the shipping area known in British shipping weather forecasts as Finisterre?
5 Which inland sea lies between the Bosporus and the Dardanelles?
6 What name has been given by seafarers to the stormy areas between latitudes 40° and 50° south, in which strong westerly winds prevail?
7 Which Elizabethan sea dog did Edmund Spenser address in a eulogy as 'the shepheard of the Ocean'?
8 What was the name of the oceanographic research ship of which Jacques Cousteau became commander in 1950 and from which he first made undersea films?
9 What is the name which the fifteenth-century Portuguese navigator Bartolomeu Diaz gave to what is now the Cape of Good Hope?
10 In which ocean is the French-owned island of Réunion?
11 Where, precisely, is the original 'Bridge over the Atlantic', built in 1792 by a local man, John Stevenson, to a design by Thomas Telford?
12 Who wrote the 1951 novel *The Cruel Sea*, based on his wartime experiences in the Royal Navy?
13 Which Spanish explorer was the first European to sight the Pacific Ocean, from a peak in Darien in 1513?
14 In Greek mythology, who was the goddess of the sea?
15 What was the name of the Nantucket whaling-boat which was rammed and sunk by a huge, 70-ton male sperm whale in the Pacific in November 1820, and inspired the writing of Herman Melville's *Moby Dick* (1851)?
16 What was the destination of the US brigantine *Mary Celeste* on its ill-fated voyage from New York in November 1872?
17 In classical mythology, what was the name of the eldest of the Titans, who was the father of all rivers and came to be associated with the water which surrounded the flat disc of the earth?
18 What is the name of the tragic Dutch merchant ship which ran aground off the unexplored coast of Western Australia in 1629, leading to mutiny and wholesale murder of the passengers and crew?
19 Who wrote the hymn *Eternal Father, Strong to Save* (1869), which begins with the following lines?

Eternal Father, strong to save,
Whose arm doth bind the restless wave,
Who bidd'st the mighty ocean deep
Its own-appointed limits keep:
O hear us when we cry to thee
For those in peril on the sea.

20 What are traditionally known as the Seven Seas?

Oceans and Seas

1 *The Blue Planet*. It was also published as a book in the same year.
2 **Ellen MacArthur**. Her time of 94 days, 4 hours and 30 minutes made her the fastest woman (and the youngest person) to circumnavigate the globe. The winner, setting a new record of 93 days, 3 hours, 57 minutes and 32 seconds, was Michel Desjoyeaux of France.
3 **Sinbad the Sailor**, in *The Arabian Nights (The Thousand and One Nights)*. The tales were told for 1001 nights by Scheherazade, the bride of the Sultan Schahriah, to avoid the usual fate of his wives (he killed them).
4 **FitzRoy**. It was named after the naval officer and meteorologist Robert FitzRoy (1805–65), who devised a storm warning system which was the prototype of the daily weather forecast.
5 **Sea of Marmara.**
6 **Roaring Forties.** The term has also been applied to the areas between 40° south and 50° north in the crossing between Europe and North America.
7 **Sir Walter Raleigh** (1552–1618), in *Colin Clouts Come Home Againe* (1595):

Whom when I asked from what place he came,
And how he hight, himselfe he did ycleepe,
The shepheard of the Ocean by name,
And said he came far from the main-sea deepe.

8 *Calypso.*
9 **Cape of Storms.**
10 **Indian Ocean**. Its capital is Saint-Denis.
11 **Between the island of Seil and the mainland of Scotland**, just south of Oban – the Clachan Bridge. The new Skye Bridge, connecting Skye to the mainland at the Kyle of Lochalsh, can now also claim to be a bridge over the Atlantic.
12 **Nicholas Monsarrat** (1910–79). It was made into an Ealing film in 1953 (produced by Leslie Norman, the father of TV film presenter Barry Norman).
13 **Vasco Núñez de Balboa** (1475–1519). He joined an expedition to Darien, on the Isthmus of Panama, as a stowaway in 1511, helped to found the town of Santa María de la Antigua and became the leader of the colony.
14 **Amphitrite** ('she who encircles the earth'), the daughter of Nereus and Doris, and wife of Poseidon (the Greek equivalent of the Roman Neptune).
15 *Essex*. Only eight of the crew survived.
16 **Genoa**. On board the *Mary Celeste*, which was carrying a cargo of 1701 barrels of neat alcohol, were the captain, Benjamin Briggs, his wife, young daughter and a crew of seven, none of whom was seen again. The ship was found deserted in December of that year, drifting half way between the Azores and the Portuguese coast.
17 **Oceanus**. As a sea-god, he is represented as an old man with a long beard and the horns of a bull.
18 *Batavia*. A reconstruction of the ship is now moored at the Australian National Maritime Museum in Sydney harbour.
19 **William Whiting** (1825–78), an English teacher who was master of the Quiristers of Winchester Cathedral from 1842.
20 **Antarctic, Arctic, Indian, North Atlantic, North Pacific, South Atlantic** and **South Pacific Oceans**.

1 What, in the writings of Julius Caesar, did the Romans call the Mediterranean?
2 Which former trade union activist in the 1972 national builders' strike stars as the layabout couch potato Jim Royle in the BBC television comedy series *The Royle Family*?
3 Which folk trio recorded *Puff the Magic Dragon* in 1963?
4 What is the Scottish bluebell (wild hyacinth) called in England?
5 Who starred as Brian Cohen, a young man whose life apparently parallels that of Jesus, in the 1979 Monty Python film *The Life of Brian*?
6 Who replaced Walter Smith as the manager of Everton FC in March 2002?
7 Of which of the Channel Islands is St Anne the capital and only town?
8 What are the names of the twins who are the main characters in Edgar Allan Poe's Gothic horror novel *The Fall of the House of Usher* (1839)?
9 Of which nineteenth-century English politician was it said, 'He is a self-made man and worships his creator'?
10 What is the derivation of the word 'pundit', meaning an expert?
11 Which mathematician and children's author wrote, in 1879, *Euclid and his Modern Rivals*?
12 Which English artist painted *St Francis and the Birds* in 1935, which is now in Tate Britain?
13 Which eighteenth-century German composer wrote the *Brandenburg Concertos*?
14 Who invented the clockwork radio, after watching a television programme about AIDS in Africa?
15 In the Old Testament, whom did David send to his death at a war front in order to marry his widow, Bathsheba?
16 What is the more common name for the medical condition known as insolation?
17 Which US zoologist demonstrated in 1940 that the ultrasound produced by bats is used in echo location to map their surroundings?
18 What kind of medieval weapon was a falchion?
19 Which seventeenth-century French philosopher wrote the phrase '*Le coeur a ses raisons que la raison ne connaît point*' ('The heart has its reasons, of which reason knows nothing')?
20 Where is the deepest point in the Atlantic Ocean?

1 *Mare nostrum* ('Our sea').
2 **Ricky Tomlinson.** He was one of the 'Shrewsbury Two' who were jailed for conspiracy to incite violence.
3 **Peter, Paul and Mary.** Peter Yarrow (b. 1938), Noel Paul Stookey (b. 1937) and Mary Travers (b. 1936) began recording in 1961.
4 **Harebell** (*Campanula rotundifolia*).
5 **Graham Chapman** (1941–89).
6 **David Moyes,** who had been manager of Preston North End. Walter Smith was formerly the manager of Glasgow Rangers.
7 **Alderney.**
8 **Roderick** and **Madeleine Usher.**
9 **Benjamin Disraeli** (1804–81), by the radical John Bright (1811–89).
10 **A Brahmin learned in Sanskrit and Hindu religion.** The word 'pundit' (also Hindi 'pandit') comes from Sanskrit *pandita*, learned.
11 **Lewis Carroll** (Charles Lutwidge Dodgson, 1832–98). It was a light-hearted defence of Euclid.
12 **Stanley Spencer** (1891–1959). The painting shows St Francis as a paunchy old man wearing bedroom slippers and a brown dressing gown tied with a cord around his middle, apparently conducting a dawn chorus of domestic fowl.
13 **Johann Sebastian Bach** (1685–1750). The six pieces were dedicated to Margrave Christian Ludwig of Brandenburg.
14 **Trevor Bayliss** (b. 1937). His first working prototype, which ran for fourteen minutes, was featured on *Tomorrow's World* in 1994. The following year corporate finance expert Christopher Staines and South African entrepreneur Rory Stear set up BayGen Power Industries in Cape Town employing disabled workers to manufacture the Freeplay radio.
15 **Uriah the Hittite.**
16 **Sunstroke.**
17 **Donald Griffin** (b. 1915).
18 **Sword** (from Latin *falx*, sickle). It was a slightly curved sword, broader at the point, like a scimitar.
19 **Blaise Pascal** (1623–62), in his *Pensées* (published posthumously in 1669).
20 **Puerto Rico Trench** (or Milwaukee Deep, 8648 metres). The deepest point in the Pacific Ocean is in the Mariana Trench (11,040 metres).

1 Who was the first official Poet Laureate, in 1668?

2 In whose *Revolting Rhymes* does Cinderella yell at her fairy godmother:

I want a dress! I want a coach!
And earrings and a diamond brooch!
And silver slippers, two of those!
And lovely nylon panty-hose!
Done up like that I'll guarantee
The handsome Prince will fall for me!

3 Which nineteenth-century English poet is sometimes known as 'the Northamptonshire peasant poet'?

4 Which seventeenth-century sonnet ends with the line, 'They also serve who only stand and wait'?

5 Who, in the poem by Charles Causley, 'bought an old castle complete with a ghost' and laughed at the spectre's attempts at haunting him?

6 Which English poet became Dean of St Paul's Cathedral in 1621?

7 In 1915 which Gloucestershire village was immortalised by Edward Thomas after his train stopped at its station 'unwontedly' one summer afternoon?

8 To which event in the late eighteenth century was William Wordsworth referring when he wrote in *The Prelude*:

Bliss it was in that dawn to be alive,
But to be young was very heaven!

9 Which Liverpool poet wrote *Eye sore*?

10 Which poet wrote the following lines?

And since to look at things in bloom
Fifty springs are little room,
About the woodlands I will go
To see the cherry hung with snow.

11 In which poem does Louis MacNeice pray for 'a white light in the back of my mind to guide me'?

12 Which nineteenth-century English poet wrote a visionary poem entitled *Queen Mab* in which the Fairy Queen, at the age of twenty-one, carries off in her chariot the soul of the maiden Ianthe?

13 *Zoom!* (1989) was the first published collection by which Yorkshire poet, drawing on his work as a probation officer and on the rhythms of the Yorkshire vernacular?

14 Which maiden, in a poem by Edgar Allan Poe, 'lived with no other thought/Than to love and be loved by me'?

15 Who set the opening of William Blake's poem *Milton* to music for the hymn *Jerusalem* in 1916?

16 In 1797 whose poetic muse was interrupted by the arrival of a 'person on business from Porlock'?

17 Which eighteenth-century English poet was nicknamed 'Namby-Pamby' for his excessively sentimental and affected poems addressed to babies?

18 Which minstrel was 'infirm and old;/His wither'd cheek and tresses grey/Seem'd to have known a better day'?

19 Which twentieth-century poet and novelist has published three volumes of poetry which explore his early life in Guyana, including *Mama Dot* (1985)?

20 Which poet wrote that 'Procrastination is the thief of time'?

1 **John Dryden** (1631–1700). Two others are thought to have been earlier 'unofficial' Poets Laureate: Ben Jonson (from 1616) and William D'Avenant (from 1638). For an annual salary of £200 and a butt of wine, Dryden was required to write for public occasions.
2 **Roald Dahl** (1916–90).
3 **John Clare** (1793–1864).
4 ***When I consider how my light is spent*** (Sonnet 16, *On His Blindness*, 1673), by John Milton (1608–74).
5 **Colonel Fazackerley Butterworth-Toast:**
But Colonel Fazackerley, just as before,
Was simply delighted and called out, 'Encore!'
At which the ghost vanished, his efforts in vain,
And never was seen at the castle again.
6 **John Donne** (c. 1572–1631).
7 **Adlestrop.** The railway station is now closed.
8 **The French Revolution.**
9 **Roger McGough** (b. 1937):
I saw
a building
soar
into the sky
making
the sky's
eye
sore.
10 **A.E. Housman** (1859–1936), in *A Shropshire Lad*, Canto II (1896).
11 ***Prayer Before Birth*** (*Collected Poems* 1925–48).
12 **Percy Bysshe Shelley** (1792–1822). He published it in 1813.
13 **Simon Armitage** (b. 1963).
14 **Annabel Lee.**
15 **Hubert Parry** (1848–1918).
16 **Samuel Taylor Coleridge** (1772–1834). In his introduction to *Kubla Khan* (1816), Coleridge described his awakening from an opium-induced dream in which he had composed some three hundred lines about Kubla Khan's palace. On waking, he began to write them, but after only fifty-four lines he was 'called out by a person on business from Porlock', and by the time he got back to his desk the vision had gone.
17 **Ambrose Philips** (c. 1674–1749). The name was coined by the dramatist Henry Carey (c. 1687–1743) and came to be applied generally to anyone considered wishy-washy or insipid.
18 **The Last Minstrel,** in Walter Scott's *The Lay of the Last Minstrel* (1805).
19 **Fred D'Aguiar** (b. 1960). The other volumes are *Airy Hall* (1989) and *British Subjects* (1993).
20 **Edward Young** (1683–1765), in *The Complaint: Night Thoughts* (1742–45).

1 In the nonsense poem by Edward Lear, what did the Pobble lose while swimming the Bristol Channel?
2 Which leguminous shrub of the genus *Ulex*, which is commonly seen in moorland areas in Britain, is also known as 'furze'?
3 Who is the presenter of BBC Radio 4's musical quiz *Counterpoint*?
4 At the estuary of which river is the Polish port of Gdansk situated?
5 At which racecourse is the Hennessy Gold Cup run at the end of November or the beginning of December?
6 Who plays the resurrected Buffy the Vampire Slayer in the BBC2 television series of that name?
7 Who was appointed Minister for the Environment (now Environment, Food and Rural Affairs) in the New Labour government which took office in 1997?
8 In Marcus Gheeraerts the Younger's portrait of Elizabeth of England, sometimes known as the *Ditchley Portrait*, on what is the queen standing?
9 Which planet (apart from the earth) was not included in Gustav Holst's seven-movement suite *The Planets* (1914–16) because it had not been discovered at the time?
10 Which London bank sacked four of its investment bankers in 2001 for running up a bill for £44,007 for a celebratory meal for six at Gordon Ramsay's Petrus restaurant in London?
11 Which monastic order was founded by St Bruno of Cologne in 1084 in the Dauphin Alps at Chartreuse, near Grenoble, in France?
12 Which nineteenth-century English author wrote two novels based on his life as a gypsy entitled *Lavengro* (1851) and its sequel *The Romany Rye* (1857)?
13 In Hinduism what is the most sacred syllable?
14 What was the stage name of the diminutive nineteenth-century US showman Charles Sherwood Stratton?
15 How was the communications satellite *Intelsat 1*, launched in 1965, more familiarly known?
16 Who was the architect of Castle Drogo, in Devon, completed in 1930 for Julius Drewe, who founded the Home and Colonial grocery chain?
17 Which Dutch-born US physician developed the first clinically useful artificial kidney?
18 In classical mythology, who were the Corybantes?
19 Which German theoretical physicist in 1900 produced a mathematical formula which correctly predicted the spectral energy distribution of radiation emitted by a black body – the original quantum theory?
20 Which English poet wrote a volume of autobiography in blank verse entitled *Summoned by Bells* (1960)?

1 **His toes** (*The Pobble Who Has No Toes*).
2 **Gorse.**
3 **Ned Sherrin** (b. 1931). He made his name in the 1960s as the producer and director of BBC TV's satirical Saturday evening show *That Was the Week That Was*.
4 **Vistula.** Warsaw is farther inland on the banks of the Vistula.
5 **Newbury.**
6 **Sarah Michelle Gellar** (b. 1977).
7 **Michael Meacher** (b. 1939), MP for Oldham West and Royton since 1970.
8 **A globe of the world** (with her feet on Oxfordshire, the location of Ditchley, the home of Sir Henry Lee, for whom Elizabeth had the portrait painted). The painting is thought to have been a gift to show him forgiveness for his becoming 'a stranger lady's thrall' (the lady was Anne Vavasour). The painting is now in the National Portrait Gallery, London.
9 **Pluto.** Pluto, the ninth and most distant planet from the sun, was discovered in 1930 by the US astronomer Clyde Tombaugh.
10 **Barclays Capital.** At £7334.50 per head, it beat the most expensive meal per head (£4363.77) recorded in the *Guinness Book of Records*, at Le Gavroche, London.
11 **Carthusian.** Chartreuse liqueur was first distilled there in 1607, but Carthusian monks practise strict abstinence and live as solitaries; lay brothers live in a community. The original monastery, La Grande Chartreuse, has been destroyed and rebuilt several times, and is now a museum.
12 **George Henry Borrow** (1803–81).
13 **Aum** (Om). The prolonged intonation of aum is linked with the creative sound through which, in Hindu belief, the universe came into existence.
14 **General Tom Thumb** (1838–83). The 101-centimetre-tall performer toured the USA and Europe with Phineas T. Barnum's circus. He married another of Barnum's performers, Lavinia Warren (1841–1919), who was just over 81 centimetres in height.
15 **Early Bird.** It was launched into stationary orbit over the Atlantic Ocean and provided telephone channels between Europe and the USA for three and a half years. In 1984 Early Bird was briefly reactivated to celebrate the twentieth anniversary of ITSO (International Telecommunications Satellite Organisation).
16 **Sir Edwin Lutyens** (1869–1944). Julius Drewe had discovered that a Norman baron named Drogo de Teigne was his ancestor and had the castle built on land in Drewsteignton which had once belonged to him.
17 **Willem Johan Kolff** (b. 1911). He treated his first patient with his 'rotating drum' artificial kidney in 1943 – a dialysis machine using a series of membranes to remove from the blood impurities which would normally be filtered out by the healthy kidney.
18 **Priests of the goddess Cybele.** Her worship was celebrated with orgiastic dances and wild music – hence the word 'corybantic', meaning frenzied.
19 **Max Planck** (1858–1947). He was awarded the Nobel Prize for physics in 1918.
20 **John Betjeman** (1906–84). He was appointed Poet Laureate in 1972. He published two further autobiographical collections: *A Nip in the Air* (1972) and *High and Low* (1976).

Queens Questions

1 Where, in a rousing speech to her troops before they faced the Spanish Armada, did Queen Elizabeth I say 'I know I have the body but of a weak and feeble woman; but I have the heart and stomach of a king'?
2 In the nursery rhyme *Sing a Song of Sixpence*, when the king was in his counting house, counting out his money, where was the queen and what was she doing?
3 In Shakespeare's *A Midsummer Night's Dream*, what is the name of the Queen of the Fairies?
4 What was the name of the statuesque queen of Tonga whose appearance attracted enormous attention at the coronation of Her Majesty the Queen in 1953?
5 Who played the role of the Queen in the 1991 TV play *A Question of Attribution* (written by Alan Bennett)?
6 To which legendary queen of Carthage did Aeneas recount the story of the fall of Troy in Virgil's *Aeneid*?
7 Who was the first husband of Catherine of Aragon, who became the first wife of Henry VIII?
8 Which granddaughter of Queen Victoria married the future Emperor Nicholas II of Russia in 1894 and was eventually executed with him and their children by the Bolsheviks in July 1918?
9 Who was known as 'the Winter Queen'?
10 Which queen of England is said to have saved her husband's life during the Crusades by sucking poison from his wound at Acre (now in Israel)?
11 Whose queen consort was Berengaria of Navarre?
12 Which Egyptian queen of the fourteenth century BC, the beautiful wife of the 'heretic Pharaoh' Akhenaton, has become the symbol of Egyptian beauty?
13 Which queen embroidered her personal motto, '*En ma fin est mon commencement*', on her chair of state?
14 Which fourteenth-century queen of England deposed her husband from the throne and then had him murdered?
15 Which profession has benefited since 1704 from 'Queen Anne's Bounty'?
16 In Greek mythology, which legendary queen's girdle did Herakles (Hercules) have to capture as one of his Twelve Labours?
17 Which queen of Sweden was a prime mover in the Peace of Westphalia, which ended the Thirty Years' War in 1648, and then abdicated in 1654 after her secret conversion to Catholicism?
18 Which queen of England, a former Empress of the Holy Roman Empire, was never crowned and was known as 'Lady of the English?
19 Which French princess was married first to Henry V of England and then to Owen Tudor of Wales?
20 To which English queen did Chaucer dedicate *The Legend of Good Women*?

Queens

1 **Tilbury**, Essex.
2 **She was in the parlour eating bread and honey.**
3 **Titania.**
4 **Queen Salote Tupou III** (r. 1918–65).
5 **Prunella Scales** (b. 1932).
6 **Dido.** According to Virgil, she fell in love with Aeneas and burned herself to death on a funeral pyre when he left her.
7 **Prince Arthur** (1486–1502), Henry's older brother. They married in 1501, but Arthur died six months later. Catherine married Henry VIII in 1509, after his accession to the throne.
8 **Alexandra** (1872–1918). She was the daughter of Alice Maud Mary and the Grand Duke Louis of Hesse-Darmstadt.
9 **Elizabeth of Bohemia** (1596–1662). She was the eldest daughter of James VI and I and wife of the Protestant Frederick V, the Elector Palatine (1596–1632); Frederick was elected to the throne of Bohemia in 1619, but held it for only a winter. Their daughter Sophia became the mother of George I, the first Hanoverian monarch of Britain.
10 **Eleanor of Castile** (1246–1290), wife of Edward I.
11 **Richard I** (Lionheart). He married her in 1191 in Limassol, Cyprus.
12 **Nefertiti.** Her face was immortalised in the superb sculptured head (now in the Berlin Museum) discovered in 1912 during excavations at Amarna.
13 **Mary Queen of Scots** (1542–87). It means 'In my end is my beginning'. Mary embroidered the motto on the chair of state which accompanied her during her captivity in England (1568–87).
14 **Isabella of France** (1292–1358). She left her husband, Edward II, for her native France in 1325 but returned with an army the following year and deposed him. She took a lover, Roger de Mortimer, and had Edward II murdered in Berkeley Castle in 1327. Eventually she and Mortimer were arrested by Edward III; Mortimer was executed, and Isabella was sent into retirement at Castle Rising, Norfolk.
15 **The clergy.** Queen Anne passed an Act which used the Crown revenue from the church (originally taxes paid to the Pope, appropriated by Henry VIII) to augment the livings of the poorer parish clergy.
16 **Hippolyta,** queen of the Amazons. She handed over her girdle, but was killed by Herakles when fighting broke out between her followers and his.
17 **Kristina** (1626–89, r. 1632–54).
18 **Matilda** ('the Empress Maud', 1102–67), the daughter of Henry I. In 1114 she married the Holy Roman Emperor (Henry V), and returned to England after his death in 1125. In 1128 she married Geoffrey Plantagenet of Anjou, by whom she had a son, the future Henry II.
19 **Catherine de Valois** (1401–37), daughter of Charles VI of France. She married Henry V in 1421, and gave birth to the future Henry VI. After her husband's death in 1422 she secretly married Owen Tudor, a Welsh squire; their eldest son (Edmund, Earl of Richmond) was the father of the first Tudor king of England, Henry VII.
20 **Anne of Bohemia** (1366–94), daughter of the Emperor Charles IV and first wife of Richard II. They married in 1382. *The Legend of Good Women* tells the story of nine women famed for their fidelity in love, as directed by the queen of love, Alceste (identified with Anne of Bohemia).

1 In the fortnightly satirical magazine *Private Eye*, what name is given to Her Majesty the Queen?
2 In the 1993 film *Schindler's List* (based on Thomas Keneally's Booker Prize-winning 1982 novel *Schindler's Ark)*, which actor played the part of Oskar Schindler?
3 Which song, composed by the nineteenth-century US musician Daniel Decatur Emmett, became the unofficial anthem of the Confederacy during the Civil War and the South thereafter?
4 Who was England's goalkeeper during the 2002 World Cup Finals?
5 What is the name of the bouffant-haired presenter on BBC1's daytime antiques show *Bargain Hunt*?
6 Which nineteenth-century English poet was so grief-stricken by the death of his wife that he buried the manuscripts of many of his unpublished poems with her, but dug them up a few years later?
7 Which red flower is also known as Poor Man's Weatherglass or Shepherd's Dial?
8 Which Scottish football stadium is the home ground of Queen's Park FC?
9 What is the collective term for a group of choughs?
10 Which British city is sometimes known as the 'City of a Thousand Trades'?
11 Which writer's most substantial work is a quintet of novels, published as *Children of Violence* between 1952 and 1969, about Martha Quest, who, like the author, grows up in southern Africa and settles in England?
12 Which Italian sculptor made the marble *Penitent Magdalen* (now in the State Hermitage Museum, Leningrad) in 1809?
13 What is the name of the first Soviet cosmonaut to walk in space, in 1965?
14 Which nineteenth-century English tycoon, known as 'the Railways King', built a huge railway empire in Britain in the mid-1840s, was three times Lord Mayor of York and MP for Sunderland (1845–59), but died ruined in 1871?
15 In a church, what is usually placed in an ambry or aumbry?
16 In 1961 what did the Czech polymer chemist Otto Wichterle contribute to the comfort of contact-lens wearers?
17 What is the derivation of the term 'to grangerise', meaning 'to illustrate books by inserting prints taken from other works'?
18 Who was the third wife of chairman Mao Zedong of China, and leader of the 'Gang of Four' which supervised the Cultural Revolution (1966–9) and tried to seize power after Mao's death?
19 Which eighteenth-century French engineer, hailed as 'the Father of Modern Automata', invented automata such as the 'Flute Player', the 'Tambourine Player' and a gold-plated duck which flapped its wings and swam (and even ate food and defecated)?
20 Which of Henry VIII's wives was the mother of Edward VI?

1 **Brenda.**
2 **Liam Neeson** (b. 1952).
3 *Dixie* (1859).
4 **David Seaman** (b. 1963) of Arsenal FC.
5 **David Dickinson** (b. 1942). He has been in the antiques business himself for more than twenty-five years.
6 **Dante Gabriel Rossetti** (1828–82).
7 **Scarlet Pimpernel** (*Anagallis arvensis*). When rain is at hand or the weather is unfavourable, its flowers do not open.
8 **Hampden Park**, in Glasgow, which is also Scotland's national stadium. Queen's Park is Scotland's oldest football club (founded in 1867).
9 **A chattering.**
10 **Birmingham.**
11 **Doris Lessing** (b. 1919). The books are *Martha Quest* (1952), *A Proper Marriage* (1954), *A Ripple from the Storm* (1958), *Landlocked* (1965) and *The Four-Gated City* (1969).
12 **Antonio Canova** (1757–1822).
13 **Alexei Leonov** (b. 1934). He performed the first 'extra-vehicular activity' for ten minutes from the spacecraft *Voskhod 2*.
14 **George Hudson** (1800–71). His biography, *A Biography of George Hudson: Railway Pioneer and Fraudster*, by Robert Beaumont, was published in 2002.
15 **The consecrated host** (usually to be taken to people who cannot attend the Communion service because of illness).
16 **Soft lenses.** Wichterle (1913–98) made a lens, which did not irritate the eye, from a jelly-like, water-absorbing 'hydrogel' plastic. From a children's construction set he assembled a prototype centrifugal casting device driven by a bicycle dynamo connected to a bell transformer, and used it to cast his first four lenses. The US company Bausch & Lomb prepared to market them but, because the US Food and Drug Administration ruled that the lens was a drug, production was delayed until 1972 by the many tests which it had to undergo.
17 From **James Granger** (1723–76), vicar of Shiplake, Oxfordshire, who in 1769 published a *Biographical History of England . . . adapted to a Methodical Catalogue of Engraved British Heads*. Later editions were published with blank interleaved pages for inserting extra illustrations. It provoked a fury of zeal among book collectors, who took engravings from every conceivable source, including valuable early books.
18 **Jiang Qing** (c. 1913–91). After Mao's death in 1976 she was sentenced to death by Mao's successor, Deng Xiaoping; this was later commuted to life imprisonment, but after her release on health grounds she is said to have taken her own life.
19 **Jacques de Vaucanson** (1709–82). He was appointed an inspector of silk factories in 1741 and developed the first fully automated loom controlled through a system of perforated cards, which was improved by Jacquard and became one of the most important inventions of the Industrial Revolution.
20 **Jane Seymour** (c. 1509–37). She died twelve days after the birth.

Rugby

Questions

1 Which veteran BBC rugby union commentator retired in April 2002 after fifty years at the microphone?
2 Which British club won the Rugby League World Club Challenge Trophy at Huddersfield's McAlpine Stadium in February 2002?
3 Which Irish-born actor starred as a miner who becomes a professional rugby player in the 1963 film *This Sporting Life*?
4 Which Edinburgh ground hosted the first rugby union international, played between England and Scotland (twenty a side) in March 1871?
5 Which national team did New Zealand defeat in 1995 by 145–17, the highest-ever score in the Rugby Union World Cup?
6 What was the original name of the Rugby Football League, formed when twenty-two clubs broke away from the Rugby Football Union in 1895?
7 Which international match in 1975 holds the official attendance record for a rugby union game, with 104,000 spectators?
8 Which rugby league player was signed by Huddersfield in 1906 as a fifteen-year-old and went on to lead his 'team of all the talents' to three championships and three Challenge Cup victories (1913, 1915 and 1920)?
9 Which Irish rugby union club won the inaugural Celtic Championship tournament by defeating Munster 24–20 in December 2001?
10 In the 1990 Grand Slam decider between Scotland and England at Murrayfield, who scored the winning try for Scotland?
11 What was the name of the Russian prince who came to England when his family fled the Russian Revolution and played for England as a wing three-quarter, scoring two tries in their first win over the All Blacks at Twickenham in 1936?
12 What was the nickname given to the all-conquering All Blacks team of 1925, who ended their tour by beating England 17–11 at Twickenham despite having a player sent off?
13 Which rugby union forward led Scotland to win the Calcutta Cup and the Five Nations Championship in 1929, won thirty-seven international caps and later stood (unsuccessfully) as a Liberal candidate for Inverness-shire?
14 Which Welsh international rugby union player for Neath and then Llanelli switched to rugby league (playing for Widnes and then Warrington), before switching back to the union code by joining Cardiff in 1995?
15 Which English rugby union threequarter dropped a goal in the seventy-sixth minute of the Lions' third match against the Springboks in 1997 to clinch a memorable series victory?
16 Which eccentric nineteenth- and twentieth-century Irish rugby union player always wore a monocle during games?
17 Which Irish rugby union wing threequarter, who won twenty-nine caps for Ireland spanning fifteen years, became President of the Heinz International Corporation?
18 Which New Zealand rugby union full back from 1956 to 1964 was known as 'the Boot'?
19 Which Sydney-born Warrington rugby league player was the most prolific try scorer in the history of the game, scoring 796 tries between 1946 and 1964 (740 for Warrington alone)?
20 Which rugby union international at Twickenham was the occasion of the first live radio commentary of any British sporting event?

1 **Bill McLaren** (b. 1923). Hawick-born McLaren, a PE teacher, played wing forward for Hawick and earned a final Scottish trial before he was struck down by a near-fatal attack of tuberculosis.
2 **Bradford Bulls.** They defeated Australia's Newcastle Knights 41–26.
3 **Richard Harris** (b. 1930).
4 **Raeburn Place.** Scotland won by one goal to nil. In the early days the only way to win was by goals (converted tries or dropped goals – a touchdown simply allowed a side to 'try' for a goal). Scoring by points was not introduced until the late 1880s.
5 **Japan.**
6 **Northern Rugby Football Union.** The name was changed to the Northern Rugby League in 1922, and to the Rugby League in 1980.
7 **Scotland v Wales at Murrayfield,** in a Five Nations championship match. Scotland won 12–10.
8 **Harold Wagstaff** (1891–1939). He was the youngest professional player in Britain, and the youngest International (17 years and 228 days).
9 **Leinster.**
10 **Tony Stanger,** the Hawick winger. The try enabled Scotland to win 13–7.
11 **Alexander Obolensky** (1916–40). England won 13–0: three tries (three points each in those days) and a dropped goal (four points). Obolensky's old school, Trent College, presents awards named after him to pupils of his former house who make outstanding contributions to the house and to the school.
12 **The Invincibles.**
13 **John M. Bannerman** (1902–69). A prominent figure in the Gaelic movement, he was made a life peer as Lord Bannerman of Kildonan in 1967.
14 **Jonathan Davies** (b. 1962). He won twenty-eight rugby union caps for Wales. He now commentates on rugby union and league football for the BBC.
15 **Jeremy Guscott** (b. 1965). The Lions won 18–15. The only Lions try was scored by scrum half Matt Dawson.
16 **D.B. Walkington.**
17 **Tony O'Reilly** (b. 1936). He was a member of the Test Series-winning British Lions Tour of South Africa in 1955 and of the Tour of New Zealand and Australia in 1959.
18 **Don Clarke,** who kicked 340 goals for the All Blacks in a career of eighty-nine matches (thirty-one Tests). He was inducted to the International Rugby Hall of Fame in 2001.
19 **Brian Bevan** (1924–91). A stoker in the Australian navy, he signed for Warrington in 1945 but had to return to Australia to be demobbed. He returned in 1946 to take up a regular place in the team. The Brian Bevan Memorial (by the sculptor Philip Bews) – a cast bronze running figure set at a height of 4 metres on three steel masts (to look like rugby goalposts) – was unveiled on a traffic roundabout in Warrington town centre in 1993.
20 **England v Wales** (11–9, 15 January 1927). The commentary was provided by Captain Teddy Wakelam, a former Harlequins player.

General Knowledge Questions

1 Which two rugby union international matches in 1951 have gone down in history as 'Murrayfield Massacres', for very different reasons?
2 Which English spin bowler took nineteen Australian wickets in the fourth Test Match at Old Trafford in 1956?
3 Which common household plant was known in Victorian times as the 'Cast-Iron Plant'?
4 Which Top Ten hit in 1971 by former Beatle George Harrison was re-released and reached No. 1 posthumously in January 2002?
5 Who played the part of Mary Beth Lacey in the 1982–8 BBC1 detective series *Cagney and Lacey*?
6 From the refining of which food is 'blackstrap' a product?
7 Who won an Academy Award for Best Original Score for the music for Steven Spielberg's block-busting 1982 film *E.T. The Extra-Terrestrial*?
8 Which antiques expert, whose name means a hot drink of port and lemon juice, was the first presenter of the BBC television programme *The Antiques Roadshow* in 1982?
9 Which English art historian and Surveyor of the Queen's Pictures was unmasked in 1979 as a former Soviet spy?
10 In which Scottish town was the £84.5-million 'Millennium Link', reconnecting the Forth & Clyde Canal and the Union Canal, opened in May 2002?
11 The first two names of which entertainer (also known as Walter Busterkeys) were Wladziu Valentino?
12 In 1937 which Pope issued encyclicals denouncing both fascism in Nazi Germany and Communism in Soviet Russia?
13 On which London structure is the massive bronze sculpture of a four-horse chariot (*quadriga*) made by Adrian Jones, a former army captain and veterinary surgeon, in 1912?
14 What name is given to the ceremony with which Hindus begin *puja* (worship)?
15 Which veteran English journalist was given a Special Award 'for his first seventy years in newspapers' at the 2002 Press Gazette Awards?
16 Which English courtier and epigrammatist penned the following couplet?
Treason doth never prosper, what's the reason?
For if it prosper, none dare call it treason.
17 What is the heraldic term for a gold roundel (flat disc)?
18 Which British-born artist and computer scientist, a former student and lecturer at the Slade School of Fine Arts, London, invented the world's first artistic computer, 'Aaron'?
19 Which Victorian novelist and founder editor of the Tory paper *John Bull* is credited with sending the world's first known postcard, in 1840, which was sold at auction in 2002 for £31,000?
20 Which rugby league Test match between Great Britain and Australia became known as the 'Rorke's Drift Test'?

General Knowledge

1 **Scotland v Wales** (February 1951) and **Scotland v South Africa** (November 1951). Scotland confounded the critics by defeating a star-studded Welsh side 19–0, but at the start of the following season they were thrashed 44–0 by the touring Springboks.

2 **Jim Laker** (1922–86).

3 **Aspidistra.** It earned the nickname because of its capacity to survive in gas-lit rooms.

4 ***My Sweet Lord.*** Profits from the re-release were given to charities.

5 **Tyne Daly.** She also played the part in the original American film, with Loretta Swit as Christine Cagney (played first by Meg Foster and then by Sharon Gless in the TV series).

6 **Sugar.** It is a thick, strong molasses taken from the final stage of the refining process and has very little crystallised sugar remaining in it.

7 **John Williams** (b. 1932).

8 **Arthur Negus** (1903–85).

9 **Anthony Blunt** (1907–83).

10 **Falkirk.** The 'Falkirk Wheel' is the world's first rotating boat lift. The massive engineering project also involved making a 145-metre tunnel under the Roman Antonine Wall.

11 **Liberace** (1919–87).

12 **Pius XI** (Achille Ratti, r. 1922–39). The Papal Encyclicals were entitled *With Burning Anxiety* and *On Atheistic Communism.*

13 **Wellington Arch**, at Hyde Park Corner.

14 ***Arti.*** The worshipper circles a lighted lamp (burning ghee, clarified butter) in front of a *murti* (image of a deity) three times in a clockwise direction while chanting a prayer or singing a hymn.

15 **W.F. (Bill) Deedes** (b. 1913). He was editor of the *Daily Telegraph* from 1974 to 1986.

16 **John Harington** (1561–1612). He was a godson of Elizabeth of England. His works included a celebrated translation of Ariosto's epic poem *Orlando furioso* (1591).

17 **Bezant** (a medieval Byzantine coin).

18 **Harold Cohen** (b. 1928). Aaron is a programme which simulates the cognitive processes underlying the human act of drawing and can be seen producing original 'freehand' drawings in museums and science centres.

19 **Theodore Hook** (1788–1841). The hand-coloured postcard, which he addressed to himself, is the only known postcard in existence with a Penny Black stamp on it. The cartoon drawn by Hook makes fun of the new uniform penny postage rate introduced by Rowland Hill in 1840.

20 **The Third Test in Sydney, Australia, in July 1914.** Injuries reduced the British team to ten men for the final half hour, but Britain still won 14–6. Rorke's Drift was the renowned battle in the Zulu War (1879) when a hundred British soldiers twice repelled onslaughts by thousands of Zulu warriors.

Science fiction Questions

1 In the title of John Wyndham's 1953 novel, what is the submarine alien which 'wakes'?
2 In Douglas Adams's radio series *The Hitchhiker's Guide to the Galaxy* (which he also wrote as a series of novels, 1979–84), the answer to the great question of life, the Universe and everything is what?
3 How is the brilliant albino chemist Griffin described in the title of an H.G. Wells sci-fi novel of 1897?
4 Which pop group, which came to prominence in 1980, took its name from a character in the cult 1968 sci-fi film *Barbarella*?
5 What name was used in the 1982 sci-fi film *Blade Runner* for a robot with a human appearance?
6 What name is used in science fiction for a theoretical cosmic dimension within which the conventional space-time relationship does not apply?
7 Which sci-fi movie blockbuster of the 1990s featured the world's major cities being violently attacked by alien spaceships?
8 To whom is the catchphrase 'Beam me up, Scotty' in *Star Trek* popularly, but wrongly, attributed?
9 Which 1977 film owed its title to Joseph Allen Hynek, an astronomer at Northwestern University?
10 Who played the Emmy-winning title role of Jaime Sommers in the 1970s ITV series *The Bionic Woman*?
11 After which US inventor and publisher are the annual Hugo Awards for the best science-fiction novel named?
12 Which US sci-fi writer's first book was *Pebble in the Sky* (1950)?
13 In which 1992 sci-fi horror film featuring Harley Stone (played by Rutger Hauer) does the man-versus-monster showdown take place in London's Cannon Street Underground Station?
14 Who composed the music for the 1936 sci-fi film *The Shape of Things to Come*, which became the first film soundtrack to be released commercially?
16 The library of which British university holds the UK Science Fiction Foundation Special Collections and Archive?
17 In 1945 which future sci-fi author wrote for *Wireless World* an article entitled 'Extra-Terrestrial Relays' predicting in detail a satellite communications system which would relay radio and television signals all over the world?
18 Which sci-fi writer has published autobiographical volumes named *Bury My Heart at W.H. Smiths* (1990) and *The Twinkling of an Eye* (1998)?
19 What was the original title which H.G. Wells gave to *The Time Machine* (1895)?
20 The 1950 book *Worlds in Collision* by which Russian-born doctor and psychologist was banned from a number of academic institutions because the scientific establishment refused to accept his challenging views relating ancient myths and legends to cosmological events?

1 **The Kraken** (*The Kraken Wakes*, alternative title *Out of the Deep*).
2 **Forty-two.**
3 ***The Invisible Man.*** The original title of the novel was *Griffin*. He discovered how to eliminate reflection and refraction from his body tissues and thus become invisible.
4 **Duran Duran.**
5 **Replicant.**
6 **Hyperspace.**
7 ***Independence Day*** (1996), starring Jeff Goldblum as the computer buff who saves the US President and the rest of the world, and Will Smith as the intrepid pilot who helps him.
8 **Captain Kirk** (William Shatner). 'Beam us up, Mr Scott' appears to be the nearest version of the sentence actually spoken by Captain Kirk.
9 ***Close Encounters of the Third Kind.*** He studied all the reports of UFO sightings in the 1960s and devised a classification system for reported sightings of aliens.
10 **Lindsay Wagner** (b. 1949). *The Bionic Woman* was a spin-off from *The Six Million Dollar Man* in which Jaime Sommers first appeared. She had a parachuting accident leading to serious injury, after which Steve Austin (the 'Six Million Dollar Man'), insisted that she be given emergency bionic surgery to save her life. She was given bionic legs, a bionic arm and a super-sensitive bionic ear.
11 **Hugo Gernsback** (1884–1967). In 1926 he founded *Amazing Stories*, one of the first magazines devoted to what he called 'scientifiction'.
12 **Isaac Asimov** (1920–92). An academic biochemist, he produced a prodigious body of science fiction, including the four *Foundation* novels. He added the word 'robotics' to the English language.
13 ***Split Second.*** An earlier version had been made in 1953 with Stephen McNally.
14 **Arthur Bliss** (1891–1975). In 1953 he was appointed Master of the Queen's Musick.
16 **Liverpool.** The Science Fiction Foundation was founded in 1970 by the writer and social activist George Hay and others, with Arthur C. Clarke and Ursula K. Le Guin as patrons.
17 **Arthur C. Clarke** (b. 1917), a former RAF radar instructor and technician. The reaction from specialists was sceptical; however, twenty years later the Early Bird satellites were launched.
18 **Brian Aldiss** (b. 1925).
19 ***The Chronic Argonauts.***
20 **Immanuel Velikovsky** (1895–1978). Efforts were made to block dissemination of Velikovsky's ideas and even to punish supporters of his investigations. The furore became known as 'the Velikovsky Affair', and was recorded in a 1966 book of that title by Alfred de Grazia.

General Knowledge

1 Who was the commander of *Stingray*, the atomic submarine of the World Aquanaut Security Patrol (WASP), in the 1960s ITV series of that name?
2 What was the name of the singer and guitarist of the group Nirvana who committed suicide at the age of twenty-seven in his lakeside mansion in Seattle?
3 Traditionally, the Flat Racing season begins and ends at which racecourse?
4 Which English author created the archetypal schoolboy character Jennings, a pupil at Linbury Hall private boarding school?
5 What was the breed of Prince Charles's favourite dog Tigga, which died in March 2002 at the age of eighteen?
6 In the Second World War, Operation Torch was the code name for which Allied landings in November 1942?
7 In David Hockney's 1967 painting *A Bigger Splash*, what is the setting in which the splash takes place?
8 What was the name of the Romanian communist dictator who was overthrown by the army in December 1989 and shot with his wife on Christmas Day?
9 Who was the first commander of the International Space Station, arriving there in November 2000 along with the other crew members?
10 Where, in medieval times, were Courts of Piepowders held?
11 What is the name of the new bridge, the first of its kind – a 'hybrid' cable-stayed bridge made of steel and concrete – across the river in Boston, Massachusetts?
12 Who, according to a poem by Leigh Hunt,
Awoke one night from a deep dream of peace,
And saw, within the moonlight in his room,
Making it rich, and like a lily in bloom,
An angel writing in a book of gold.
13 In which state of the USA did Huey Long (nicknamed 'Kingfish') secure the support of the poor by his intensive 'Share the Wealth' programmes, only to be assassinated in 1935 by Carl Austin Weiss, a man he had vilified?
14 In Greek mythology, which flowers were said to carpet the Fields of Elysium, the abode of the blessed departed?
15 Which prominent Italian director made a series of films in the 1960s and 1970s lambasting the corruption and crime at the heart of Italian political life?
16 In a classical Roman house, what was the *triclinium*?
17 Which Scotsman patented the first telefax machine ('chemical telegraph') in 1846 and demonstrated it at the Great Exhibition of 1851 by sending a facsimile transmission to Paris?
18 Which library, which used to be in the Fawcett Library in London's Guildhall, is now housed in a former washhouse in the city's East End?
19 What was the name of the first chess-playing 'automaton', unveiled by the Hungarian nobleman Wolfgang von Kempelen to the imperial court in Vienna in 1770?
20 Which fantasy and science fiction author wrote the *Discworld* series?

General Knowledge Answers

1 **Troy Tempest** (played by Don Mason).
2 **Kurt Cobain** (1967–94). A biography, *Heavier than Heaven*, by Charles R. Cross, was published in 2001.
3 **Doncaster.** It begins in March and ends in November.
4 **Anthony Buckeridge** (b. 1912). A former boarding-school pupil and prep-school teacher, he wrote twenty-four volumes of Jennings stories, starting with *Jennings Goes to School* (1950).
5 **Jack Russell.**
6 **The North Africa campaign.**
7 **A swimming pool.** It is the last of three paintings in which Hockney tried to capture on canvas the sudden splash of water just after a diver has broken the still surface of the swimming pool. The others are *The Little Splash* and *The Splash* (both 1966 and in private collections). *A Bigger Splash* is in Tate Modern, London.
8 **Nicolai Ceausescu** (1918–89). He had been elected to the newly created post of President in 1974.
9 **William Shepherd** of NASA. The other crew members to arrive with him in a *Soyuz* capsule were the Russian cosmonauts Sergei Krikalev and Yuri Gidzenko.
10 **At fairs and markets**, to settle disputes involving itinerant traders. A piepowder was a travelling merchant; the word derives from an Anglo-Norman word meaning 'dusty-footed'.
11 **Charles River Bridge** (Leonard P. Zakim Bunker Hill Bridge, designed by HNTB). It carries eight lines of traffic across the river, with a further two cantilevered off to the side, and is claimed to be the 'widest cable-stayed bridge in the world'.
12 **Abou Ben Adam**, in a poem of that name (1838).
13 **Louisiana.**
14 **Asphodel.**
15 **Francesco Rosi** (b. 1922). His films included *Salvatore Giuliano* (1962), *The Mattei Affair* (1972) and *Illustrious Corpses* (1975).
16 **Dining room.**
17 **Alexander Bain** (1811–77).
18 **Women's Library**, designed by Sandy Wright of Wright & Wright. Its collection aims to evoke 'a witty, forceful, and often moving, view of women's campaigns and lives over the last 300 years'. It includes women's magazines, larger-than-life posters from the 1970s and 1980s on Greenham Common, abortion and domestic violence, and suffrage propaganda items used in the campaign for the vote.
19 **'The Turk'.** The contraption consisted of a wooden cabinet behind which was seated a life-sized wooden figure of a Turk, run by clockwork. The cabinet housed an elaborate mechanism of densely packed wheels, cogs and levers. The 'machine' defeated many players, including the Emperor Napoleon. In 1863, however, Edgar Allan Poe exposed the fact that 'the Turk' also had an expert chess player hidden in the cabinet.
20 **Terry Pratchett** (b. 1948).

Toys — Questions

1 Which optical toy was first patented in 1817 by the Scottish physicist David Brewster?
2 Which pop singer's first No. 1 hit, in 1959, was *Livin' Doll*?
3 Which children's book by Enid Blyton, published in 1949, gave rise to a range of toys which is now a worldwide industry?
4 Which toy was created in 1956 by Fred Francis, proprietor of a small company named Minimodels, as a simulation of Formula One racing?
5 What is the name of the symphony, now thought to have been written by either Leopold Mozart or Michael Haydn but formerly attributed to Franz Joseph Haydn, which makes use of toy instruments to imitate the sounds of a cuckoo, a quail and a nightingale?
6 Which 'instant fad' toy, inspired by Hawaiian dancing, was first marketed in 1958 by two US entrepreneurs, Richard Knerr and 'Spud' Melin, founders of the Wham-O Company?
7 What was the name of the British-made vinyl teenage doll which was Toy of the Year in 1968, but which disappeared in 1997 after she was sold by Pedigree to Hasbro?
8 In 1923, which traditional plaything, reputed to be based on a hunting weapon used in the Philippines, was introduced to the USA by Pedro Flores, a Filipino bellboy in a Santa Monica hotel?
9 What type of toy was produced by Pelham of Marlborough from 1947 to 1992?
10 Which 'make-your-own' toy character, created by New York designer George Lerner, came as a package of twenty-eight plastic face and body parts, including ears, noses and mouths?
11 Who is the 'dolls expert' on BBC television's *The Antiques Roadshow*?
12 Which make of car was represented by the first die-cast model vehicle, produced by the Dowst Manufacturing Company of Chicago in 1910 in their Tootsie Toys (later Tootsietoys) range?
13 What is the name of the tabletop football game developed in 1947 by Englishman Peter Adolph which still has worldwide devotees of all ages who compete in various leagues and knockouts?
14 Under what trade name did Coleco market from 1983 the handmade cloth dolls which Xavier Roberts designed in 1976 as 'Little People'?
15 Which brand of coloured wax crayons was first marketed by a US chemical company (Binney & Smith) in 1903?
16 Which toy car won the first annual Toy of the Year award, in 1965?
17 Which British doll designer made cloth-and-felt airman and sailor mascots in the 1920s and 1930s?
18 Which toys, now in the Victoria and Albert Museum, are known as 'Lord and Lady Clapham'?
19 Of which popular plaything and sports item was the 'volito', patented in London in 1823, a forerunner?
20 What was the name of the German doll which contributed to the creation of the Barbie doll, which made its debut at the New York Toy Fair in 1959?

1 **Kaleidoscope.** The name is derived from the Greek *kalos* (beautiful), *eidos* (shape) and *skopein* (to see).
2 **Cliff Richard** (b. 1940).
3 ***Little Noddy Goes to Toyland.***
4 **Scalextric.** In 1952 Fred Francis had produced metal racing cars containing a unique type of clockwork motor trademarked 'Scalex'. In 1956 he made an electric motor and modified Scalex to run on a rubber-based track system with two parallel grooves containing metal rails (carrying an electric current) to guide the cars by means of a gimbal wheel suspended beneath them.
5 *Toy Symphony.* Other toy instruments featured are the trumpet, drum, rattle and triangle.
6 **Hula hoop.**
7 **Sindy.**
8 **Yo-yo.** It means 'come-come' in Filipino. Flores started a company to make the toy; it was first mass-produced by the Frank R. Duncan in 1930.
9 **Stringed puppets.** The characters included Noddy, Andy Pandy and Mickey Mouse.
10 **Mr Potato Head.** The parts were for sticking into a potato. In 1964 plastic potato bodies were produced to replace real potatoes.
11 **Bunny Campione.** She first appeared on the programme in 1985, and now runs a fine-art consultancy company covering all antiques.
12 **Model T Ford.**
13 **Subbuteo.** He developed it from a game called Newfooty devised by William Keeling in the 1920s in Liverpool. He was refused a patent for it under the name of 'Hobby'; as a keen birdwatcher, he used instead the Latin name for the hobby falcon, *Falco subbuteo*.
14 **Cabbage Patch Kids.** Each doll had a unique name and birth certificate and came with adoption papers, so that children felt that they were getting a real baby. Xavier Roberts's signature was written on the doll's bottom (in a different colour each year).
15 **Crayola.** The name was coined by Alice Binney, wife of one of the company's founders; it combined the French word for chalk (*craie*) with the Latin *oleum*, olive tree.
16 **James Bond's Aston Martin DB5** (Corgi).
17 **Norah Wellings.** She established the Victoria Toy Works at Wellington, Shropshire, in 1926, making pressed-felt and velveteen-faced dolls with painted features. Many were made as mascots to be sold on the Atlantic liners.
18 **Two William and Mary painted wooden dolls** (c. 1690). They were sold at Sotheby's in 1974 for £16,000, and earned the name because the vendor's family originally lived in Clapham, south London.
19 **Roller skate.** The patent, granted to Robert John Tyers, described the volito as 'an apparatus to be attached to boots, shoes or other covering for the feet for the purpose of travelling or for pleasure'.
20 **Lilli.** Lilli was modelled in 1955 on a sultry caricature in a comic strip in the German magazine *Bild*. Ruth and Elliot Handler formed the Mattel company with Harold Mattson to market a more innocent-looking adult doll; 'Barbie' was the name of the Handlers' daughter, whose paper dolls had originally inspired Ruth to create an adult doll.

General Knowledge Questions

1 After which US President was the 'Teddy Bear', first marketed in 1902 in the USA, named?
2 About what did Wordsworth write a poem whose subtitle is *Sept. 3, 1802* and which begins 'Earth has not anything to show more fair'?
3 Which berries are used for flavouring gin?
4 Which Anglo-Irish author and nationalist wrote a popular spy story about a German invasion of Britain entitled *The Riddle of the Sands* (1903)?
5 Thomas Derbyshire and Robert Harper are the real names of which TV comedy duo?
6 Which former Sussex and England cricket captain was appointed Bishop of Liverpool in 1975?
7 Who was the producer of the 1968 film *The Producers*, which revolved around a deliberately tasteless Broadway production of a musical entitled *Springtime for Hitler*, which it was hoped would fail?
8 In the reign of which British king was the maze at Hampton Court Palace planted?
9 What was the pen name, meaning 'bitter', of the Russian writer Aleksei Maksimovich Peshkov?
10 What is the name of Prince Charles's organic food company?
11 What are the names of the two British medical researchers who developed *in vitro* fertilisation (IVF) of the human egg, and whose work led to the birth of Louise Brown, the world's first test-tube baby, in 1978?
12 The name for which eighteenth-century style of design in art and architecture is derived from a French word for shell-covered rockwork used in the decoration of artificial grottoes?
13 What is the name of the long-distance footpath, one of twelve designated National Trails, which runs 290 kilometres from Sedbury, near Chepstow, to Prestatyn in Flintshire, on the coast of North Wales?
14 Which US pioneer of the solid-bodied electric guitar created the Broadcaster (later Telecaster) and Stratocaster guitars?
15 What is the name of the collapsible baby buggy, replacing the pushchair, which was first produced in 1967?
16 Which British composer wrote the orchestral work *Fantasia on a Theme by Thomas Tallis* in 1910?
17 Which human disaster, according to a report by medical masters at the University of Paris in 1348, was caused by a celestial conjunction of Saturn, Jupiter and Mars in the moist sign of Aquarius at 1pm on 20 March 1345?
18 In mathematical physics, which series, developed in 1822 and named after a French mathematician, is used for analysing the conduction of heat in solid bodies?
19 Who sets the tortuous and torturing crossword puzzle in the *Observer* under the pseudonym Azed?
20 What name was given to the series of miniature toy cars first manufactured by Lesney of London in 1953?

General Knowledge Answers

1 **Theodore ('Teddy') Roosevelt** (1858–1919), President from 1901 to 1909. A Russian immigrant, Morris Mitchtom, saw a newspaper cartoon, by the political cartoonist Clifford Berryman, of Roosevelt refusing to shoot a bear cub while out hunting, and launched a range of Teddy Bears in his small novelty shop in Brooklyn, New York.

2 **London in the early morning** (*Composed Upon Westminster Bridge*).

3 **Juniper** (French *genièvre*, altered by the Dutch to *genever* and shortened by the English to 'gin').

4 **Erskine Childers** (1870–1922). The novel was turned into a 1979 film starring Simon MacCorkindale, Michael York and Jenny Agutter.

5 **Cannon and Ball.**

6 **David Sheppard** (b. 1929). He retired as bishop in 1997.

7 **Mel Brooks.** In the film, Mel Brooks impersonated Hitler. The spoof musical in the film opened for real on Broadway in April 2001 and won a record twelve Tony Awards.

8 **William III** (r. with Mary 1689–94 and alone 1694–1702). It is believed to have been planted with hornbeam, which was replaced by hollies, yews and other evergreens.

9 **(Maxim) Gorky** (1868–1936).

10 **Duchy Originals.** In 1990 the Prince of Wales commissioned some research into the feasibility of a small range of agricultural marketing initiatives, aiming 'to encourage responsible husbandry of the land and environmentally friendly manufacture' and to generate funds for his charitable causes.

11 **Patrick Steptoe** (1913–88) and **Robert Edwards** (b. 1925). Their work was carried out at the Centre for Human Reproduction in Oldham, Lancashire.

12 **Rococo** (from French *rocaille*, rock).

13 **Offa's Dyke Path.** Offa's Dyke was built as a demarcation line (rather than a fortification) between England and Wales by Offa, king of Mercia (r. 757–96). Men from the border country along the Mercian (English) side had to contribute by providing food or building a section of dyke.

14 **Leo Fender** (1909–91).

15 **Maclaren Stroller.** It was invented by Owen Maclaren and first produced in his converted stables. It was revolutionary in its mobility and also that it fits easily into a car or luggage compartment.

16 **Ralph Vaughan Williams** (1872–1958). Thomas Tallis (c. 1510–85) was a significant composer of Tudor sacred music.

17 **The outbreak of the Black Death.** The celestial conjunction was thought to make the earth exhale poisonous vapours; flea-carrying rats, the real cause, went unsuspected.

18 **Fourier series**, after Jean-Baptiste Fourier (1768–1830), who wrote *Théorie analytique de la chaleur* (*Analytical Theory of Heat*, 1822).

19 **Jonathan Crowther.** The pseudonym is the reverse spelling of Deza, one of the Spanish Inquisitors – like his *Observer* predecessors Torquemada and Ximenes.

20 **Matchbox.** When former school friends Rodney Smith and Leslie Smith returned from the Second World War in 1947 they rented a condemned public house from which to run a casting business (Lesney). Their first order was for 20,000 string-cutters. In 1948 they began producing die-cast model cars which used the brand name Moko.

1 Which future Prime Minister 'wrote the whole outline of a proposal for a University of the Air' between church and lunch on Easter Sunday, 1963, and oversaw the launch of the Open University in 1969?
2 What was the University of Newcastle upon Tyne called when it was a college of Durham University?
3 In which 1987 Channel 4 television drama serial, based on a 1974 novel by Tom Sharpe, did David Jason play the role of Skullion, a janitor at a Cambridge college?
4 At which British university was Churchill College established in 1960?
5 Who played the part of the hairdresser who becomes a mature university student in the 1983 film *Educating Rita*, based on the play by Willy Russell?
6 After which famous engineer is the university at Uxbridge named?
7 Where did the Holy Roman Emperor, Charles IV, found the first university in central Europe in 1348?
8 At Oxford, who are familiarly known as 'bulldogs'?
9 At which university is a first-year student called a 'bejan' or 'bajan'?
10 What are the names of the two universities in Leeds?
11 Which English novelist wrote *The Masters* (1951), set in a Cambridge college, and coined the phrase 'The Two Cultures' to highlight the divide between science and the humanities in British culture?
12 In which fictional south-coast English 'plate-glass' university did Malcolm Bradbury set his 1975 novel *The History Man*, later dramatised for TV?
13 Which is the oldest university in Germany?
14 Which Cambridge college has a famous sundial dating from 1642 about which the antiquary Cole recorded in about 1733: 'on ye Wall of ye Chapel and over ye Door wch leads to it is also lately painted a very elegant Sun Dial with all ye signs. This is no small ornam^{t} to ye Court to enliven it'?
15 Which ancient Italian university, founded in the ninth century, housed what was considered the finest medical school in early-medieval times?
16 A campus of which university is based at Ivy House, which was once the home of ballerina Anna Pavlova and still houses her archives?
17 Which British university college has a 'Mathematical Bridge'?
18 At which German university was the religious reformer Martin Luther the professor of biblical exegesis when he nailed his 'Ninety-Five Theses' to the door of the Schlosskirche in 1517?
19 The campus of which university in California consists largely of the former Palo Alto farm of its founders, after whom it is named – a railroad magnate and his wife, who dedicated the university to their deceased only child, Leland?
20 Which Ancient Greek philosopher founded the Academy in Athens on the site of an olive grove sacred to the legendary Attic hero Academus, after whom the Academy was named?

1 **Harold Wilson** (1916–95). He was Prime Minister from 1964 to 1970 and 1974 to 1976.

2 **King's College.** The University originated in a School of Medicine and Surgery (later the College of Medicine, established in 1834) and Armstrong College (1871) for the teaching of physical sciences. The Newcastle colleges merged to form King's College, Durham, in 1937 and in 1963 King's College became the University of Newcastle upon Tyne.

3 ***Porterhouse Blue.***

4 **Cambridge.** Churchill College is the national and Commonwealth memorial to Winston Spencer Churchill (1874–1965).

5 **Julie Walters** (b. 1950). Her tutor was played by Michael Caine.

6 **Isambard Kingdom Brunel** (1806–59) – Brunel University.

7 **Prague** (Universita Karlova, Charles University).

8 **A proctor's bowler-hatted assistants.** Proctors are college tutors with the duties of enforcing discipline; 'bulldogs' are college porters appointed to accompany them on patrols through the streets, and to assist them on ceremonial occasions.

9 **St Andrews.** The word derives from the Anglo-Norman *bec jaune*, a young bird.

10 **University of Leeds** and **Leeds Metropolitan University.**

11 **C.P. Snow** (1905–80).

12 **Watermouth.** The 1981 serial adapted for television by Christopher Hampton starred Anthony Sher in the title role.

13 **Heidelberg.** It was founded in 1386 by the Elector Rupert I.

14 **Queens' College, Cambridge.** It is not known whether the design was new in 1733, or merely repainted.

15 **Salerno.** The university was so prestigious that in 1221 the Holy Roman Emperor Frederick II decreed that no doctor in the kingdom could practise medicine legally until he had been examined and approved by the school at Salerno.

16 **Middlesex.** At Ivy House, near Hampstead Heath, London, Anna Pavlova had an ornamental lake on which she kept swans. The library now resides in what was once her bedroom; adjoining this is her mirror-lined rehearsal studio.

17 **Cambridge.** The original wooden bridge over the Cam at Queens' College was built in 1749 by James Essex the Younger (1722–1784) to the design of William Etheridge (1709–1776). It was rebuilt in 1866 and again in 1905 to the same design.

18 **Wittenberg.**

19 **Stanford.** It was founded in 1885 and opened in 1891 by Leland Stanford (senior) and his wife, Jane.

20 **Plato** (c. 428–c. 348 BC).

1 In *Jude the Obscure* what name did Thomas Hardy give to the university city of Oxford?
2 Who wrote the 1987 children's book *Madame Doubtfire*, on which the 1993 film *Mrs Doubtfire* was based, starring Robin Williams and Sally Field?
3 Which spice is obtained from the stigmas of the crocus?
4 Which group had a UK No. 1 hit in 1967 with *Silence Is Golden*?
5 Who played the part of Oz, one of the three unemployed Tyneside bricklayers in the 1983–6 ITV series *Auf Wiedersehen Pet*, which was revived by the BBC in 2002?
6 In which island prison off the coast of Cape Province, in South Africa, was Nelson Mandela jailed for treason between 1964 and 1982?
7 Which popular workbench for DIY enthusiasts was patented as the 'Minibench' in 1968 by Lotus car engineer Ron Hickman?
8 What is a 'magnus hitch'?
9 Who was appointed Minister for Sport in 2001 in succession to Kate Hoey?
10 Which British monarch lost his throne in the 'Glorious Revolution' of 1688?
11 Which popular Greek singer was one of the hostages held in Beirut when terrorists hijacked a TWA airliner after take-off from Athens in June 1985?
12 The feast day of which fourth-century French bishop, regarded as the patron saint of lawyers, was the first day of the term named after him at the Inns of Court and old universities?
13 Who was the designer-engineer of the magnificent iron-trough Pontcysyllte aqueduct near Llangollen in North Wales, which carries the Llangollen Canal over the River Dee?
14 The spicy Chinese soup known as 'bird's-nest soup' is made from the nests of which bird?
15 In ecclesiastical architecture, what is the name given to a porch or chapel at the west end of some medieval churches and cathedrals in England?
16 Which seventeenth-century Dutch painter's *The Art of Painting* depicts an artist at his easel, with his back to the viewer, painting a young woman posing as Clio, the Muse of History?
17 In February 1957 which television current affairs programme broke the so-called 'toddlers' truce' – the break in television programmes between 6 and 7pm which gave parents time to get their children to bed?
18 Who was the commander of the French fleet which was defeated by Nelson at the Battle of Trafalgar in 1805?
19 For what is an *abra* used in Dubai?
20 At which British university is the Cavendish Laboratory, the centre for experimental physics founded by the Duke of Devonshire in 1871?

General Knowledge Answers

1 **Christminster.**
2 **Anne Fine** (b. 1947), who was nominated Children's Laureate in 2001.
3 **Saffron.** British towns which have been named after the crocuses grown around them included Saffron Walden (Essex) and Croydon (Greater London), from *Crogedene* (meaning a valley where wild saffron grows).
4 **The Tremeloes**, formerly the backing group of Brian Poole.
5 **Jimmy Nail.** The other bricklayers were Dennis (Tim Healy) and Neville (Kevin Whately).
6 **Robben Island.** In 1982 Nelson Mandela was moved to the maximum-security Pollsmoor Prison, where he remained until 1988, when he was admitted to hospital with tuberculosis. The South African government under President F.W. de Klerk released him on 11 February 1990.
7 **Black and Decker Workmate.** Ron Hickman had approached Black and Decker with his idea in 1967 but had been turned down. He began to manufacture it himself, but Black and Decker changed their mind and began producing the Workmate in 1972.
8 **A knot**, similar to a clove hitch but having one more turn.
9 **Richard Caborn** (b. 1943), MP for Sheffield Central and formerly Minister for Trade at the Department for Trade and Industry (1999–2001).
10 **James II and VII**, the last male monarch of the Stewart dynasty. He fled to France after William of Orange (his son-in-law, the future William III) landed unopposed at Torbay in November 1688.
11 **Demis Roussos** (b. 1946).
12 **St Hilary of Poitiers** (c. 315–c. 368). His feast day is on 13 or 14 January.
13 **Thomas Telford** (1757–1834). It is 307 metres long and 38 metres high.
14 **Asian swift**, of the genus *Collocalia*. Recipe: soak nests overnight, wash thoroughly and clean with peanut oil; drain, rinse and leave to dry. Remove feathers, twigs and other debris. Pound a chicken breast and mince to pulp. Mix 2 tbsp cornflour with 2 tbsp chicken stock. Bring 150ml chicken stock to boil. Add 100g bird's nest and simmer for 30 minutes. Dribble 1 tbsp dry sherry into minced chicken. Lightly beat 2 egg whites and fold into chicken (do not blend completely). Bring soup back to boil. Slowly add chicken stock mixture. Add salt and bring to boil.
15 **Galilee.**
16 **Jan Vermeer** (1632–75). The painting is in the Kunsthistorisches Museum, Vienna.
17 ***Tonight***, a pioneering early-evening news magazine which ran from 1957 to 1965, with Cliff Michelmore as the front man and Alan Whicker, Derek Hart and Fyfe Robertson among its roving reporters.
18 **Pierre Charles Jean Baptiste Sylvestre de Villeneuve** (1763–1806). Villeneuve had been ordered to sail from Cadiz into the Mediterranean for an attack on Naples, but, hearing of his imminent replacement by another officer, he led his fleet to face that of Nelson in the Battle of Trafalgar. He was taken prisoner by the British but released in 1806; he committed suicide on his way to Paris to report to Napoleon.
19 **Crossing the creek which divides the city in two.** An *abra* is a basic water bus which plies non-stop from bank to bank.
20 **Cambridge.** It was founded in memory of the physicist Henry Cavendish (1731–1810), who first identified hydrogen as a distinct substance.

Viking Age

1 Which momentous event in 793 is said to mark the onset of the Viking Age?
2 What name was given to the eastern region of England, conquered and occupied by Danish armies in the ninth century, which had its own legal customs and laws?
3 Which viking raider founded the duchy of Normandy in the tenth century?
4 What is the name given to the tribute with which the Anglo-Saxon king Ethelred II bought off the Danish invaders during his reign (978–1016)?
5 What is the name of the annual fire festival in Shetland, held in Lerwick on the last Tuesday of January?
6 Which naval battle off the south-west of Norway late in the ninth century enabled Harald Fine-Hair (*hárfagri*) to unite the whole of Norway under a single crown?
7 What was the name of the fortified military encampment on the Baltic coast which was the headquarters of the Jómsvikings, the semi-legendary professional warriors in the tenth century whose adventures are recounted in *Jómsvíkinga Saga*?
8 Which Scottish historical novelist published, in 1817, a long narrative poem set in Viking times, *Harold the Dauntless*?
9 What name was given to the elite unit of Scandinavian mercenaries of the tenth and eleventh centuries who served as part of the imperial guard of the Byzantine emperors in Constantinople?
10 Which warrior king of Norway invaded the north of England in September 1066, only to be defeated and killed by Harold of England three weeks before the Battle of Hastings?
11 What is the name of the excavated site in Newfoundland which has been identified as a small viking settlement dating from the Norse discovery and attempted colonisation of North America c. 1000?
12 What is the name of the Neolithic burial mound on the Mainland of Orkney which contains twenty-four runic inscriptions dating from the twelfth century?
13 Which tenth-century king of Denmark erected the great three-sided rune-stone at Jelling, in Jutland, in memory of his father Gorm *gamli* ('the Old') and mother Thyri, whom he describes as 'Denmark's Glory'?
14 Which US actor and director provided the narration for the 1958 film *The Vikings*, starring Kirk Douglas, Tony Curtis, Janet Leigh and Ernest Borgnine?
15 What was the name of the adventurer who was outlawed from Iceland in 1084 and explored the unknown island of Greenland, where he founded a Norse colony?
16 In which Danish fjord were five eleventh-century viking ships discovered and excavated in the 1960s?
17 According to the *Russian Primary Chronicle* (c. 860), who was the Scandinavian founder of the 'Rus' state at Novgorod?
18 At which battle in Essex in 991 did Byrhtnoth, the noble *ealdorman* of Essex, lose his life in an epic stand against an invading viking army?
19 Which island in the Baltic holds a unique collection of 370 carved 'picture stones' dating from the fifth century onwards, as well as some 50,000 silver Arabic (Kufic) coins?
20 What was the title of the saga-novel published in 1891 by Rider Haggard after a long visit to Iceland in 1888?

Viking Age

Answers

1 **The raid on the church and monastery on the 'Holy Island' of Lindisfarne on 7 June 793.** It was the earliest securely dated viking raid, from Hordaland, in western Norway.

2 **The Danelaw** (from the Anglo-Saxon *Dena lagu*). In 886 Alfred the Great signed a peace treaty with the Danes which effectively partitioned England.

3 **Rollo**, known in Icelandic sources as Hrólfur, nicknamed Göngu-Hrólfur (Walker-Hrólfur) because he was so huge that no horse could carry him and he had to walk. In 911, King Charles III ('The Simple') granted him the lands of Normandy in exchange for his promise to defend France against further viking inroads.

4 **Danegeld** (from the Old Norse *Dana*, of Danes, and *gjald*, payment).

5 **Up-Helly-Aa** (derived from 'Uphalliday', when the holidays of Yuletide were 'up', or over). Up-Helly-Aa is a late-Victorian development of a boisterous celebration of Twelfth Night, refined into a 'viking' fire festival which culminates in the torchlight ceremonial burning of a viking galley.

6 **Havrsfjord** (known as *Hafrsfjörður* in the Icelandic sources). Harald faced, c. 890, a confederate fleet of Norwegian chieftains and independent 'kings' off Stavanger and won a resounding victory.

7 **Jómsborg**. Archaeologists have identified it with the port and island of Wolin near the mouth of the River Oder in Poland.

8 **Walter Scott** (1771–1832). Scott published a précis in English of one of the Icelandic sagas (*Eyrbyggja Saga*, 1813) and wrote a novel set in the Northern Isles of Scotland but rooted in their viking past, *The Pirate* (1822).

9 **Varangian Guard**. It was a type of viking Foreign Legion.

10 **Harald *harðráði*** ('Hard-Ruler'), sole ruler of Norway from 1047 to 1066.

11 **L'Anse aux Meadows**. It was excavated in the 1960s by Helgi Ingstad and his wife Anne Stine; the site has been reconstructed by Parks Canada as a National Historic Park.

12 **Maeshowe**. Most of the runic graffiti were incised by a band of 'Jerusalem-farers' (crusaders) who broke into the mound in search of treasure.

13 **Harald *blátönn* ('Bluetooth') Gormsson** (c. 910–85), the first Christian king of Denmark. On the rune-stone he said that 'he won for himself all Denmark and Norway, and made the Danes Christian'.

14 **Orson Welles** (1915–85).

15 **Eiríkur *rauði*** (Eirik the Red). He was the father of Leifur Eiríksson (Leifur *heppni*, Leif the Lucky).

16 **Roskilde**, at Skuldelev. The ships had been filled with boulders and scuttled in order to block the main navigational channel as a defence against Harald *harðráði*, king of Norway, around 1045. They have been restored and are on display in the Viking Ship Museum at Roskilde.

17 **Rurik**.

18 **Maldon**. A celebrated Old English poem, *The Battle of Maldon*, movingly expresses the old Germanic warrior ethic of heroic valour:

Mind must be mightier, heart the fiercer
Courage the greater, as our strength lessens.

19 **Gotland**.

20 ***Eric Brighteyes***.

General Knowledge Questions

1 What is the literal meaning of the Old Icelandic word 'saga'?
2 On 2 April 2002 which jockey beat the record of 269 winners ridden in a season set by Gordon Richards in 1947?
3 Which veteran TV comedian emerged from fourteen years of retirement in 2002 to play the role of Winston Churchill's butler in the biographical drama *Churchill – The Gathering Storm*?
4 What is the title of the first musical on which Andrew Lloyd Webber and Tim Rice collaborated?
5 Which fruit releases the gas ethylene (ethene), which promotes the ripening of other fruits placed close to it and is used commercially for ripening stored fruit which has been harvested while unripe?
6 What is the popular Swiss dish made from grated potatoes, sautéed, pressed into a frying pan in pancake form and cooked on the hob?
7 Which leading Conservative politician was assassinated by a car bomb within the precincts of the Palace of Westminster in April 1979?
8 The title of which novel by H.E. Bates was the first line of Michael Drayton's 1606 poem *Agincourt*?
9 What is the more familiar name for Hansen's disease, named after the Norwegian physician and bacteriologist who discovered, in 1869, the bacillus which causes it?
10 Who succeeded the late Donald Dewar as First Minister of Scotland in October 2000, only to resign in November 2001 during a media scandal over his office expenses?
11 Which institution in London has been the location for the annual televised Christmas Science lectures since 1966?
12 What is the present name of the Middle Eastern capital city once known as Philadelphia?
13 In which language was France's entry in the 1996 Eurovision Song Contest, *Diwanit Bugale (May the Children Be Born)*, sung by Dan ar Braz et l'Héritage des Celtes?
14 Of which British tribe in Yorkshire was Cartimandua the pro-Roman queen?
15 What is the name of the three-legged symbol of the Isle of Man?
16 Which Oxford college, founded in 1438 by Henry VI and Henry Chichele (fellow of New College and Archbishop of Canterbury), is limited to forty graduates who win a place by competitive examination?
17 Which seventh-century saint, whose feast day is 2 March, was the younger brother of St Cedd and moved the bishopric of Mercia from Repton to Lichfield?
18 Which Atlantic fish is sometimes known as 'sailor's choice'?
19 In the 'Long Parliament' of Charles I's reign, who were the 'Five Members' of the opposition whom the king tried unsuccessfully to arrest in January 1642?
20 Which archaeologist presented the TV series *Blood of the Vikings* on BBC2 in 2001?

1 **Saying** (something told, from the verb *segja*, to say). It now refers specifically to the medieval prose narratives written in Iceland about historical or legendry characters from the Nordic past.
2 **Tony McCoy**, riding Valfonic in the Wooton Novices' Handicap Hurdle at Leek, Staffordshire.
3 **Ronnie Barker** (b. 1929). He retired from show business in 1988 to run an antiques shop in Chipping Sodbury in the Cotswolds.
4 ***Joseph and the Amazing Technicolor Dreamcoat*** (1968).
5 **Banana.**
6 **Rösti.**
7 **Airey Neave** (1916–79). A former Army intelligence officer, he masterminded Margaret Thatcher's bid for the leadership of the Conservative Party in 1975, and was appointed Shadow Secretary of State for Northern Ireland.
8 ***Fair Stood the Wind for France*** (1944):
Fair stood the wind for France
When we our sails advance,
Nor now to prove our chance
Longer will tarry.
9 **Leprosy.** It was named after Gerhard Hansen (1841–1912).
10 **Henry McLeish.** Donald Dewar, Scotland's first First Minister, died on 11 October 2000.
11 **Royal Institution of Great Britain**, in Albemarle Street, Mayfair. The Royal Institution was founded in 1799 'for diffusing the Knowledge, and facilitating the General Introduction, of Useful Mechanical Inventions and Improvements; and for teaching, by Courses of Philosophical Lectures and Experiments, the application of Science to the common Purposes of Life'.
12 **Amman**, the capital of Jordan. By about 1200 BC it was the Ammonite capital Rabbath-Ammon, and was renamed Philadelphia after the Ptolemaic ruler Philadelphus in the third century BC. The city was captured by the Arabian armies of Islam around 635, after which the name of the city reverted to Ammon or Amman.
13 **Breton.**
14 **Brigantes.**
15 **Triskelion** (from Greek *triskeles*, three-legged).
16 **All Souls** (The College of All Souls of the Faithful Departed). The fellows take Holy Orders: twenty-four study arts, philosophy and theology; and sixteen study civil or canon law.
17 **St Chad** (d. 672). He was the first bishop of Mercia and Lindsey at Lichfield, Staffordshire.
18 **Pinfish**, a small porgy (*Lagodon rhomboides*). The nickname apparently derives from its spines.
19 **John Pym, John Hampden, Arthur Heselrig, Denzil Holles** and **William Strode**. The king forcibly entered the House of Commons with four hundred soldiers, but 'the birds had flown'. The Speaker, William Lenthall (1591–1662), refused to answer any questions about them with the classic riposte, 'I have neither eye to see, nor tongue to speak here, but as the House is pleased to direct me.'
20 **Julian Richards.**

1 In which medieval bastion in Gwynedd was Prince Charles invested as Prince of Wales in 1969?
2 The 40-hectare estate of which Tudor mansion near Cardiff, donated by the Earl of Plymouth, is now home to the Museum of Welsh Life?
3 At which ruined abbey in the Wye Valley in Monmouthshire did Wordsworth write the following elegiac lines?

. . . I have learned
To look on nature, not as in the hour
Of thoughtless youth, but hearing often-times
The still, sad music of humanity . . .

4 Which town in the Rhymney Valley in Mid-Glamorgan, superintended by a great medieval castle, is famous for its creamy, white cheese?
5 Who was the first Welsh-born actor to win a Academy Award for Best Actor?
6 Where in Carmarthenshire did the poet Dylan Thomas and his wife Caitlin make their home from 1949 until his death in 1953?
7 Which Romano-British historian and monk wrote the sixth-century treatise *De Excidio et Conquestu Britanniae*, the only contemporary British account of events from the invasion of the Romans down to his own time?
8 What is the Welsh name for 'plate cake', made on a bakestone from a traditional Glamorgan recipe?
9 Which Welsh buccaneer famously captured Porto Bello and Panama in 1671, was knighted in 1674 and became Deputy Governor of Jamaica?
10 Which native tribe in mid-Wales, eventually conquered by the Romans in the first century AD, has given its name to a geological period in the Palaeozoic Era?
11 To which sixth-century Welsh bard, considered the founder of the Welsh poetic tradition, is there a monument on the banks of Llyn Geirionydd in Caernarfonshire, where he is thought to have been born?
12 Which artist, born in Haverfordwest, Pembrokeshire, set off in 1903 with her friend Dorelia McNeill to walk to Rome, but got only as far as Paris, where she settled and produced works including a series of ten pictures of a neighbour entitled *The Convalescent*?
13 What is the terminus of the narrow-gauge Ffestiniog railway, which crosses The Cob from the slate town of Blaenau Ffestiniog to the sea?
14 In which small Welsh town near Criccieth, Gwynedd, was David Lloyd George (Prime Minister from 1916 to 1922) brought up by his mother and his uncle, the village cobbler?
15 What name was given to the bands of Welsh tenant farmers disguised as women who demolished toll gates and rioted against rates and rents between 1839 and 1844?
16 Who wrote the 1940 classic novel *Owen Glendower*, which was reissued in paperback in 2002?
17 Which Dublin-born society lady settled in Plas Newydd in the Vale of Llangollen in 1778 with her friend Sarah Ponsonby, where they became known as 'the Queens of Llangollen'?
18 What is the term for the Welsh bagpipe?
19 What is the name of the twelfth-century Welsh prince who was long believed to have discovered America in 1170?
20 According to the old rhyme, which are the Seven Wonders of Wales?

1 **Caernarfon Castle**. It was built by Edward I in the 1280s.
2 **St Fagans Castle**. The museum has a collection of vernacular buildings from all over Wales which have been rescued from demolition.
3 **Tintern Abbey** (*Lines Composed a Few Miles above Tintern Abbey*, 1798).
4 **Caerphilly**.
5 **Ray Milland** (Reginald Truscott-Jones, 1905–86). Born in Neath, he won his Academy Award for his role in the 1945 film *The Lost Weekend*.
6 **Laugharne** (at the Boat House). The house, overlooking the 'heron-priested' shore, and Dylan's nearby 'writing shed', have become popular tourist attractions.
7 **St Gildas** (c. 500–c. 570). He was born in Strathclyde, in Scotland, and became a monk in South Wales.
8 ***Teisen lap***.
9 **Henry Morgan** (c. 1635–88). Born in Llanrhymney, Glamorgan, he was kidnapped as a child and shipped to Barbados, where he joined the buccaneers.
10 **Silures**. In 1835 Roderick Impey Murchison (1792–1871) named a sequence of rocks in Wales and its borderland with England 'Silurian' in honour of the Silures, who had resisted Roman conquest for many years.
11 **Taliesin** (fl. 550).
12 **Gwen John** (1876–1939), sister of the flamboyant Augustus John (1878–1961). One of the paintings entitled *The Convalescent* (1918–19) is in Tate Britain, London.
13 **Porthmadog Harbour station**. The station buildings house a small museum whose prize exhibit is a railway hearse.
14 **Llanystumdwy**. He was born in Manchester, where his father, a Welshman from Pembrokeshire, was a headmaster; his mother moved to Llanystumdwy after his father died.
15 **Daughters of Rebecca** (the sister of Laban in Genesis). The 'Rebecca Rioters' took their name from Genesis 24:60: 'And they blessed Rebecca and said unto her, "Thou art our sister, be thou the mother of thousands of millions, and let thy seed possess the gate of those which hate them".'
16 **John Cowper Powys** (1872–1963).
17 **Lady Eleanor Butler** (1739–1829).
18 ***Pibacwd*** (Welsh *piba*, tube or pipe, and *cwd*, bag or pouch).
19 **Madoc** (Madog ap Owain Gwynedd, c. 1150–80). The story of his voyage appeared in Richard Hakluyt's *Divers Voyages Touching the Discoverie of America* (1582), but has since been proved to be fictitious. At Rhos, in North Wales, there is a plaque which announces that 'Prince Madoc sailed from here to Mobile, Alabama'.
20 ***Pistyll Rhaedr and Wrexham steeple,***
Snowdon's mountain without its people,
Overton yew trees, St Winifred's Wells,
Llangollen Bridge and Gresford bells.

The 'Seven Wonders' are all in North Wales. Pistyll Rhaedr ('the spring of the waterfall'), in the Tanat Valley, is the highest waterfall in Wales (74 metres). Wrexham Steeple is not a steeple at all, but the sixteenth-century tower of the Church of St Giles. Yew trees in the churchyard at Overton (near Bangor-on-Dee) date back to at least the twelfth century.

General Knowledge Questions

1 Which industrial area in South Wales became a World Heritage Site in 2000?

2 Which football club was the first English team to win a European trophy?

3 Which Gilbert and Sullivan operetta is set in the Tower of London?

4 Which actors portrayed the rival barristers in the 2002 ITV drama series *The Jury*?

5 By what name is the pop singer Marvin Lee Aday, whose album *Bat Out of Hell* (1977) was one of the best-selling albums ever, better known?

6 About what was Sylvia Plath writing in the following lines?

Overnight, very
Whitely, discreetly,
Very quietly
Our toes, our noses
Take hold on the loam,
Acquire the air.

7 Who starred in the 1997 British comedy film *The Full Monty* as an unemployed Sheffield steelworker named Gaz leading a group of five others in a striptease show?

8 Which Hebridean island was purchased in a community buyout in 2001?

9 Which outsize star of silent movies was charged with the manslaughter of a starlet after she died of complications following an alleged sexual assault by him?

10 In 1899 which German company patented the anti-inflammatory and pain-relief drug aspirin, which had been developed in a usable form from salicylic acid in 1853 by the French chemist Charles Frédéric Gerhardt but never marketed?

11 In which Cornish town is the second of the Prince's Foundation's 'urban villages', popularly dubbed 'Charlie Town 2'?

12 Which French Existentialist philosopher and writer was awarded the Nobel Prize for literature in 1964 but declined to accept it?

13 Who was the Danish architect of the Sydney Opera House, which has been called the 'Eighth Wonder of the Modern World'?

14 Which English Quaker and philanthropist was a pioneering prison reformer who combined this work with looking after a large family?

15 What is the more common name of the purple-flowered herbaceous vine sometimes known as bittersweet?

16 What name has been given to the diptych, by an unknown fourteenth-century artist and now in the National Gallery, London, in which one panel depicts Richard II as one of the three kings in the Adoration of the Magi?

17 Which province of Uzbekistan is thought to be the origin of the word 'buckram', now used for a type of stiffened cloth?

18 Which advertising copywriter devised the evocative (but ultimately ineffective) slogan 'You're never alone with a Strand' in 1960?

19 Which saint, whose feast day is 4 February in Northampton and 16 February in Nottingham, was the founder of the only English monastic order?

20 Built on the west bank of the River Wye in Monmouthshire in about 1070, which is considered to be the oldest stone castle in the UK?

General Knowledge Answers

1 **Blaenafon.** The Blaenafon Ironworks, founded in 1757, grew into one of the largest in Wales but closed down in 1980. It forms the centrepiece of the Big Pit Mining Museum, which was opened in 1983.
2 **Tottenham Hotspur** (1963). Spurs won the European Cup Winners Cup that year, beating Atletico Madrid 5–1 in Rotterdam.
3 ***The Yeomen of the Guard*** (1888).
4 **Antony Sher** (Gerald Lewis, prosecution QC) and **Derek Jacobi** (George Cording, defence QC).
5 **Meatloaf.** The name originated when he was at school, when a football coach bestowed it on him because of his great size and ungainly movements.
6 **Mushrooms** (in *Mushrooms*, first published in *The Colossus*, 1960).
7 **Robert Carlyle** (b. 1961).
8 **Gigha.**
9 **Roscoe ('Fatty') Arbuckle** (1887–1933). He was acquitted, but his screen career was ended by the publicity. Later he returned to film-making as a director under the pseudonym 'William B. Goodrich'.
10 **Bayer.** The painkilling properties of salicin, derived from willow, had long been known, and Gerhardt was the first to find a way of 'buffering' salicylic acid (using acetyl chloride) to prevent damage to the stomach, but he did not market it. Felix Hoffmann of Bayer rediscovered Gerhardt's formula and made it up to treat his father's arthritis. Hoffmann then persuaded Bayer to market the drug, which they named 'Aspirin': 'a' from acetyl chloride, 'spir' from *Spiraea ulmaria* (the plant source of salicylic acid) and 'in' (the common suffix for medicines).
11 **St Austell.** The first was Poundbury, Dorset.
12 **Jean-Paul Sartre** (1905–80).
13 **Jørn Utzon** (b. 1918).
14 **Elizabeth Fry** (1780–1845). Her reports and recommendations led to radical changes in prison conditions throughout most of Europe.
15 **Woody nightshade** (*Solanum dulcamara*).
16 ***Wilton Diptych.*** It takes its name from Wilton House, near Salisbury, Wiltshire, seat of the earls of Pembroke, who once owned the diptych.
17 **Bukhara,** once an important source of textiles. In the fifteenth century attorneys carried green briefcases made of buckram, and the word came to be associated with stiff pomposity.
18 **John May** (1926–2002). He also devised the 'Mars 1970' campaign for Shell/BP's promotion of oil-fired central heating in the 1950s.
19 **St Gilbert of Sempringham** (c. 1083–1189), in Lincolnshire, founder of the Gilbertine Order of nuns and monks. He was canonised by Pope Innocent III in 1202. The Gilbertine Order was dissolved at the Reformation.
20 **Chepstow.** It was built by William FitzOsbern, Earl of Hereford (d. 1071) one of William the Conqueror's closest circle of friends. The castle is now a ruin.

Youth

Questions

1 Which US paediatrician influenced generations of post-war parents with his *Common Sense Book of Baby and Child Care* (1946)?
2 Which children's charity was launched in 1986 by Esther Rantzen?
3 Whose recording of *Young Hearts Run Free* reached No. 2 in the UK charts in 1976?
4 Which US perfume house created *Youth Dew* in 1952?
5 In Greek mythology, what was the name of the beautiful youth, loved by both Aphrodite and Persephone, who was gored to death by a wild boar?
6 Which religious movement in Europe in 1212 was led by a French shepherd boy named Stephen, from Cloyes-sur-le-Loir, near Vendôme, after he had a vision in which Jesus appeared to him disguised as a pilgrim?
7 Who became the youngest person to graduate from Oxford University (St Hugh's College) when she gained a first-class degree in maths at thirteen, having also been the youngest person to pass O-level maths at eight?
8 Which First World War poet wrote *Anthem for Doomed Youth* in 1917?
9 Which Shakespearian character sings:

Then come kiss me, sweet and twenty,
Youth's a stuff will not endure.

10 What name is given to the symbolic drink taken during the initiation ceremony when Sikh boys and girls are admitted to the Khalsa (the 'brotherhood', founded by Guru Gobind Singh in 1699)?
11 The establishment of which London hospital, by the philanthropist shipbuilder and seafarer Thomas Coram, assisted by the artist William Hogarth, was given a Royal Charter by George II in 1739?
12 Which garden plant of the aster family, which originated in Mexico, is known as 'Youth and Old Age'?
13 To which French statesman of the early twentieth century is attributed the apophthegm 'Anyone who is not a radical at sixteen has no heart – anyone who is not a conservative at sixty has no head'?
14 What was the name of the nine-year-old girl who wrote the comic classic *The Young Visiters* – a child's-eye view of romance and high society?
15 In 1844 who formed a club in London for the 'improvement of the spiritual condition of young men in the drapery and other trades', which led to the development of the YMCA (Young Men's Christian Association)?
16 In 1907 which Italian physician and educationist opened the first Casa dei Bambini (Children's House), a school for young slum children in Rome, and established the educational system which bears her name?
17 Which sixteenth-century French philosopher wrote, '*Si jeunesse savait, si vieillesse pouvait*' ('If youth but knew, if old age but could')?
18 Who was venerated as the Norse goddess of spring and rejuvenation?
19 Which English poet wrote the following lines?

Oh, talk not to me of a name great in story;
The days of our youth are the days of our glory;
And the myrtle and ivy of sweet two-and-twenty
Are worth all your laurels, though ever so plenty.

20 According to Ovid's *Metamorphoses*, which Phrygian youth was loved by Cybele with a chaste passion on condition that he remained a virgin, but was driven mad by her jealousy and castrated himself?

1 **Benjamin Spock** (1903–98).
2 **ChildLine.** Esther Rantzen is chairman of ChildLine, which is a free national helpline for children in trouble or danger.
3 **Candi Staton** (b. 1943).
4 **Estée Lauder.** The ingredients include top notes of orange and spices, with a heart of floral fragrances such as rose, ylang-ylang, orange blossom and mandarin, modified by cassie, cinnamon and carnation, and balsamic base notes such as amber and balsam of Tolu.
5 **Adonis.**
6 **The Children's Crusade.** Some 30,000 children set out to wrest the Holy Land from the Muslims by love instead of by force; none of them reached their destination – at Marseilles they were carried off by merchants and sold to slave markets. However, the religious fervour excited by the Children's Crusade helped to initiate the Fifth Crusade (1218).
7 **Ruth Lawrence.** She became a professor by the age of nineteen, and now lectures at the Institute of Mathematics of the Hebrew University in Jerusalem.
8 **Wilfred Owen** (1893–1918):
What passing-bells for those who die as cattle?
Only the monstrous anger of the guns.
9 **The Clown**, in *Twelfth Night* (Act II, scene iii), in the song 'O mistress mine, where are you roaming?'
10 ***Amrit.*** It is made from sugar and water and stirred (using a ceremonial steel sword) in a steel bowl.
11 **The Foundling Hospital.**
12 **Zinnia** (*Zinnia elegans*). It was named after the German botanist Johann Zinn, a friend of Linnaeus, who collected the plants during expeditions to Mexico.
13 **Georges Clemenceau** (1841–1929), Prime Minister of France from 1906 to 1909 and 1917 to 1920.
14 **Daisy Ashford** (1881–1972). She wrote it in 1890 and the manuscript lay forgotten in a drawer until 1919, when it was published with a preface by J.M. Barrie. Unpunctuated and wonderfully misspelt, it tells of the adventures of Ethel Monticue and her admirer Mr Salteena ('I am parshial to ladies if they are nice I suppose it is my nature').
15 **George Williams** (1821–1905). He was an employee in the drapery firm of Hitchcock & Rogers at the time, and subsequently became a wealthy draper.
16 **Maria Montessori** (1870–1952), There are now Montessori schools throughout the world, based on stimulating children's interest and, through the use of simple materials, enabling sustained concentration.
17 **Henri Estienne** (c. 1531–1698), in *Les Prémices* (1594).
18 **Iðunn** ('the rejuvenating one'). She was the wife of Bragi, the god of poetry, and the keeper of the magic apples of immortality, which the gods had to eat to preserve their youth.
19 **Lord Byron** (1788–1824), *Stanzas Written on the Road between Florence and Pisa, November 1821.*
20 **Attis** (Atys). Cybele (the mother goddess of Phrygia) changed him into a pine tree when he was about to commit suicide.

1 In classical mythology, which beautiful youth was carried off to Olympus, by Zeus in the form of an eagle, to become the cupbearer to the gods?
2 Which US blues singer, composer and guitarist developed the electric urban blues style and had hits with *Hoochie Coochie Man* (1954) and *I've Got My Mojo Working* (1957)?
3 Who plays the role of Inspector Pat Chappel in the ITV series *The Vice*?
4 Which common garden flower gets its name from the Latin word for a small sword?
5 Which music was identified as the most popular choice of the 'castaways' on BBC Radio 4's *Desert Island Discs*, which celebrated its sixtieth anniversary in March 2002?
6 During the Irish 'Land Wars' of the late nineteenth century, which English land agent unwittingly gave his name to a form of ostracism and isolation?
7 What is the literal meaning of the Japanese word 'karaoke'?
8 In which Italian city is the Brera Art Gallery (Pinacoteca di Brera), founded by Napoleon I in 1809?
9 To which order of insects does the European glow-worm (*Lampyris noctiluca*) belong?
10 What was the name of the royal house of France from 1328 to 1589?
11 Which Austrian composer wrote the symphony nicknamed 'The Schoolmaster'?
12 Which comic-strip cartoon hero inspired the invention of ankle tags for monitoring the movements of criminal offenders released early from prison?
13 What was the stage name of the Italian comic actor Antonio de Curtis, who starred in many films including *The Poor and the Noble* (1954, with Sophia Loren) and *Hawks and Sparrows* (1966, with Ninetto Davoli)?
14 What is the title of the memoirs of the Labour politician Mo Mowlam, published in 2002?
15 What is the name of the longest and tallest suspension bridge in the world, connecting Kobe with Awaji-shima Island in Japan?
16 Who wrote the seventeenth-century poem *A Song of a Young Lady to Her Ancient Lover*, which begins with the following lines?

Ancient Person, for whom I
All the flattering Youth defy,
Long be it ere thou grow Old,
Aching, shaking, crazy Cold;
But still continue as thou art,
Ancient Person of My Heart.

17 In 1927 which Austrian zoologist published *The Dancing Bees*, in which he explained the ways in which honeybees communicate to one another the distance and direction of a food supply?
18 Which British treasure ship, which sank in a storm off Cadiz in January 1694 on its way to help the Duke of Savoy with 10 tons of gold or silver, has recently been discovered by the US salvage company Odyssey Marine?
19 The oldest-known photograph in the world, of a Flemish print of a boy leading a horse, taken in 1826, was sold at auction in France in March 2002 for £278,000: who was the photographer?
20 Which former editor of the *Independent on Sunday* is the pioneer of 'yoof' television (early-evening broadcasts for younger viewers)?

1 **Ganymede.**
2 **Muddy Waters** (McKinley Morganfield, 1915–83).
3 **Ken Stott** (b. 1955).
4 **Gladiolus.** It is also known as the sword lily.
5 **Beethoven's *Ode to Joy***, in the last movement of his Symphony No. 9.
6 **Charles Boycott** (1832–97). Boycott, a retired army captain and land agent for the 3rd Earl of Erne's estates in County Mayo, tried to evict three tenants who demanded rent reductions. Charles Parnell, president of the Land League, started a campaign against him, and Boycott was eventually hounded out of the country.
7 **'Empty orchestra'.**
8 **Milan.** Its original collection was that of Milan's Academy of Fine Arts. The gallery is housed in the Palazzo Brera, an eighteenth-century Neoclassical building which was originally a Jesuit college.
9 **Beetles** (Coleoptera). The luminescence is caused by substances known as luciferins (organic compounds which oxidise in the presence of the enzyme luciferase).
10 **Valois.** The first ruler in the dynasty was Philip VI (r. 1328–50). One of the later Valois kings, François II (1544–60, eldest son of Henri II and Catherine de Médicis), married Mary Queen of Scots when he was Dauphin, but died within a year of ascending the French throne in 1559.
11 **Franz Joseph Haydn** (1732–1809). It is properly known as Symphony No. 55 (1774). The nickname arose because, on the score of the slow movement, the repeated oblique strokes marked on the notes suggest the minatory finger of a schoolmaster.
12 **Spiderman,** in a 1970 story about how Spiderman was electronically tagged by Big Boy. John Love, a district judge in Albuquerque, New Mexico, persuaded a computer expert to develop the idea, which was first tried out in Britain in 1988.
13 **Totò** (1898–1967).
14 ***MoMentum.*** Mo (Marjorie) Mowlam (b. 1949) was appointed Secretary of State for Northern Ireland when Labour won the 1997 General Election; in the October 1999 reshuffle she became Minister for the Cabinet Office and Chancellor of the Duchy of Lancaster until she stepped down from Parliament in 2001.
15 **Akashi Kaikyo Bridge.** It weighs 100,000 tonnes and the central span is 1990 metres long; it is built to withstand hurricanes, earthquakes and tidal waves.
16 **John Wilmot, Earl of Rochester** (1647–80).
17 **Karl von Frisch** (1886–1982). He shared the 1973 Nobel Prize for physiology or medicine with the animal behaviourists Konrad Lorenz and Nikolaas Tinbergen.
18 **HMS *Sussex*** (built in 1693).
19 **Joseph Nicéphore Niépce** (1765–1833).
20 **Janet Street-Porter.**

MAGNUS MAGNUSSON'S QUIZ BOOK

Magnus Magnusson

Magnus Magnusson's first quiz book is perfect for both the serious contestant and for the light-hearted quiz fan. Echoing the show's classic twin formula of specialist subjects and general knowledge, the book contains more than one thousand carefully graded questions and their answers, including a smattering of old favourites from *Mastermind* itself.

0 7515 3065 4

I'VE STARTED SO I'LL FINISH

Magnus Magnusson

'You passed on just the one.' *Mastermind*, the BBC television contest, has subjected more than 1,400 would-be Brains of Britain to its rapid-fire interrogation. But after twenty-five years, the programme was broadcast on television for the last time in September 1997. At its zenith *Mastermind* attracted twelve million viewers. Its winners – taxi drivers, diplomats and teachers – became national celebrities and the programme spawned an obsession with general knowledge, from Trivial Pursuit to pub quizzes. Its success has been due to a simple formula, the consistency of its standards and in large measure to the gravitas, courtesy and humour of its Icelandic born question-master, Magnus Magnusson. His book of behind-the-scenes and in-the-chair anecdotes is a valedictory celebration of a much-loved programme.

0 7515 2585 5

BRAIN MEN

Marcus Berkmann

Marcus Berkmann is a competitive obsessive but a brilliantly knowledgeable nerd and a great success at pub quizzes. He's possibly the only man in Britain that Nick Hornby is jealous of – because his team beat Hornby's in a pub quiz and went on to win the knockout tournament.

This hilarious book does for quiz culture – from *Mastermind* to *Fifteen to One* to the quiz in your local – what *Lost in Music* did for bad rock bands. Thousands of people take part in quizzes every week answering questions like, who won the League Cup in 1972? (Stoke City beat Chelsea 3-2); which of Henry VIII's wives was both a widow and a virgin when she married him? (Catherine of Aragon)

Funny, informative, original – this book has all the answers.

0 349 11299 1

THE A TO Z OF (ALMOST) EVERYTHING

Trevor Montague

This extraordinary work of reference is nothing less than an A to Z of everything – from Abbreviations to Zip Codes. Painstaking in its quest for accuracy and comprehensiveness, the book contains nothing superfluous – it is pure fact. Many of the sections stand up as reference works in their own right: the music section encompasses more information than many specialist music books; the history section contains a detailed chronology of world history, listing every major event; the geography section includes the only fully comprehensive list of every known capital city, even those on tiny Pacific islands.

Trevor Montague has appeared on various TV quiz shows, including *Mastermind*, and his labour of love is the fruit of many years' studying.

0 316 84953 7

Notes